Brewery Planner

Brewery Planner

A Guide to Opening and Running Your Own Small Brewery
• Second Edition •

Compiled by Brewers Publications

Brewers Publications: Boulder, Colorado

Copyright 1996 by Brewers Publications

Managing editor: Elizabeth Gold
Copy editors: Theresa Duggan and Kim Adams
Cover design by Michelle Ludt
Interior design by Carolyn Robertson

Printed in the United States of America
10 9 8 7 6 5 4 3 2 1

Published by Brewers Publications, a division of the Association of Brewers, PO Box 1679, Boulder, Colorado 80306-1679, USA; (303) 447-0816; info@aob.org or FAX (303) 447-2825.

Direct all inquiries/orders to the above address.

Library of Congress Cataloging-in-Publication Data
Brewery planner : a guide to opening and running your own small
    brewery / compiled by Brewers Publications. — 2nd ed.
        p.   cm.
    Includes bibliographical references and index.
    ISBN 0-937381-51-9 (alk. paper)
    1. Brewing.   I. Brewers Publications (Firm)
TP570.B826   1996
663'.3' 068--dc20

                                                                96-30655
                                                                    CIP

Table of Contents

Foreword

by David Edgar
Director of the Institute for Brewing Studies

The craft-brewing industry continues to grow and prosper at a level that few predicted possible. New microbreweries and brewpubs opened in the United States at a rate of five per week during 1995, accelerating to six per week during the first half of 1996. (Two-thirds of the new openings are brewpubs, one-third are microbreweries.) Welcome to the new golden age of brewing in North America.

In charting the course for your successful brewing voyage, it is important to study the information contained inside this second edition of the *Brewery Planner: A Guide to Opening and Running Your Own Small Brewery*. The staff of Brewers Publications has compiled a strong collection of testimonials and advice from individuals who have proven track records of success in craft brewing.

Total craft-brewing industry sales volume may be decades from leveling off. Craft brewing is about changing America's tastes and it is about supporting local companies. Just as people feel comfortable knowing the people who own their local bakery or run their neighborhood coffee shop, beer drinkers like to know that the brewer of the beer they drink is part of their local community too.

If you plan carefully, you, too, can be a part of this vibrant community of young breweries. However, don't fool yourself into believing that the launch of a new brewing venture is a simple endeavor or that your success in some other field will automatically translate to success in this industry.

If you're starting a brewpub, you're entering the restaurant business — a very competitive business. Doing so without professional advice or assistance from someone experienced in running restaurants is an invitation to failure.

If you're starting a microbrewery, welcome to the beer business, also a very tough business. While you'll no doubt discover the brewing and packaging of your product to be challenging, the distribution end of the equation is where most new breweries find the steepest learning curve. You will need a thorough understanding of the beer distribution business if you intend to navigate the tangled web of different sets of regulations governing distribution in different states. That being stated, the best formula for microbrewery success is to focus on building your brand's penetration of your home territory, gradually establishing its reputation as "the beer of (insert your city/county/state here)" — before venturing hundreds of miles away (and increasing the possibility of your product being mishandled before it reaches the customer).

Brewers can ensure a future stake in this business by (1) "sticking with the program" — continuing to produce full-flavored, distinctive, all-malt beers; (2) understanding that a well-planned (and appropriately executed) marketing and sales program are vital to competing in this market; and (3) staying creative — in marketing as well as brewing — and not being afraid to experiment or to take a few risks, whether with innovative products or with new ways of introducing them to a broader market. Keep in mind, as well, that beer is part of the cultural fabric of your community, or region, and thus deserves the same respect and "place" in the community as other forms of culture.

As an educational association for the craft-brewing industry, the Institute for Brewing Studies is here to help with your brewing journey. We wish you all the best in your brewing pursuit and look forward to tasting the fruits of your efforts!

Contact (303) 447-0816, FAX (303) 447-2825, info@aob.org or http://www.aob.org/aob for more information on the Institute for Brewing Studies.

Chapter 1
Overview of Designing a Brewery

by Eric Warner
Founder and Brewmaster of Tabernash Brewing Company

Planning

Brewers have to be some of the most crazed individuals on the planet, with long hours, horrendous working conditions, and poor pay. Why would anyone in their right mind sell the car, the house, liquidate all other assets, and go deeply into debt to wallow in such lowly conditions? Having a ready supply of good beer on hand is certainly one motivating factor, and owning a business is a dream many people have considered. But the mystique of brewing and the respect brewers receive are the strong drives that really inspire us to open our own breweries.

Owning and operating a brewery is one of the most multifaceted undertakings imaginable. The owner of a microbrewery needs sufficient knowledge in chemistry, physics, microbiology, mathematics, accounting, finance, marketing and sales, advertising, and promotion and programming. This individual should have experience brewing, welding, plumbing, and building, as well as other good mechanical skills. This person should be strong, enjoy waking up at 5 a.m., and have a love of temperature extremes. Since very few people have a résumé that corresponds to these demands, this information has been written to help answer the deluge of questions on the minds of everyone who considers opening and operating a brewery — even those who are sound of mind.

Be Realistic

Jumping from brewing five gallons of beer in the basement to owning and operating a brewery that produces thousands of barrels of beer annually should be taken *very* seriously. Before getting started with all of the logistical aspects of building your brewery you have to visualize your future. Some of you who read this are in places very far away from North America, but most of you will think about opening your brewery in the United States, and I believe America is still the land of unlimited opportunities. You can make your brewery whatever you want it to be, but the plain fact is you will need to have better people, aquire more capital, get your message across more effectively, and be better organized than your competitors. Your beer will also have to be ten times better than what's available to your potential customers.

If you just won the lottery, skip down a couple of paragraphs. If not, pay close attention to what follows. You will not be the next Pete's or Sam Adams and probably not the next Redhook or Sierra Nevada. It's also highly unlikely that you will be the next Gordon-Biersch or Wynkoop. This phenomenon of microbreweries and brewpubs is exciting, unique, and growing at an explosive rate. Craft beer is here to stay and so are basic principles of economics. There are still many relatively untapped craft-brew markets in the United States, but there are also many where elbow room is getting tighter.

By the time you open your brewery, the North American craft-brew industry will be somewhere beyond adolescence and either in maturity or the golden years. Just about everybody will have at least heard of a "micro-brew" or a local brewpub. Some consumers will have graduated beyond mass-marketed "faux" microbrews, or cookie-cutter brewpubs, but most will be prone to the allure of brand or concept identity, not the inherently better attributes of your beer or your restaurant. Essentially the following scenario will unfold. This is reality for the next ten years, and it is critical that you understand where you want to fit in and how you need to be competitive in that segment.

There will be twenty-odd national craft-brew brands and line extensions of these brands. Some of them will be faux microbrews and some of them will be made by companies that truly believe in great beer. Some will be contract brews, some will come from the majors, and some will come from first or second generation microbrewers. Unless you work for a major brewing company or have stacks of money, this won't apply to you.

There will be somewhat more regional or select market microbrews scattered across the United States and Canada. Many of these will be owned or managed by companies in the national brand category. Some of these will be content with the markets they are in and the volume of business they have, while others will aspire to be national brands. Few will die; they will either grow, stay put, and be content, or they will succumb to the allure of acquisition. If you are not afraid to raise capital, understand what it takes to build a brand, make great beer, and are extremely well organized, you can compete in this category.

There will also be hundreds to thousands of local microbreweries. Many will be new. Many will be on the brink of insolvency. Even more will aspire to reach the regional status. A select few will be happy to stay small and local, and if they've planned right, they will have a successful business. Anybody who wants to can play in this category, and many

will. The trick here will be to realistically assess what you can eke out of your market and build your brewery around that volume of beer, so it is profitable. You'll have to make great beer to be competitive but you'll also be able to enjoy a "lifestyle" business.

By the year 2007 there will be thousands of brewpubs in America. If you want to start a brewpub, it is critical to understand something very simple: *You are operating a restaurant, not a manufacturing facility.* There will nonetheless be examples of breweries that have small restaurants attached, but brewpub owners have to understand restaurant operations or they will perish. I personally believe that brewpubs will be more of a trend or fad, but then again, which restaurant concept doesn't have an element of built-in obsolescence? The future is probably the brightest for the brewpubs, if for no other reason than they can sell a glass of beer for ten times what it costs to make. Brewpubs in my state have padded their bottom line even more by distributing bottled or keg beer. If you're lucky enough to be in a state that allows that, by all means do it.

If you're still up to the challenge after reading the last few paragraphs, now comes the *really* sobering part: building your management team and raising capital. An economics professor in Germany told me an interesting anecdote. Andrew Carnegie has written on his gravestone something to the effect of "he always surrounded himself with people who were better than he." I'm sure this isn't verbatim, and it may not even be true, but it made a lot of sense then and it still does today. I think you know where I'm going with this, so I'll simply say make sure you have partners and key employees who complement each other and share the same vision. If you want to start a family business, make sure you have openly and honestly communicated with your relatives about the required commitment and about how you each foresee it impacting your relationships with one another. I think the best thing to do when starting a business is to have everyone complete a task to get the ball rolling. Someone can do market research, someone can put together spreadsheets, someone can brew prototype beers. See how the group dynamic is and how effectively everything is being accomplished. Examine the willingness to cooperate among those involved, as well as their willingness to take advice and criticism from others. Think about how project members deal with adversity and how they react when mistakes are made. Finally, plan who will set up and operate the brewery and who will handle the detailed areas where expertise is lacking. It's much easier to do all of this in the early stages than it is once you're off the ground.

I will not go into great detail about raising capital. Unless you've got a buddy who is worth a fortune or a lot of rich relatives, plan for a lot of disappointment. This doesn't mean that it can't be done, but be realistic about how you plan to do it. Be realistic about how long it will take, how you will make your presentation to banks and investors, what percentage of the company you need to sell, and above all, how much capital you will need to get through development and at least one year of operation. Remember the golden rule: Start-up businesses always underestimate expenses and overestimate revenue. The other thing to keep in mind is you will burn through a lot of cash, not only as you start but during high growth years as well.

Market Research

Although sales of microbrewed beers are still on the rise, their combined market share is still very small. Large North American breweries collectively spend over $1 billion a year on advertising, with certain breweries passing the $100 million figure. One thing should be clear: it is *extremely* unlikely that microbreweries will directly compete with the pale, light lager megabrands dominating the market. By the same token, the big boys are really taking notice of microbreweries' presence. Look at their faux beers, look at their ads that poke fun at microbrews, and most notably of all, their cloaked or direct efforts to limit the amounts of

beer small brewers can produce or distribute. The truth is the giants will continue to lose market share, and as this affects their financial performance more and more, they will scrap for any piece of the micro market they can get. They do not care about the blood and sweat you have put into your brewery. They do not care about the life savings you have invested in your brewery. They do not care that your beer tastes great and that you're very proud of it. The trick is to find the consumers who *do* care about these things and let them know your independent, local, handcrafted beer is available. These consumers are out there, they're curious, and they want to try your beer. All you have to do is locate them, make sure there are enough of them to make your business viable, and then communicate your message to them.

In most cases, a small brewery will make so-called specialty beers, which do not emulate mass-produced North American pale lagers. It is wise to begin by investigating the beer sales structure in the proposed market areas. If the per capita consumption of beer in these areas is low compared to figures from other regions, then consider other markets as alternatives. If beer sales in the target areas are solid, further differentiate market structure. The percentage of draft beer sold versus bottled beer sold strongly indicates what packaging considerations must be made when distributing the beer.

Since the type of packaging greatly influences brewery cost structure, conclusions about feasibility can be made early on simply by determining whether potential customers drink draft beer in bars and restaurants or if liquor store sales of bottled beer dominate that market. This can be helpful if the decision isn't clear whether a microbrewery or a brewpub would work best locally. If specialty beers have a market share that is at or above the national level, this market may have good potential. If specialty beer sales are low, this doesn't preclude successful marketing of such products, but determine why those sales are low in the area. If imports sell well and few microbrewed beers are available, the area may be ripe for a microbrewery or a brewpub. The next step would be investigating the breakdown of these specialty beers in terms of beer style, the outlets where they are sold, and the demographic profiles of those who purchase the beers.

A profile of beer drinkers in the target area helps determine where the beer would sell best and what styles would have the most consumer appeal. If the typical local beer drinker takes advantage of happy hour specials on mass-produced beers, a lighter draft product may be best. If the drinker willingly shells out $8 for a six-pack of specialty beer and consumes it at home, a heavier, bottled product might work best. This touches on another issue — product pricing. Will the market tolerate a price on your product that will be higher than well-established name brands? If the local market has a large base of working class beer drinkers due to the nature of the local economy, it may be difficult to sell the product for 50 to 100 percent more than lower-priced brands. If the area is a financial center or one where service or tourism industries dominate local economies, it may be feasible to ask $3 for a pint of beer at the local tavern.

This leads into the question of if the beer will be marketed locally, regionally, or nationwide? Aside from the technological aspects of shelf life in marketing the product over an extended area, consider the demographic make-up of market areas. A microbrewed beer that sells very well on the West Coast may not sell well in the Midwest, or vice versa. Do not underestimate the climate of the brewery location. Marketing a double bock as the flagship beer in south Florida could be dangerous, and a pale, light lager probably won't hit the spot on a winter's day in the Yukon.

Looking at existing models and drawing conclusions to help determine feasibility is a useful market research tool. Examine successful as well as failed microbreweries to determine the keys to success and the elements of failure. Be sure to notice where successes or failures have hinged on marketing

decisions as opposed to product quality, distribution aspects, or company structure. If such models operate locally where the project is planned, the question of saturation will arise. Can that area support another microbrewery or brewpub? If the product by virtue of its style, package, or advertising resembles a well-established beer, locals may criticize the new product. On the other hand, what works well for one may also work well for another. One thing we've noticed at Tabernash Brewing Company is we're still the only brewery in Colorado dedicated to making lager beers and real weissbier. It provides for great differentiation but it also means we have to work harder to make that clear to consumers. We recently came to the painful conclusion that amber ales make up a pretty good chunk of the micro market in Colorado. As lager brewers, we weren't about to make a beer using a common ale yeast and a bunch of Cascade hops, so we decided to make a California common–style beer. So far it's been a huge success.

The point is we got in the game with a competitive product but we didn't copy the other guy or compromise what we're about. Ultimately, your product should express the individuality of what you're trying to do. Herein lies the beauty of opening and operating a microbrewery. The product you make and ultimately sell should reflect the type of beer you enjoy and your personality, however, the realities of operating a business also dictate. How and where you will sell your beer will conclude in a compromise between personal taste and market forces. If proper market research is conducted and a communication strategy is developed based on that research, you can make the beer you want and realize financial success as well.

The Brewery and the Beer

As important as planning, distribution, marketing, and sales may be, the cornerstone of any successful brewing company remains the brewing facility and the beer it produces.

Consistency and quality control are the paramount concerns to the brewer, particularly if the beer is packaged and distributed over a large area. Achieving this is simplified and ensured by having the best brewing equipment money can buy. As is true with everything in life, compromises must be made. As a general rule, I advise people to save money on tanks and peripheral equipment. At Tabernash we've saved hundreds of thousands of dollars on fermentation and storage tanks by purchasing reconditioned stainless steel tanks. We've also bought second-hand refrigeration equipment, chemical tanks, fork lifts, etc. Try not to skimp on the equipment that has a lot of moving parts and a direct impact on the quality of your beer. We purchased our brew house, filter, pumps, hoses, and packaging equipment new.

The same probably holds true for the building your brewery will be housed in. Everybody would love to have a tiled, copper brew house with a beautiful pub nestled in some pristine mountain valley. Again, reality means you'll probably end up renting space in "the up and coming" part of town. Unless you're an expert at balancing unlimited desires, financial reality, and what it really takes to make great beer, you'll have to find somebody to help you sort it all out. In order to operate a safe, efficient brewery that makes great beer, it is crucial to have somebody on board who is capable of evaluating and selecting the right facility, the best equipment your money can buy, and the raw materials needed to make your beer. Suppliers and consultants can be of service here, but it is essential that at least one individual in the organization has sufficient knowledge of the technological parameters involved in the brewing and packaging process. It helps if this person has an understanding of what architectural and engineering issues are involved with building a brewery. If this person is also familiar with laws and regulations governing the brewery and production processes, as well as the ever-increasing role of waste and environmental issues involved

in brewing, that is a bonus. And, if this dream brewer has been through it all once before at another brewery, hire him or her right away.

Site Selection

If you choose to build a brewery from the ground up, you must consider several things. Observe zoning requirements before seriously examining a prospective site. If a brewpub is planned, determine if the site is zoned for a restaurant. If a microbrewery is planned, will it be zoned industrially or commercially in that locality? Upon doing this a number of sites can be quickly eliminated from the selection process.

Predict growth in the area of consideration, as it applies to future zoning changes. Examine the neighborhood surrounding the brewery in terms of its character, demographic history, and attitude toward the brewing/bar business. This is particularly important when a brewpub is planned. Building a brewery in an area of economic decline could be detrimental. Selecting a site in an area of heavy industry could conjure up negative images in the minds of potential customers. Erecting a brewery near a school or church could result in unwarranted and unwanted bad press.

The physical location of the brewery can also influence the brewing procedures, equipment choice, process steps, and ultimately the quality of the beer itself. If a possible site lies seven thousand feet above sea level, consider the reduced boiling temperature of water at this elevation. Overlooking this simple law of physics can result in improper equipment choices and/or bad beer. Or let's say you want to start your dream brewery on a tropical island. Water could be very expensive, or you may find you have to desalinate ocean water or build huge catch basins for rain water. Evaluate a site in terms of water quantity, quality, and accessibility, all of which greatly influence production costs. A brewery I consulted in extreme northern Canada had to actually pump water from a local river for its water. In January this meant they also had to have an ice auger in addition to their tanker truck, hoses, and pump.

Ambient microflora cannot be taken lightly. Building a brewery in a rural area near vineyards or next to an orchard can result in infection problems. The higher concentration of bacteria and wild yeast in these areas will increase the chances of a random infection. Incorporate the area's climate into the evaluation of possible brewery locations. The difference between refrigeration costs for a brewery in Phoenix and one in Toronto are staggering.

Again, I can't recommend enough the value of having somebody involved in the start-up project who has knowledge of how to design the facility and get the most bang for the buck. You can really get your clock cleaned on engineering and architectural expenses if you're not careful. The worst case scenario is to have architects and engineers overcharge you *and* overdesign the facility. Overdesigning will usually result in higher architectural and engineering fees, a larger bill from the contractor(s), and higher than necessary permit and construction fees.

If your head brewer is capable of managing the entire brewery construction process, including budgeting, working with architects and engineers, managing contractors, and selecting the right equipment, you can actually save money by employing that brewer six to twelve months before you make your first batch of beer. Another way to think of it is if the brewer is going to work in the brewery, then it probably makes more sense that he or she designs it. If your expertise is in sales, marketing, finance, or something other than manufacturing, consider investing the money up front and finding somebody who can build a brewery that will require the least amount of capital to make the best beer as economically as possible.

The Building

In all likelihood, you won't be building your brewery from the ground up; and unless a brewery is built from scratch, it is unlikely the building will be ready-made for brewing and packaging. In some cases major alterations must be made to adapt the structure to the brewing process. It's a good idea to consult with engineers, contractors, equipment suppliers, and building inspectors before acquiring a building. These people can evaluate the building in terms of its stability (remember, one barrel of water at 60 degrees F weighs 258 pounds!), adaptability, and suitability as a brewery. Such consultation will also indicate what it will cost to modify the building to a brewery and comply with local building codes.

Some of the finer points involved in the selection process are: height of ceilings, insulation, width of doors and entryways, structure of floors, shipping and receiving areas (dock-high doors!), and composition of floors. Are the floors able to withstand stress, beer, caustic or corrosive substances, and traffic? Are the floors leak proof? Determine if the building is free of insects and rodents, as these pests are costly to eradicate. Determine the soundness and dimensions of the facility for plumbing, electricity, gas, sewage, etc. In some areas, buildings must also meet the standards of applicable seismic codes.

Don't take the available *cubic* footage in a building choice lightly. A building with a high cubic to square foot ratio becomes attractive when its rent is lower than other buildings in the area, square footage is somewhat smaller than optimally desired, or when taller pieces of brewery equipment like cylindro-conical fermentation tanks are planned in the brewery design. With a little imagination and reconstruction, a building that is seemingly too small can be designed to utilize all of the space the building has to offer.

One element of brewery design that is constantly bungled is dry and finished goods storage. It's easy to tell how much space you will need for brewing equipment, but projecting storage needs for malt, empty kegs, bottles, pallets, and finished goods is a much different story. This is where high cubic to square footage is extremely advantageous.

Storing raw materials or finished goods off-site is fine. Companies do it all the time all over the world, and it's not a frustrating "gotcha" if you plan for it.

Oh, did I forget the biggest consideration in selecting the best location for your brewery? Rent is crucial. You have to remember that in all likelihood your brewery (I'm talking about micros, not pubs here) will not be profitable for at least two to three years. The difference between $2 and $5 per square foot over that period for a five-thousand-square-foot facility is $30,000 to $45,000. Theoretically, if you're paying that much more in rent, you should get more out of your facility. Maybe some refrigeration equipment, floor drains, sanitary finishes on the floors, walls, and ceiling. My theory is start-ups are better off raising a little more money to begin with to transform a low-rent shell of a brewery into the basic facility needed to make beer than to have a huge nut to crack every month. Assuming you've done your homework on both your start-up costs and your sales projections, you will come much closer to hitting your start-up budget than achieving your monthly sales and expenses. Remember, start-up businesses always overestimate revenue and underestimate expenses. A lot of start-up micros will go under because they think they'll have the sales curves that micros in virgin markets have had. Most of the meaningful markets will have at least a couple of micros as you read this. Competition will be intense and market share will not come as easily as it has, so the breweries that can weather the storm (low overhead, efficient production, aggressive sales and marketing) will survive.

A lot of what I just related also applies to brewpubs, however it's important to remember that you're opening a restaurant, not a brewery. Restaurants have a much greater chance of succeeding if they are at the right location. You can pay high rent if you can charge a lot for your products, and if customers will frequent your establishment. Look at a brewpub facility for its aesthetic qualities, as well as its practical qualities. Selecting a building with historical significance can possibly help create a unique pub atmosphere. Government grants and loans are often available to businesses that help preserve such landmarks.

Finally, the building selected should meet the expansion needs of the brewery. Obviously a brewpub is less concerned with extra square footage than a microbrewery with lofty plans for the future. Weigh the extra costs of excess floor space against the capital costs of building an entire new brewery. I think the days of triple-digit annual sales growth for individual breweries are coming to an end, so plan to be in your brewery for a while. Our brewery is located in a multi-unit building that has a lot of month-to-month tenants. It's a dream scenario for short-term expansion.

Design and Equipment for the Brewery

I constantly chide my wife for her zealous pursuit of shopping, but I must admit, it is quite an exciting moment when you put down five- or six-figure deposits on brewing equipment. There is a lot of hard work and diligence that goes into deciding which equipment to buy. Even when you think you've made the best choice, you can still get burned. Sometimes your beers will not be of the ideal quality you're striving for. A lot of the equipment suppliers to the microbrewing industry struggle with the exact same problem. Sure, you could buy the fancy European equipment but you probably can't afford it. The most important criterion in making your final decision about which supplier to use is your faith in their commitment to helping you resolve the problems you will encounter when using their equipment. Sometimes malfunctions are due to the equipment, but other times your or your brewer's ineptitude or confusion cause them. Most suppliers warranty their equipment, but the guys who will walk you through a problem that is no fault of the equipment are your best bets.

This rule assumes you've decided on two or three potential suppliers. If there's only one game in town for a certain piece of equipment, then your decision is easy. In most cases you will decide between these two to three suppliers, and the following criteria will help you choose. I definitely recommend checking the equipment manufacturer's reputation. This is best done by calling breweries who have purchased equipment from your prospective suppliers. Remember, if you ask the suppliers for a reference list, it is unlikely they will refer you to unsatisfied customers. Do some digging on your own and answer the following questions: Has the equipment been reliable and economical? Are the beers from breweries using this equipment flavorful and clean (although this is not entirely dependent on the brewery itself)? Is the service and support from this supplier good? Are they charging different customers the same price for the same equipment? Are they timely with their production and delivery schedules? Are they truly a turnkey supplier, if they tout that? Does the equipment do what they say it will?

Other things to bear in mind are the flexibility or expandability of the equipment or system. A total turnkey brewery or a metrically fitted brewery may not be compatible with future equipment purchases. Spare parts should be readily available for the system. The Italian filters are the worst in this regard — stock spare parts for these filters. Finally, the equipment should meet all electrical, health, construction, plumbing, and safety standards before being purchased.

A common question among beginning breweries is whether or not to go turnkey. My advice is this: if you're a brewpub and you don't have anybody who is knowledgeable with system design and orchestration, go turnkey. If you're a micro, you will be forced to a certain extent to piece together your brewery using a variety of suppliers, because companies that make brew houses don't usually make bottling lines. It usually gets cloudy when it comes to accessory parts. Equipment manufacturers may try to sell you hoses, pumps, valves, etc., that you might be able to locate for a less expensive price. In either case

it's important to make sure that the size of the equipment is matched in each step of the brewing process. Going turnkey, you will usually get a malt mill that matches the mash tun, which matches the brew kettle, which matches the fermenter, and so on. Designing the brewery on your own definitely necessitates having someone who is at least familiar with the big picture.

Orchestrating Beer Styles with Brewery Design

The style of beer you want to brew is largely a decision to make on your own. Market research can give some indication of this style, but cases can be made for brewing ales, lagers, or both. Don't make this decision without considering the costs of both. Common arguments for brewing ales are lower production time and reduced refrigeration costs. Though this is a valid rule of thumb, note that a thoroughly attenuated, high-quality lager beer can be produced in four to five weeks at temperatures only slightly lower than those of top-fermented beers.

What must be clear from the outset are the chosen fermentation parameters. A classically brewed lager could take up to ten weeks to ferment and condition, whereas a more modern fermentation might require only twenty-four days to produce the same style of beer. This difference forces the brewery to consider the capacity of the fermentation and lager tank. It also means refrigeration costs will differ in these two cases. Though ales generally require less time to attenuate than lagers, fermentation parameters of top-fermented beers must also be matched with projected output in terms of fermentation and storage vessels and the cost structure of the planned brewery.

Also consider brew-house design when deciding on the beer styles. If adjunct brewing is a consideration, the brew house must be capable of mashing more intensely than a brew house designed for a single-step infusion mash using highly modified malt. If dark, full-bodied lagers are desired, the system should be capable of decoction mashing. If light Pilsener-style beers are on tap, the system should have as little oxygen uptake as possible to avoid unwanted deepening of color and taste.

Brewery Departments

The brew house. This is the altar of any brewery and is, therefore, often one of the more ornately designed areas in a brewery. In a brewpub it is well worth considering copper or copper-clad brew kettles, as this can only increase the mystique of the brewery, especially if it will be visible to the public. If tours are part of the promotional campaign, the brew house should be as neat and accessible as possible. This will also benefit the brewers in the course of their daily ritual. A brewery that has a good design and remains tidy is easier to work in than one that is crowded and unkempt.

Ultimately, give the technical factors of designing the brew house top priority. Just because a brew house is opulently beautiful does not mean it will yield the highest quantity and quality of wort. Keep in mind these two parameters are the most important when selecting the brew-house equipment. The quantity and quality of wort yielded is dependent upon a host of factors including malt quality, brewing water, the malt mill, brew-house design, and the mash procedure. The malt mill can greatly influence the final cast out wort as well as the lauter time and efficiency, and as such should be of proper design. In most cases, a two-roller mill is satisfactory, although four-, five-, or six-roller mills will improve the quality of the grist, and with it the quality and quantity of the wort. The malt can be crushed dry or wet or be conditioned with steam just prior to milling. In most small North American breweries a dry grist, two-roller mill is employed, as this variation is the least expensive.

In a traditional, classically designed brewery the malt mill is situated above the mash tun, so gravity can feed the grist to the main floor of the brew house. This isn't always feasible, and some alternate means of conveying the crushed grain must be used — either pneumatically, mechanically, or manually. The same options apply to transporting the unmilled grain to the malt mill. As is true with the storage and handling of any cereal grain, the danger of dust explosions is present, and consequently necessary precautions must be taken to avoid this potentially lethal and costly hazard. Occupational Safety and Health Administration standards provide guidelines for alleviating such a mishap, as well as guidelines for protection from the dust and flour that arises during the milling process. Always design milling operations to be as ventilated and as dust free as possible. This protects you and your employees, and also reduces the amount of time spent sweeping and dusting the grist room.

Grain for the brew will seldomly be delivered in synchronization with the production process, which necessitates some type of grain storage. If the grain is delivered in bulk form, a silo is best. Most small breweries receive their grain in bagged form, so their brewery design includes a storeroom to house the supply of brewing grains. If grain storage is on an upper level, it's important to remember a pallet of malt weighs anywhere from two thousand to three thousand pounds. Ideally this room should be cool, dry, free of mice and insects, and located close to the malt mill.

Consider the brew-house design at length and in great detail. As previously mentioned, this part of the brewery is often the showpiece of any brewing operation, therefore aesthetic qualities also merit attention. The decision-making process involved in purchasing a brew-house can be compared to purchasing an automobile. The brew house represents a major capital expenditure for the brewery, as does the purchase of an automobile for an individual. Often the brewer or potential car owner contemplates his or her needs.

Efficiency, power, safety, ease of operation, appearance, service and support, guarantees and warranties, delivery time, and market position of the manufacturer are all applicable criteria for buying a brew house as well as a new car. As is the case with automobiles, there is also a market for used breweries. The benefits and risks are also similar. You can save a lot of money purchasing a used brew house, but you can also get burned. Often a used brew house is considered for its antique value, though technologically it may be obsolete. Renovations and repairs may be necessary, and dependability may be questionable.

Ideally, weigh the needs of your brewing operation against your brew-house budget and also consider your company's cost structure. Shelling out a bit more for an efficient brew house that will result in a higher extract yield might pay off down the road in reduced malt costs. Spending more money on a more versatile brew house will enable you to brew a greater number of beer styles. Buying a used brew house can result in lower capital expenditure, but running costs such as malt, energy, and repair may be higher.

One major aspect of brew-house design is the source of heat. If a single-step-infusion or a step-infusion process is planned, only the brew kettle will have to be heatable. This can also apply to a decoction system if the lauter tun will double as a rest mash vessel. If a classic three-vessel decoction system or adjunct brewing is planned, then two vessels need to be heatable. The simplest option for brew-house heat is electric. Using electric heating for boiling is only applicable in the smallest of operations due to the inefficient heat transfer, in the case of direct coil heaters, which causes mash scalding.

One of the most common choices for small breweries is to directly fire the kettles with coal, oil, or more popularly, with natural gas. Coal and oil, though cheaper than gas, are more complicated to use and usually result in higher emissions than gas. Natural gas is clean, readily accessible, consistent in quality, and easy to employ as a fuel. If a microbrewery is planned, using steam to heat the brewing vessels may be the best choice. Process steam can be used not only for this purpose, but also to sterilize pipelines, kegs, bottlers, or for other heating purposes. Another option is using hot water to heat brewing vessels. Hot water heating is only viable for very small operations since the heat of cooling water is less than condensed steam (based on equal masses of water and steam). Naturally, all motors will have to be electrically powered, and the brew house must be equipped with the necessary electrical outlets and wired accordingly.

To initiate the brew, the grist must be mixed with brewing water of a desired mash-in temperature. Usually the water and grist are mixed in a separate section to reduce dust clouds and to ensure a sufficient mix of the two. If such an installation isn't budgeted for in your brewery, you can mix the water and grist in the mash tun. The mash-in process should proceed as quickly as possible, so the water lines and mixing section must be amply sized. If a brewery is conscientious of its energy economics, a sufficient amount of warm brewing water will be on hand to mash-in with. This water is obtained from the wort cooling process and is stored in a well-insulated warm water tank. In this case, a used tank is a good choice. Many smaller breweries like to use the brew kettle as a hot liquor back for mashing in and then they will transfer the hot liquor for sparging to a fermenter, thus saving the expense of a tank.

Design the mash tun in accordance with the planned volume and amount of cast-out wort. This is particularly important if a combination mash-lauter tun is going to be used, as too thin or too thick a grain bed will result in less than ideal lautering conditions. Insulate the mash tun well and, in the case of the mash tun that isn't doubling as a lauter tun, equip it with an agitator to evenly distribute the mash across the areas where heat transfer occurs. The agitator blade is usually propeller-shaped and should rotate at speeds that will mix the mash, not purée it. The form of the mash tun is normally cylindrical, and the bottom is convexly curved or conical.

The lauter tun, though not the sole means of separating the sweet wort from the mash, is the most commonly used method for wort separation. Most North American small brewing systems have an integrated mash-lauter tun. Small breweries rarely apply other methods of wort separation such as the mash filter. The lauter tun is made of stainless steel or copper and is also well insulated to prevent a drop in temperature during the run-off. It needs to be perfectly level to ensure proper run-off and maximum yield. The form of the lauter tun is cylindrical, and its capacity is sized according to the size of the mash, which is determined by the amount of milled grain. Grain bed depths of one to two feet are common, with the deeper beds used in mash-lauter tuns. Modern lautering technology prescribes grain bed depths of as little as eight to ten inches. The design of the false bottom facilitates a steady, efficient run-off that yields a clear wort. It is often made of stainless steel and is laid into the lauter tun on a system of supports. The false bottom is either slitted or holed, and the plate(s) of the false bottom is milled or punched. A wire, V-screen-type bottom is also commonly used. In either case, the false bottom should be removable, yet firmly secured in place during usage, particularly if rakes are used in the lauter tun. If the lauter tun is a dedicated lauter tun, then the mash should be pumped into the lauter tun at the bottom to minimize oxidation of the mash.

Do not overload the lauter tun, as this will bend the false bottom, resulting in an uneven run-off and decreased yield. To clarify the initial run-off, employ some method of wort recirculation to pump the first runnings back onto the top of the mash so the grain bed filters them. A sparger is aligned somewhere above the surface of the mash and has the form of either a rotating sprinkler arm or a fixed ring with spray balls or jets attached to it. Some lauter tuns are equipped with cutting rakes to loosen the grain bed during the lautering process and thereby reduce the resistance the grain bed subjects the wort to. Such lauter tuns are also equipped with a

plow parallel to the false bottom that can be raised and lowered to discharge the spent grains from a hole in the bottom of the tun. This automates the process of removing spent grains from the lauter tun and is a real time-saver if there is a large amount of grain. Generally speaking, if your brew house is larger than fifty barrels you probably want to have rakes and a spent-grain discharge system. Particularly large systems should also have an automated means of moving the spent grains to a silo or storage vessel. The sweet wort is obtained from the bottom of the lauter tun via one centrally located run-off pipe or in larger tuns via several run-offs evenly distributed on the bottom. From here the sweet wort is either recirculated into the lauter tun or pumped into the kettle by an open or closed wort collecting grant.

The brew kettle must have the capacity to hold the lautered wort plus sufficient headroom for foaming during the boil. To avoid oxidation of the wort, the lautered run-off should be underlet into the brew kettle. Like the other vessels in the brew house, insulate the kettle well. The shapes of the kettles are extremely varied, but the most common form is a cylindrical kettle with a slightly concave or slightly convex bottom. Copper kettles conduct heat better than stainless-steel ones, but the latter are less expensive and easier to clean and maintain. The top of the kettle must have a dome and vent to lead the steam away from the brew house. The kettle is fitted with a manway through which the hops are also often dosed.

Kettles can be heated in a variety of ways. The most traditional method is with a direct fire, in which case the flame is directed at the concave bottom of the brew kettle. Kettles heated with steam are fitted with jackets through which the steam circulates and condenses. To ensure a rolling boil the jackets, offset them in some manner or segregate them into areas having two different steam pressures, resulting in two different steam temperatures. The kettles can also be fitted with an internal boiler — placed inside the kettle to circulate steam — or with an external boiler. Located outside the actual brew kettle, the external boiler is comprised of plates or pipes where steam and wort circulate. The walls of the plates or pipes separate the two media and serve as the surface through which the heat transfer occurs. With this system the kettle can be fitted with a flat bottom and double as a whirlpool.

Brew kettles have a few, key design criteria, otherwise they are pretty simple. For one, the kettle must be sized so the wort comes to a boil quickly and can maintain this boil for the prescribed time. Obviously, a good boil is predicated on the heat source being adequate. Steam boilers are generally more efficient than direct fire burners, and in either case, it's important to consider factors (such as altitude) that can affect the net efficiency of the system, as it will be operating in your facility. To this end, the kettle must achieve the desired evaporation rate during the boil. It is important to establish the evaporation rate from the outset so the necessary calculations for energy usage and cast-out quantity can be made. Secondly, the boil must be rolling and vigorous, so that *all* parts of the wort have equal contact time with the heating surfaces, otherwise off-flavors may result and protein coagulation will be less. Avoid dead zones in the boil to alleviate these problems.

After the boil is complete, remove the trub matter from the wort. If natural hop cones have been used, they will also have to be removed. In this case employ a hop strainer or hop separator to separate the hops from the cast-out wort. The hot trub — comprised of protein matter, bitter substances, polyphenols, and other organic matter — can be separated from the wort in a number of ways. The most rudimentary method is sedimentation. The wort can remain in the brew kettle if this is the case, provided an outlet is installed on the side of the kettle. Sedimentation tanks, separate from the brew kettle, can also be employed. This method is simple, yet not entirely effective. There are different schools of thought regarding the necessary degree of

hot-trub separation, and some will argue it isn't even necessary. One of the most famed Belgian monastic breweries believes hot-trub removal robs the yeast of essential nutrients. Suffice it to say, the standard in the industry today is to strive for complete hot-trub separation. To achieve this, the wort can be filtered, centrifuged, and run through a whirlpool; these steps can be combined in certain cases. Because filtering and/or centrifuging the wort are costly endeavors, the use of the whirlpool has become the standard in the North American small-brewing industry.

For the whirlpool to function optimally, certain dimensions must be observed in its design. The whirlpool must be perfectly cylindrical, and the inlet(s) should run tangentially into the side of it. The whirlpool should have two outlets. One should be high enough above the bottom of the whirlpool to remove the first one-half to two-thirds of the wort. The lower outlet should be mounted on the lower side near the edge of the bottom. The height to width ratio of the whirlpool must also be within a certain range for the physical forces acting on the trub particles to have their maximum effect. To get the best whirlpooling effect, the diameter to height ratio of the wort in the whirlpool needs to be at least 1:1. This is why I'm not a huge fan of combination brew kettle–whirlpools. The design elements of a good whirlpool and a good brew kettle are basically mutually exclusive. The lone exception to this is the combination brew kettle–whirlpool with an external boiler that I mentioned earlier. This design, however, isn't the most realistic option for start-up micros or brewpubs. Have the bottom of the whirlpool properly designed for complete (as possible) trub removal. Flat bottoms or whirlpools with a slightly raised center sloping toward a trough around the perimeter have proven very effective.

In order for yeast to ferment and reproduce, wort needs to cool to a certain temperature (depending on beer style), and indeed the temperature at which the yeast is pitched can greatly influence the course of the fermentation and the character of the finished beer. In many older breweries around the world a cool ship is used to cool the wort, but the risk of infection, the deepening of color, and the lack of heat recovery have precluded the installation of cool ships in new breweries. Baudelot or surface coolers have also been subjected to the same fate, though a clear advantage of this type of cooler is the aeration of the wort occuring in the process. Tube coolers are also no longer state of the art, though they represent a viable alternative to the plate heat exchanger that is found in the majority of the North American breweries today. The plate cooler can be single stage or dual stage, with brewing water serving as the coolant in the first stage and cold water, alcohols, or other coolants in the second stage. With this type of system, it is essential that the number of plates be sufficient to cool the wort in less than one hour, that the energy recovery from the hot wort be as complete as possible, and the amount of hot brewing water obtained in the process be of the proper temperature and amount. I constantly see small breweries with under-dimensioned plate heat exchangers. If your system is designed right, you should be able to cool your wort in less than an hour and have a hot liquor tank full of sparge-temperature water. I've never been a big proponent of the cold liquor tank. It takes up space, and a two-stage heat exchanger doesn't cost much more than a single-stage cooler.

Post-boil wort aeration is also critical for a speedy fermentation with the right balance of aromas and flavors. The aeration of the wort can be carried out at any temperature. Venturi tubes, aerating candles made of ceramic or a sintered metal, or metal platelets can be used to aerate the wort. Use either sterilized air or pure oxygen for aeration, though in the latter case, take precautions to avoid over-oxygenating the wort, which has a toxic effect on the yeast. It is useful to have a gauge integrated into the aeration device to monitor the amount of oxygen or air taken up by the wort. This gauge is particularly advantageous when the wort is aerated with pure oxygen to ensure that the wort is not under-aerated or to simply control more precisely this parameter of the fermentation.

Whether or not to remove cold trub is more open to debate than that of hot trub separation. Although less common in ale breweries, a good portion of lager breweries undertake cold trub separation, with the desired end being a smoother, rounder, and pleasantly bitter beer. The simplest way to remove cold trub is cold sedimentation, which requires only a vessel in which sedimentation takes place. Employ cold filtration to obtain the most effective degree of cold trub separation. Take caution not to remove too much trub, otherwise the resulting beers may taste empty and lack character. Most small brewers won't be confronted with this problem, as this practice usually is unaffordable. The same holds true for the centrifuge.

One of the most innovative technologies to develop in the modern brewing world is flotation. The cooled wort is heavily aerated, and as the air bubbles rise in the flotation tank, air bubbles carry cold trub particles to the surface of the wort. A layer of foam forms on the surface of the wort, and the wort is subsequently pumped from the bottom of the tank and the foam-trub layer remains in the tank.

The preceding elements of the brew house represent only the core components, and there are many accessories which have to be planned for. Pumps, motors, piping, valves, meters and gauges, analytical devices, hoses, cleaning equipment, a hot liquor tank, and a hop-dosing device are all examples of what this could entail.

The fermentation and maturation cellars. Any room in which fermentations take place should be well ventilated, clean, and cool, particularly for open fermenters. If expansion is on the horizon, liberally size this room to make room for additional fermenters. The walls and ceiling of the fermentation cellar should be smooth and devoid of cracks or slits in which microorganisms could grow. Indeed, the local health department inspector will probably insist that you have food-grade surface finishes in most of the brewery areas. The floor should be structurally stable enough to hold fermenters and aging tanks and be able to withstand water, detergents, and other chemicals, as well as be easy to clean. The floor should be sloped, and install drains to avoid areas of standing water. Ventilators are best placed on the ceiling, otherwise microorganisms can be blown upward from the floor into the air.

The decision to go with open or closed fermenters is a difficult one, as there are advantages and disadvantages to both. Unfortunately, the advantage of one is often the disadvantage of the other! The open fermenter is the more traditional fermentation vessel, and many small European brewers swear by them. In open fermenters, craft brewers are able to watch over their fermentations and note their progress. Harvesting ale yeast or removing the post-kraeusen layer on the surface of the green beer is easily done with an open fermenter. In open fermenters ale yeast comes in contact with the air above the fermenter, making the yeast more virile and increasing the number of times it can be pitched. The open fermenter does *not* need to be designed to withstand pressures other than atmospheric, which translates to less tank expense. This is accentuated by the fact that all of the closed fermenters' accessories to (pressure regulators, sight glasses, manways, etc.) are superfluous. Finally, taste tests have shown beers from open fermentations are often preferred to the control beers from closed fermentations.

Despite these advantages, closed fermenters have gained popularity over the last couple of decades and have become the standard in large breweries the world over. In a closed fermenter, the risk of infection is reduced. Secondly, the advent of CO_2 recovery systems has warranted a change over to closed fermentation, although most micros won't be able to justify this expense. Also changes in fermentation technologies have run parallel to the advent of closed fermentations. There are

just as many good beers brewed in open fermenters as in closed. Clean in place (CIP) cleaning and sanitizing procedures are only usable if the fermenter is closed (although some open fermenters can be fitted with lids that allow both CIP and CO_2 recovery), thus automated cleaning is made possible by closed fermentation.

Regardless of the type of fermenter used, it will have to be cooled. The days of hauling ice into the fermentation cellar filled with wooden fermentation vats are over, and fermenters today are jacketed, or in the case of open fermenters, sometimes internally cooled with a cooling tube or plate. The jackets are sometimes divided into zones, especially for cylindro-conical tanks. The coolant circulates through the jacket, and the flow rate is regulated either manually or automatically. Regulating the temperature by hand can be tricky. If the brewer lacks experience in this area, an automatic temperature control is a worthwhile investment. This control is standard technology today. Larger breweries have controllers linked to a PC that captures data and refines fermentation parameters.

Equip fermenters with stand pipes to prevent yeast and other sedimentous matter from being carried with the beer when it is transferred. If the fermenters are cylindro-conical with a steep enough cone angle, then stand pipes are obviated. Closed fermenters should be fitted with pressure regulators and pressure/vacuum relief valves. Most small breweries use hoses to connect fermenters with maturation tanks, the brew house, the CIP equipment, etc., but many breweries opt for hard plumbed installations. While this may be cost effective for larger, automated plants, most brewpubs and start-up microbreweries find this manner of connecting tanks with other parts of the brewery too costly.

After primary fermentation, most beers mature for some period of time before being packaged and distributed. More traditional conditioning procedures involve transferring the beer from the fermentation tank to some kind of storage tank. Some modern fermentation techniques prescribe a single-tank fermentation and maturation process in standing, cylindrical-shaped tanks. This method yields perfectly satisfactory beers, yet such techniques require a fair degree of experience with fermentations.

The storage cellar is traditionally a subterranean basement where large stores of beer are kept to mature and preserve. The beer is subject to the ambient temperature of the cellar. More modern cellars have to be centrally cooled. Present-day North American microbrewers aren't always able to design a brewery from the ground up, and thus the concept of the dark, cobwebbed, musty storage cellar has been modified to that of a large meat cooler or warehouse filled with jacket-cooled storage tanks. At Tabernash we have single-wall tanks that are cooled in a giant cellar at 32 degrees F. Inevitably you'll spend money on insulating a storage-tank room or the tanks themselves. The nice thing about an ambient-cooled aging cellar is you don't have to worry about separate controls for each tank, you only have to hold the temperature of the cellar. You also save some money on pumps, piping, and controllers. In either case, the tanks have to be fitted with pressure-regulating devices if the beer is to be naturally carbonated. Pressure gauges are necessary as well. Like the fermenters, place stand pipes in the outlets to prevent sedimentous matter from flowing with the beer to the packaging department. The tanks themselves are made of stainless steel or aluminum, although it would be nice to see a North American do some aging in wood. The tanks most traditional form is cylindrical, and it is usually in a lying position. The greater ratio of surface area to beer depth in the lying position provides a distinct advantage in the beer's clarification and maturation compared to standing the tanks on end.

Clarifying and packaging the beer. Even if unfiltered beers are produced, the green beer must be conditioned and clarified to some degree. An *overly* turbid beer can be objectionable to the customer, and most classic cask or bottle-conditioned beers in the world are only slightly opaque. If brilliantly clear beers are desired, augment the natural clarification process. To achieve this, filter or centrifuge the beer. If semi-clarification is desired, clarifying agents will reach the desired degree of clarity.

Natural sedimentation involved in the fermentation and conditioning process is usually effective in yielding pleasantly turbid beer, provided it hasn't been rushed through fermentation and maturation. Clarifying agents such as wood chips, isinglass, or gelatin can be added to the beer just before or during the maturation process. To achieve brilliance, employ a centrifuge to clarify the beer. For the highest degree of brilliance, apply filtration techniques. Originally cotton pad filters were used. Although some breweries still use this type of filter, the process is too costly, messy, and complicated for microbrewers. Most filtered beer in the world achieves its luster through filter systems that use diatomaceous earth (DE) and/or filter sheets. Describing the variety of systems in depth transcends the scope of this book, but I will highlight the pros and cons of DE and sheet filtration.

When the system is properly used, DE filters clarify beers to a high degree of brilliance. The DE filter is relatively easy to operate and maintain, though practice is required. The DE filter is clearly the most difficult piece of brewing equipment to master. In addition to this frustration, there are a few other things to consider when using DE filtration. DE represents a running cost. Low-quality DE can affect beer flavor, and disposal of DE can present a problem in the future. DE is also a hazardous material causing eye and lung irritation and it is possibly carcinogenic. The biggest drawback of DE filtration for microbrewers is all the filters come from Italy, and it's a pain in the you-know-what to get spare parts for them!

Sheet filter systems "polish" beer by lowering turbidity and increasing biological stability. Sheet filter systems require an unfiltrate that has already been clarified to a great degree, otherwise the filter would clog quickly and the increased costs of filter sheets would not justify their use. Both diatomaceous earth and filter sheets are one-way and, at present, non-recyclable products. Low-porosity filter sheets, though beneficial in maintaining biological stability, remove bitter substances and proteins from the beer, which can damage head retention.

If filtered or non-bottle-conditioned beer is going to be shipped long distances (such as out of the States), consider the biological and chemical-physical stability of the beer, as reclamations can close any brewery's doors very quickly. Biological stability can be obtained through filtration, pasteurization, or by adding preservatives to the beer. The use of filtration techniques to achieve biological stability is effective provided aseptic conditions are maintained when packaging the beer. Membrane filters are usually employed, and over-filtration must be avoided to prevent flavor stripping. Pasteurization has become a controversial issue over the last few years. Recently many breweries have advertised that they don't pasteurize their products. Though chamber and tunnel pasteurizers significantly affect beer flavor, the same cannot always be said for flash pasteurization. I think we'll see more and more micros flash pasteurizing in the future.

When considering pasteurization techniques, observe the energy recovery possibilities involved. If chamber pasteurizers are used, or if the beer is warmed before it is bottled, the heat used to warm the product is not recoverable. Tunnel pasteurizers recover a certain degree of heat, however flash pasteurizers recover more because they are essentially a closed heat exchanger. Another option for achieving biological stability is using additives that preserve the beer. Naturally this practice is contradictory to the idea of producing fresh, natural beer that is free from additives and preservatives. So in light of present public awareness, it is not the best choice.

To ensure that the flavor of the packaged beer changes as little as possible after it leaves the brewery, maintain chemical-physical stability. Again, this issue concerns brewers who distribute across a larger geographic area more than those who concentrate on local or on-premise beer sales. The main elements affecting chemical-physical stability are oxygen, polyphenolic compounds, protein compounds, carbohydrates, and minerals, as well as heavy metals. Keeping air away from the beer after it leaves the fermentation cellar and until it is in the glass is one of the most effective ways of maintaining not only chemical-physical stability but flavor stability as well. This stability can be achieved by using CO_2 as a counter pressure gas instead of sterilized air and also by using bottlers that fill with minimal air uptake. Reducing troublesome polyphenol and protein fractions in the beer also increases the shelf life. Selecting quality raw materials and observing certain technological parameters in the brewing process — such as mashing intensively, boiling the wort long enough, and lagering the beer for a sufficient amount of time — postpones the onset of colloidal haze in the finished beer. However, some means of increasing product stability may be required. The application of adsorptive products is a popular choice for reducing either the polyphenol or the protein fractions in beer. In some cases both are reduced by the same product. These products vary in cost and manner of application, so investigate before deciding which to use. Also, use Irish moss or other kettle coagulants in the brew kettle to help increase chemical-physical stability. Alternatives to adsorptive products are chemical ones such as tannin, proteolytic enzymes, or reducing agents. These agents, though effective in improving chemical-physical stability, require precise dosing and proper application because some may affect the quality of the finished beer.

Once beer has been conditioned, clarified, and in some cases stabilized, package it as soon as possible. Before getting to that point, make sure the right amount of the beer's "fifth" ingredient is there: carbonation. My least favorite, yet the most commonly used method for carbonating microbrewed beer, is the carbonating stone. Diffusing CO_2 into finished beer takes place in the bright beer tank, which serves as a buffer between the filter and the packaging equipment. There are also in-line carbonation systems available that can carbonate beer as it's moved into the bright beer tank. At Tabernash, we use the other two methods of carbonating beer: tank carbonation and package conditioning. With tank carbonation the green beer is transferred to aging tanks with a small amount of residual fermentable sugar. The aging tank is capped off, and as this residual sugar ferments in the tank, the beer is carbonated. Package-conditioned beer achieves its carbonation by adding priming sugar or wort to relatively flat beer just prior to packaging. This beer must have yeast in it for the secondary fermentation to take place. Bar none, the best beers in the world are tank or package conditioned.

Editorial biases aside, we come back to packaging. There are basically three containers microbrewed beer is packaged in: the keg, the bottle, or the serving tank. Kegging is by far the best answer for microbreweries concentrating on local sales to restaurants, pubs, nightclubs, or hotels. This method fits very well into the cost structure of a brewery with limited start-up capital, and product quality is easier to maintain because of the larger container size of a keg reduces oxygen uptake. Kegging lines can be as simple as washing, inspecting, and filling each keg by hand to fully automated systems requiring virtually no human attendance. The choice of kegs ranges from very simple and inexpensive (Golden Gate type) to very sophisticated (Sankey type). The current trend is toward the straight-wall Sankey keg. Fewer new breweries use the Hoff Stevens–type kegs over the Sankey, while only a handful of breweries still use Golden Gates. Unless you're really scraping for start-up cash, I suggest making the investment in the Sankeys. To some extent the Sankey keg also conveys an image of quality to the bar manager — its greater ease of use and storage may increase the likelihood that an account will carry your draft product.

There are numerous choices to get your beer into the keg. Many small breweries have used homemade kegging systems that work fine. If you want to save on labor and maintain high product quality and consistency, I recommend purchasing a more automated kegging line. Remember draft to bottle ratios for micros are about 50:50 so don't underestimate the importance of your kegs and kegging equipment. Once craft-beer consumers try your bottled product and like it, they will seek out the draft version because they perceive draft beer as representing your product at its freshest and highest quality.

Bottling beer is becoming more and more of a reality for microbreweries. As I write this, Tabernash is the last microbrewery in Colorado not to bottle, and that is about to change. Bottling is something we all hate, but it's a necessary evil. It can be like opening Pandora's box if experienced and trained personnel are not on hand, if the equipment is of inferior quality, if the packaging container is unsuitable, or if the fixed and running costs have not been *carefully* calculated. Running a bottling line is one of the most complex aspects of brewery operations. Even if everything has been planned and organized, *something* will go wrong. To minimize the effect this will have at bottling time, it is best for someone with extensive experience to plan, organize, and oversee the bottling plant.

Selecting the rinsing, conveying, bottling, labeling, and packaging equipment for a brewery is one of the most painstaking decisions since so much capital will be tied up in this investment. There is nothing wrong with purchasing used equipment, but again someone must evaluate and appraise the equipment in a knowledgeable manner. I don't want to digress into a lengthy discussion about packaging equipment, but I will say that I've seen some of the biggest mistakes made by breweries who have purchased inferior equipment or the Rolls Royce when a Honda would have sufficed. If distributing in a one-hundred-mile radius and/or your beer's shelf life doesn't have to be that long, don't be oversold on unneeded technology. Always buy a good labeler. First impressions are critical.

Carefully chose your bottle, as it can affect cost structure and the taste of the beer. The chosen bottle must appeal to the target market as well. Have an experienced person accurately calculate the costs of operating and installing the bottling line. Account for various scenarios and make calculations for all situations, including the worst case, which foresees the packaging line operating at its least efficient state.

Packaging beer in larger containers is not common, but there are a few noteworthy applications. Serving beer directly from storage tanks is common in North American brewpubs and presents several advantages. For one, the beer is freshest when served in this manner. Next, product losses encountered when kegging or bottling are not a factor when serving from a tank. Costs involved with kegging or bottling — such as labor, water, energy, containers, cleansers and disinfectants, depreciation — all fall by the wayside when serving from the tank. Time spent changing kegs on a busy night is not a worry to the publican who staffs a brewpub serving beer from tanks.

However, there are a few important points to observe if the brewpub plans to dispense beer directly from the tank. If the beers are pumped to the taps under pressure, the tanks must be rated according to the operating pressure necessary to move beer to the taps. Make sure to clean the lines regularly to prevent the spread of microorganisms from the lines into the tanks. Beers which are slow sellers and remain in the serving tanks for extended periods of time also become infection prone.

In certain cases beer is "packaged" in large dairy-type trucks for transport to a packaging line (contract bottling), or the truck itself can serve as the dispensing unit at large-scale events. Both practices occur commonly in Europe and have potential for microbrewers in North America.

Aside from the packaging equipment itself, the design of the packaging area must be well thought out. A bottling line requires a lot of electrical power, so install outlets and wiring accordingly. A packaging area can get very warm, so appropriately ventilate or air-condition it. Lay out the machines in a sensible manner so product and package flow lines are as efficient as possible. Also, place them in a manner that keeps the noise intensity to a minimum for the workers. Don't forget about warehousing both empty and filled bottles. Like I said earlier, I've seen a lot of breweries underestimate this area's storage space.

Powering and Cooling the Brewery

A common preliminary budgeting mistake is to plan for all the brewing equipment, and even some of the peripheral accessories, but to neglect steam, air, CO_2, electricity, fossil fuels, and water which makes it all work. Refrigeration equipment, a steam boiler, an air compressor, and a water treatment system were 15 percent of Tabernash's start-up budget. Utilities and CO_2 make up well over 10 percent of the variable cost of producing our beer. Larger breweries have made great strides to operate more effectively and efficiently in terms of energy usage and recovery. Microbrewers aren't able to operate as efficiently as large breweries, but a small brewery can take certain measures to conserve energy, water, and raw materials. Sometimes this involves a capital expenditure that may seem unjustified, but often the extra expense is amortized in a short period of time by decreased energy and water costs.

Brewery size dictates to a great extent how it will be powered. A small brewpub might have a direct, gas-fired brew kettle and a hot-water heater, and a large, multi-million-barrel breweries might have their own power plants. For microbreweries the best answer lies somewhere in between. A steam boiler is a good choice for larger microbreweries, as process steam is needed not only for heating the brewing vessels, but also for packaging lines and sterilization. Steam boilers come in a variety of shapes and sizes. Keep a few things in mind when deciding on what type of steam boiler to install. High-pressure steam boilers are more efficient, but they also cost more. In most places local codes require a full-time certified boiler operator be on hand when the boiler is operating. There's no reason why one or more of the brewers can't obtain certification. High-pressure (i.e., high-temperature) steam is also better for sterilizing than low-pressure steam. If you're a brewpub or small-scale micro, a low-pressure boiler is adequate. Boilers usually require water treatment of some kind, particularly high-pressure boilers. By the time you add in piping, a condensate system, insulation, and a chemical feed system, you can easily double the price of what you would have paid for the boiler alone.

With refrigeration systems the choices are more limited because using ammonia as a refrigerant is out of the question for small breweries. Ammonia has a very high volumetric cooling capacity, and it is difficult for small systems to regulate. Most small brewers use chloroflourocarbons as refrigerants. Despite the bad press these refrigerants have received in the last few years, there aren't any alternatives at the moment. The best thing the brewery owner can do is make sure the cooling plant is free from leaks, and that if any leaks do arise, they are repaired quickly to avoid contributing to ozone depletion and to save on the cost of constantly refilling the system with refrigerant.

The brewer has a choice when selecting the condenser, evaporator, and coolant. If the cost of water is prohibitively high, an air-cooled condenser is the best option. In Colorado we're obligated to use air-cooled or evaporative systems. Otherwise, water-cooled condensers are standard equipment. Water at the freezing point is a good coolant because it is cheap, chemically inert, and can be stored in large quantities in an ice bath. This is advantageous when it is time to cool the wort. Brine mixtures are often implemented, and alcohol-water mixtures are a very popular coolant choice among micro-brewers to lower the coolant temperature well below 32 degrees F (0 degrees C). In either case, take precautions to avoid corrosion of the cooling system. Non-corrosive brines are available, but they are more expensive than the chloride-based brines. Add inhibitors added to alcohol-water mixtures to prevent corrosion.

All but the tiniest and simplest micro-breweries will need a source of compressed air. At Tabernash we use compressed air to operate pneumatic valves, to raise and lower our lauter tun rakes, to operate our kegging machine, and to aerate our wort. To preserve the life of our equipment we have water coalescers for the compressed air. To preserve the integrity of our beer, we also have an oil coalescer and an in-line sterile filter just prior to wort aeration.

A source of CO_2 is also necessary for large and small breweries. This CO_2 is used for dispensing keg beer, pressurizing tanks, purging equipment and transfer lines of air, operating packaging equipment, and carbonating beer. Unless your brewery is tiny, you probably want to avoid using fifty-pound cylinders. Bulk tanks usually offer a less expensive way of having five hundred pounds on reserve. Some brewers consider tanks larger than this. The investment won't be cheap, but if you use a lot of CO_2, it will pay for itself quickly through lower CO_2 cost per pound. It's also critical to have appropriate gauges and regulators at each point that the CO_2 is used.

The Laboratory

No matter how small or simple a brewery may be, some sort of analyses are conducted. I've actually heard some brewpubs don't have thermometers or hydrometers. This is incomprehensible, and I'm sure those outfits won't be around long enough to read this. Measuring density and temperature are the bare bones minimum that every brewery, large or small, needs to have. Some means of measuring pH is also extremely useful. A lot can be done to improve quality and consistency if pH is measured at a few key steps in the beermaking process. Every brewery should also do some basic microscopy to determine the biological quality of its beer. Using culture media to screen for wild yeast and beer-spoiling bacteria is another way of monitoring quality and consistency and is also a good reason to have a microscope. At the bare minimum, use microscopy in conjunction with media tests to evaluate the yeast culture, green beer, filtered beer, and packaged beer. Ideally, conduct culture tests at each step of the post–brew house production process to ensure the brewery and beer are free from infection.

Also consider malt analyses, and if you lack the equipment needed to analyze your malt, independent labs are of service. If even only periodical, these tests help monitor the quality of brewing ingredients and serve as a basis for comparing the lab values that the suppliers provide against those found in an independent analysis. Analyses of the grist are both inexpensive and insightful if yields are off or if conversion isn't achieved in the brew house. Analyses of spent grains are also simple and very insightful in this regard.

If you bottle or keg beer, it is wise to conduct tests to indicate the foreseeable shelf life of the beer, air uptake during the filtering and bottling processes, and if the desired degree of carbonation has been achieved. The possible analyses don't end here, but a microbrewery's budget probably won't include more complicated and specific analyses.

Raw Materials for Brewing Beer

Water. Beer is more than 90 percent water, so brewing water must be at least of drinking-water quality. Unless a brewery is lucky enough to have its own water source, it must be purchased from the local water works. The ion composition of water varies greatly from region to region, and indeed this has had a great influence on the character of classic beer styles throughout the world. Consider this when deciding which beer styles your brewery will produce. In some cases the water is either completely unacceptable or the water quality isn't suitable for the beer type to be brewed, so it must be treated.

One popular option among microbrewers is adding mineral salts to the brewing water to adjust its composition. If the water is too hard for the desired beer style, it can be softened in a number of ways. The addition of slaked lime is a cheap and simple method of softening water, though its application has limitations and is messy. A modern alternative is the use of an ion exchanger. Depending on the type of exchanger, it can soften water and remove undesirable ions such as nitrate or completely desalinate the water. Electro- or reverse-osmosis systems are usually too costly for small brewers. Aeration can remove troublesome ions such as iron or manganese. This helps precipitate these ions out of solution in hydroxide form, and the water can be subsequently filtered. Chlorinated water is best treated by active charcoal filtration.

If the water's biological quality is doubtful or sterile process water is desired, there are a number of possibilities. One of the most common water-sterilization practices is to use chlorine gas or hypochlorite solutions. Although this is a relatively cheap procedure, the taste of the water can be affected. Using ozone or ultraviolet radiation to improve the biological quality of the water will not affect the flavor, but these procedures are more expensive. Filtering can also be very effective for water sterilization. If the local water supply is being tapped for brewing water, chances are it will be biologically sound; however, to achieve maximum shelf life out of bottled beer, I recommend sterilizing process water.

At any rate, an analysis of the brewing water is necessary to decide which type of beer to make and how to treat the water. It is also important to make sure that your water is free from harmful substances. If a consumer or the press discovers the beer contains cadmium, plutonium, or pesticide residues before you do, you might have to close the doors for awhile. I strongly recommend having at least an activated charcoal filter for your source of brewing water. If your water is heavily contaminated, this won't cure your problem but it can help to catch unwanted trace compounds and microbes in your brewing water. It is also important to conduct water analyses on a running basis to monitor the effect of water treatment and to compensate for possible fluctuations in the water supply's quality.

Malt and cereal grains. The supply of malt is quite large, simply because it is a commodity that has been modified to suit the needs of the brewing, distilling, and food industries worldwide. Because it is a commodity, malt prices are fairly consistent within a given market. Pale malt is the least expensive and most widely used type of malt, and if you pay more than thirty cents to thirty-five cents per pound for it, you're being taken for a ride. Nonetheless, not all malted barley is the same, and the brewer must carefully select grains for the desired type of beer to ensure the quality of the finished beer is at its highest.

To select a malt supplier, establish a set of criteria — including parameters such as malt quality, cost, terms of delivery, minimum order requirement, terms of payment, etc. — and determine which suppliers fulfill those needs. Other factors to consider are the supplier's market reputation, rebates, and support. If you plan to use unmalted cereal grains, the selection process needn't be as intense, as those items are pure commodities. Consider only those grains suitable for brewing. In certain cases it may be wise to test grains from different suppliers by doing small-scale brews.

Hops. Since hops are also a commodity, such factors as the year, the growing region, and the type influence the quality. Prices from different suppliers won't vary greatly, so mainly consider the hop type and in which form it is used and your comfort level with the supplier you choose. More and more hop suppliers that ignored the craft-beer industry five years ago are now concentrating their sales efforts on the growing number of small customers. The style of beer to be made greatly dictates which type of hop to use. Bittering hops are usually used in the main boil, and aroma hops are added toward the end. Some brewers make certain beers using either bittering or aroma hops exclusively. There are a variety of hop products available, but they are all derivatives of the three main products: the natural hop cone, pellets, or hop extract. These products present a variety of advantages and disadvantages depending on the brewer's needs, and hop suppliers willingly discuss these points in detail with the brewer. If hop cones or pellets are used, refrigeration is essential during storage, particularly if they are stored for long periods of time.

Yeast. The type of yeast used to ferment wort greatly influences the flavor, body, color, and foam of the finished beer. The physiological condition of the yeast also greatly affects the character of the final product. Yeast management is a complex science. Don't underestimate it when operating a large or small brewery.

The two main groups of yeast are divided into top-fermenting *Saccharomyces cerevisiae* and bottom-fermenting *Saccharomyces uvarum* (*S. carlsbergensis*). Within these two large groups of yeast, there are countless species that the brewer can select. They vary in fermentation power; fermentation speed; their production of fermentation byproducts and flavors; their influence on beer pH, foam, and color; and their ability to flocculate and sediment. Several strains have proven themselves well in breweries around the world, and the microbrewer should consider one of these before experimenting with less proven strains. Several labs, some of which are reputable, culture and sell pure strains of brewing yeast. Selecting the yeast type and source is a decision that should be well thought out and researched.

Yeast propagation and management are serious considerations. The larger the brewery, the more involved the propagation facility must be. But even in the simplest breweries, some sort of equipment is needed to propagate yeast. There are varying schools of thought regarding self propagation of yeast (not to be confused with self-determination of man). Propagating the yeast yourself allows you to completely monitor the yeast from start to finish. If a problem does arise during propagation, adjustments can be made. Another big advantage to propagating your own yeast is you can grow exactly the quantity you need. As far as I'm concerned, if you have to propagate yeast once after you get a "ready to pitch" amount from a yeast supplier, you might as well start from a test tube. The two big drawbacks to self propagation of yeast are the labor intensiveness and the risk of infection every time you transfer the yeast to the next vessel in the propagation scheme. I'm biased toward self propagation, probably because that's what I implemented at Tabernash. My general recommendation is: If you're a micro, self propagate. If you're a brewpub, buy the ready pitch stuff.

Once the yeast is used for brewing, store it properly. Store yeast at certain temperatures, in certain substrates, and for a given length of time to ensure optimal performance. Store yeast in a sterile environment. Use a microscope and a culture test to control the purity of all pitched yeast. Controlling yeast virility is also a good idea.

Staffing the Brewery

Microbreweries often begin as small operations that are unable to budget for staffing each individual department, area of accountability, or specific job. Sometimes owners and investors work long hours performing a variety of tasks in every department of the brewery. Ideally this is part of the impetus for owning and operating your own brewery. However, hard work alone is seldom enough to start and maintain a successful brewery. Knowledge and experience are essential for planning and making decisions, not only on the technical end of the brewery but on the business side as well.

Brewing is an art requiring a bit of feeling and touch but is also a science requiring some insight into the technology involved in making and packaging beer. Individuals who have little more than extensive homebrewing experience operate many successful breweries. Just as many breweries have encountered difficulties because of inexperience in operating a facility in which hundreds of thousands (if not millions) of dollars have been invested. Just because someone has extensive experience or education as a brewer doesn't mean they are the best person for the job. There are a number of possibilities for staffing a brewery, and in the end no one solution may be any better or worse than the next. Do an extensive analysis of what tasks must be performed, what qualifications are necessary, what the labor cost structure of the company can tolerate, and most importantly, who will receive a paycheck from the brewery for working there.

If certain tasks in the brewery remain uncovered, someone within the company must augment their knowledge and skill, or you must tap some external source. In this case there are a number of options. For one, equipment suppliers often provide a great deal of support to their customers if they are service oriented and financially compensated for providing this service. Buying more expensive brewery equipment may be justified if the equipment suppliers are helpful and supportive not only during brewery installation, but after the operation is up and running.

Another option is to hire a consultant to help design and install the brewery, formulate the beers, educate the personnel, provide troubleshooting assistance, or locate qualified brewers. Caution must be taken, as dishonest consultants have burned many. Research the background of any consultant or supplier you may employ. A popular option is to hire a "brewmaster" to plan, organize, and operate the brewery. As with suppliers and consultants, brewmasters come in all shapes and sizes with varying degrees of education, experience, and success. It is best to seek out a brewer or brewmaster who is affordable and best qualified to execute the tasks required.

The microbrewing industry has a high potential for growth, otherwise you probably wouldn't be reading this. You will obviously hand select your first employees, but where a lot of growing companies drop the ball is how and who they hire during the hyper-growth years. I've built the finest production team in the country by using a combination of good draft choices and key free-agent acquisitions. I "scouted" my draft choices by letting people "apprentice" in the brewery for a short period of time. I can see how they work, and the other brewers can see what they're like to work with. It's not always easy to build a winning team on draft picks alone, so occasionally I'll pick up a free agent. Sometimes direct experience is great, but other times relevant experience is just as good, if not better. Promoting from within is also something we try to do as much as possible. One of my brewers used to be a delivery driver. They key thing is to select the best people possible who are in strong accord with the mission or goal of the company.

Of course brewers don't work for beer and smiles alone. Usually the best people also get paid the most, but balance this with maintaining production efficiency. One strategy we employ at Tabernash is an employee stock option plan. If departments and the entire company meets certain goals, we grant options. This is a good way of conserving cash, keeping key people, and most importantly, giving employees a feeling of being critical to the company accomplishing its goals. What type of wage you pay your brewery personnel all comes down to your business philosophies. Remember, however, that labor will be one of your top three cost areas for beer production. But before you get any ideas of paying your brewers minimum wage, remember it is very expensive to train new people.

The supply of trained brewers is catching up with the industry's demand in North America. Five years ago it was a much different story, but now there's a good crop of journeymen brewers and those who have completed brewing programs at universities or institutes. Take your time, there's a big pool of good people. Ultimately your brewer has to be qualified, a team player, and you have to be able to work with him or her.

One final tip: If you run across someone who can weld, has experience as a plumber, carpenter, mechanic, mason, and electrician, can fix your car, makes great coffee, and knows where all the best fishing holes are, hire him or her on the spot. A brewery is full of all kinds of machines, plumbing, and structures that will require repair at some inopportune time. If a full-time and capable employee is on hand at the moment of malfunction, hundreds if not thousands of dollars can be saved.

The First Brews

Once you have installed the equipment, placated the building inspectors (Notice how I didn't say you have your certificate of occupancy. "We're not brewing Mr./Ms. inspector. We're testing the equipment." One thing to always keep in mind on your development project is tradesmen and inspectors usually all love beer.), and can't stand another day of all that money going out with none coming in, experimental brewing can begin. Design the recipe formulation for the system installed and modify the recipes based on empirical observations of initial brews. Recipes should not be scaled upward linearly from small-scale experimental brews, as yields will increase with brew house size and sophistication. This is particularly true with hop yields. Our first batch of our assertively hopped helles ended up like a Pils, even after I had compensated for an increase in hop yield. If you buy a small brewery, don't expect to get stellar yields from your malt. If your brewery is larger and has been built by a top manufacturer, expect your yield difference to be 2 percent or less. This percentage is the difference between laboratory yield and the yield of the system using the same malt.

If your brewery produces a number of different beers, it is inconceivable to make test brews for every style but make a few brews to ensure the production process will run smoothly and the finished beers will be of the desired taste and quality. The type of brewery warrants the intensity of test brewing to a large extent. Even if equipment is able to be cleaned in place, it is best to manually clean as much of the equipment as possible before CIPing the systems. Some like to conduct water brews prior to brewing. Test brews don't necessarily have to be dumped — unacceptable ones can be blended. Common problems to look for in test brews are poor head retention, metallic flavors, and a rubbery-plastic taste. At Tabernash we perform a thorough manual cleaning before CIPing, and some still say the first batch of weiss was our best. A freestanding brewery making one product to be marketed over a large area must perfect the process until product consistency is achieved. The allure of local brewpubs lies in the fact that each brew is a bit different from the next, so the test brews themselves can usually be sold unless they have yielded an undrinkable beer. Touting the beer as the "very first beer ever made from our brewpub" should generate sufficient interest in the product.

As is the case with everything in life, and as you will certainly notice during your construction phase, stuff takes longer to get done than you think. Remember this when testing your equipment. If you're lucky, delays may only be a few hours or a day. With bigger systems like a high-tech bottling line, it may take months before the system has all of the bugs worked out of it. The key thing to know is how long it will take before the system is functional enough to do what it's supposed to and produce the quality product you look for. Whenever I bring a new system on board I do a few things to make sure everything goes "relatively" smoothly, and start-up delays are kept to a minimum.

Brewery Byproducts and Environmental Issues

The brewing process generates many byproducts and waste that occur in all three physical states of matter: solid, liquid, and gaseous. Consider how to use, recycle, or dispose of these products. Brewing and packaging beer also require much energy. Take measures to recover heat and reduce energy consumption wherever possible.

The most readily apparent brewery byproducts are the solid ones, most notably spent grains, grain dust, hot trub, spent hop cones, excess yeast, and DE. All of these can be used as livestock feed, which is the most common procedure for disposing of these byproducts. The spent grains have long been used as an inexpensive source of protein and carbohydrates for livestock. Many breweries sell spent grains to local farmers or feed producers, and even if local farmers don't pay for the spent grains, they will at least come and remove them at no charge, saving the brewery disposal costs. Breweries nestled in the midst of urban sprawl may have difficulties with disposal, as farmers are not often interested in a long drive to the city for a small amount of grain. One solution is to store the grains until enough have accumulated to make it worth the drive. A spent grain silo is typically used for storage, but it must be hosed out and cleaned regularly, as rotting spent grains host large, offensive-smelling colonies of microorganisms.

Trub matter from the brew house is rich in protein and is a valuable agricultural product. Due to the extreme bitterness of the hot trub, it must be sparingly dosed into the rest of the feed or else the animals will reject it. Some breweries even use the hot trub in the next mash to leach the remaining extract and bittering substances from it. Farmer or the pharmaceutical and cosmetics industries can also use spent or excess yeast. Smaller breweries have to rely on giving the yeast to farmers for it to be meted into the feed in small amounts. An overdose of yeast will give livestock stomach problems and deplete the animals' vitamin supply. Do not simply waste the yeast down the drain. Any brewer who does so and also claims to be an environmentalist speaks with a forked tongue, as the extremely high biological oxygen demand (BOD) of yeast makes it very troublesome to the friends down at the local wastewater treatment facility. If the yeast is put directly into a local stream or lake, it will contribute to the oxygen depletion of these waterways. DE is basically like sand, and washing it down the drain is not the best idea. Stock can digest the yeast/DE mixture, or it can be disposed of as solid waste.

One of the most troublesome brewery byproducts is the liquid waste, namely waste water and beer. The brewing process requires five to ten times more water than the amount of beer produced. An efficient, conscientious brewery strives for five times the water, while a sloppy, poorly managed operation will use ten times. Even if fresh water is cheap and waste water isn't taxed by volume, the brewery should strive for minimal water usage. The day will soon come when water is no longer cheap, and bad habits are hard to change. There are a number of ways to decrease water usage without compromising beer quality. One easy way to save water is repair all leaks immediately. "We'll take care of that tomorrow" turns into next week, then next month, and so on. Another solution is to avoid oversparging. Also, a properly sized heat exchanger for wort cooling yields only as much water (or slightly more) as the amount of wort being cooled. CIP systems that recycle detergent and rinse water for pre-wash purposes can reduce usage of cleaning water. The water hog in any brewery is the bottle washer. The water can be recycled for first rinse water, cleaning vehicles, flushing toilets, washing floors, etc. Bear in mind the more fresh water that is used, the higher the effluent will be.

Gaseous brewery byproducts come in two main forms: CO_2 from fermentation and smoke from the boiler or direct fire burner. Unfortunately, CO_2 recovery plants are only amortizable for breweries whose production exceeds fifty thousand barrels of beer per annum. This should not worry the environmentally conscious brewer, as CO_2 in the atmosphere from fermentation is negligible when compared to the amount of CO_2 generated from burning fossil fuels. Breweries, large and small, *can* have an impact on air pollution in the latter area, however. Local and federal laws dictate how clean boiler vapors must be. Natural gas is currently the cleanest fuel used to power breweries, as it produces virtually no sulfur dioxide, a leading cause of acid rain. The boiler should also operate with the proper air to fuel ratio in the burn. If it is not optimal, nitrous oxide and hydrocarbon emissions will be higher than needed, and fuel consumption will increase. Catalytic converters, filters, and desulfrication plants are a few examples of how emissions can be reduced or converted into less harmful compounds.

Ensuring efficient boiler function is only one of many ways to reduce energy usage. Boilers can be designed very efficiently in terms of primary energy usage. Designs that maximize the thoroughness of burn and use flue gases to preheat the air or feed water are helpful in this area. Brew-house design has the greatest influence on primary energy usage of any brewery department. Basic insulation of vessels and piping is an easy way to save energy. Boiling under atmospheric pressure with no type of vapor recovery system is very consumptive.

Simple designs that either boil under pressure and/or recover the heat in vapors from the brew kettle will reduce primary energy input. Overboiling increases energy usage and only under certain conditions — such as high coagulable protein amounts in the wort, high altitude breweries, or a dangerously high level of DMS precursor — should wort be boiled longer than one hundred minutes. Larger breweries may consider a system that incorporates an external boiler with vapor compression. A properly designed wort chiller attains maximal heat recovery. If pasteurization is considered, then flash pasteurization is the clear choice. It is the most efficient form of pasteurization in terms of heat recovery and is the least detrimental to beer flavor.

With increasing public awareness of environmental issues, every brewery must be concerned with public reaction to the facility and soundness of the brewing procedures. It also makes good bottom-line sense to operate as efficiently as possible.

Bibliography

Narziss, Ludwig. *Abriss der Bierbrauerei.* Ferdinand Enke Verlag, Stuttgart: Federal Republic of Germany, 1986.

Pensel, S. Kaelteanlagen. Prepared reading for lecture on cooling plants, 1990.

Chapter 2
Building a Microbrewery: Planning, Appropriate Financing, Feasibility

by Will Kemper
Independent Contractor

A great deal of work goes into each and every brewery before any beer reaches the consumer. The nature of this work involves planning, financing, and feasibility studies. This work requires thousands of hours for virtually every brewery. The magnitude of this commitment as well as the implications for success or failure make these preoperational activities extremely important.

Planning

Pasteur said, "Chance favors those who plan." Whether through chance, luck, or sheer persistence, a microbrewery's degree of success is greatly influenced by the quality and thoroughness of the planning. Insufficient planning can lead to its demise.

A successful microbrewery, like all successful manufacturing entities, combines three critical components into a powerful and effective force. These components are a commercially acceptable product(s), the sales capability necessary to establish ongoing sales to bring in necessary revenues, and the business savvy to manage the survival and growth of the business. The overall strength is mostly determined by which quality is weakest. Like a chain, it is only as strong as the weakest link. Certainly the best scenario is when all three entities are strong and working in a synergistic fashion.

In the first edition of the *Brewery Planner*, Mike Coulter presented a nine-step sequential approach to the planning and implementation of a start-up brewery. The nine steps are:

1. Conceptual examination
2. Market examination
3. Feasibility examination
4. Project justification
5. Financing
6. Project planning
7. Construction and implementation
8. Final inspection and testing, and
9. Operational management (commissioning, start-up, and operations)

While each of these sequences can be further broken down, and there is an overlapping of the various steps, this approach is certainly valid. Each existing microbrewery has gone through these steps in one form or another, and the degree of success or failure can often be attributed to how well each of these steps has been addressed.

With any new business there are questions as to functional adequacy and market share possibility. Also, the issue for any potential microbrewer should be whether or not a new brewery can fit into the existing and expanding marketplace. If a brewery is competent and professional in the important ways business is conducted, there should be a high level of success, whether it is a new brewery or a well-established one. A highly expanding market presents opportunity for those best suited to address the desires of the market. Planning should strive to be thorough in answering those important questions.

Financing

Microbreweries exist within a wide range of start-up structures. There are multimillion-dollar, state-of-the-art breweries as well as scavenged, bare-bone-budgeted facilities. There are success and failure stories with either extreme as well as in between.

Whether or not a microbrewery is successful depends on objectives of the people involved. There can be distinctly different agendas and goals for the many different microbreweries. Some breweries are being established solely to capitalize on the economic growth within the industry — thinking they will make a fast buck. Still others are created from an extreme passion for brewing or the romantic idea of just establishing a brewery. The journey for one side is to leverage the situation into as much profit as fast as possible. The journey for the other side is to have a life within a brewery. If success is defined as the attainment of goals then success is obviously very different for the two extremes identified herein.

The appropriate financing necessary to accomplish the intended goals can also be very different. Besides the basic operational philosophies addressed above, issues such as sizing, return on investment, and feasibility have to be addressed in order to determine the appropriate financing.

How funds are spent or misspent go a long way in determining the quality of the end result. As with worker performance, there is an extremely wide range of efficiency in how brewery expenditures work. The cliché "You get what you pay for" has been proven valid time and again. A cheap approach will likely lead to a cheap product. There are also many cases whereby moneys were lavishly spent on inadequate equipment or extravagantly wasted within other areas. Inappropriate usage of funds goes with a lack of knowledge of how money can be effectively used within a given area.

For example, a key funding element is site identification. Microbreweries can obviously spend a considerable amount for brewing equipment, but they will spend as much as, less than, and at times, more for site preparation than for equipment. Excessive site spending is usually realized well within the project and at a point of no turning back. This can impact whether or not the venture is underfinanced or if significant changes have to be made in other areas. Significant changes or compromises to offset excessive site spending may affect efficiency or product quality.

For a base funding level the amount should be such that the venture is not underfinanced. This is the reason most businesses, including breweries, fail. Therefore, a fundamental question for anyone trying to establish a microbrewery is, what is that amount? Because of the many ways in which funds are used or misused, it is easy to see how a minimum funding level for one venture might be twice as much as a similar venture even though there is a comparable scale and scope of operations.

The funding needed is ultimately determined by the adequacy or know-how of the individuals involved in the project. Competent people can do a lot more with fewer resources than less competent people. Normally, people have varying degrees of capability regarding business, sales, and production. Highly competent individuals in one area can be useless or even counterproductive in other areas.

The craft-brewing industry has evolved into a much more sophisticated industry than what it was only a few years ago. If a company does not have a professional level of understanding for the various aspects of business, sales, and production, this will result in added costs stemming from mistakes. Knowledge costs, either by acquisition or the lack thereof.

Feasibility

Feasibility in planning addresses the likelihood of a proposed project being successful. Proper planning should ultimately lead to a conclusion that success is both realistic and likely. A feasible business plan should thus be realistic and likely to succeed.

In the planning stages it can be difficult to correctly gauge feasibility. Most feasibility assessments are based on information which is assumed to be pertinent or valid. If the base information is false, misleading, or not applicable to the project or the issues at hand, feasibility is affected. There are often significant differences between a proposed microbrewery, as addressed within a business plan, and the actual microbrewery. Because of these pitfalls, knowledge and familiarity become the valuable tools used for business planning and feasibility studies.

Feasibility studies by potential microbreweries are often not realistic. While such studies may provide a general overview of a microbrewery within the industry, they generally lack the specificity necessary to provide a meaningful evaluation for the intended facility's practicality. It is impossible to forecast all the circumstances and conditions which a microbrewery will face, but it is foolhardy to waste time and money establishing a business plan that is not workable.

A feasible plan cannot be created without adequately addressing the three main areas necessary for the success of the operating microbrewery — business, sales, and brewing expertise. When operations commence, if any one of these main areas is not ultimately conducted in a professional and competent manner, the venture is quite likely doomed. It is far better to realize shortcomings during planning instead of afterwards.

Business. The business planning side of the operation will work to establish the initial financial structure of the business and later to maintain the necessary ongoing financial needs. A business plan also serves as the coordinating influence for sales and production.

The sales side of the microbrewery has to work to find and maintain accounts. A microbrewery is established to sell its products to others for them to sell. Assuming adequate sales without a competent sales strategy is one of the quickest ways to grind to a sudden halt.

The production side has to work to supply a consistently good commercial product for the consumer. If this is not adequately done, the business and sales sides will not be able to thrive due to the obvious limitations.

Until production commences, much of the planning stages are strictly business evaluations. Wise business decisions are based on input from the sales and production areas. If there are disregards as to the importance of sales or production along the way, the eventual operating microbrewery will suffer. Any neglected area will likely become inadequate within the overall business operations.

Sales. The sales projections originate from existing sales information. Fortunately such information is readily available. What is not shown within those numbers is the effort involved in realizing such sales. The significant numbers posted by the successful microbreweries are a result of sophisticated marketing by experienced sales people. With virtually all cases, those numbers are the result of internal company sales.

A common scenario is that new microbreweries are approached and asked to be represented by distributors. This is an exciting time for a new microbrewery when it seems as if a distributor will take the company brands and open up all sorts of accounts. After all, the distributor already serves the accounts, and the microbrewery's brands will be easy to add to the existing accounts. Because of this rosy situation it hardly seems necessary to even add a sales force.

With that thinking many a microbrewery has been content to wait for those orders that never came. The reality is that distributors wish to expand their line, and while certain accounts will be added by the distributor, the microbrewery needs to promote its own products in order to survive and grow. It should be thought that the distributor simply stores and delivers beer. Sales and promotion have to be accomplished internally. Whatever the distributor is able to add in terms of accounts is a bonus. Survival depends on sales generated by the microbrewery.

Pricing considerations can have a big impact on survivability. In the early and mid-1980s the microbreweries in the Pacific Northwest were selling their beers to distributors for approximately $60 to $70 per half-barrel. In other areas of the country microbreweries were selling their beers for around $40 per half-barrel. Costs of production for all the microbreweries were similar. Several of those Pacific Northwest microbreweries are now quite large while the lower priced microbreweries, if they are still around, are not nearly as large. Lower prices did not translate into more demand, and any profit margin was easily absorbed if and when an unforeseen problem arose. Nowadays, pricing within a region is fairly well established, and it would be difficult to reestablish higher levels.

However, arguments will always be proposed for price lowering. The theory of price versus demand will always be used whether for a start-up or during slow sales times. For the microbrewery segment, slight price variations do not make a difference. What does make a difference with lower pricing is how price-off promotions work. These are well calculated and reoccurring events designed to give consumers the impression that they are getting a bargain. By being priced too low a brewery's options concerning price promotions or other price changes are limited.

Brewing expertise. Oversimplification with equipment purchases and production will also affect feasibility. Without an intelligent regard for production, shortcomings will occur in efficiency and product quality. Lack of efficiency detracts from capacity or production-level capabilities. A lower quality product results when technical considerations are not addressed. Both shortcomings will obviously affect bottom-line results or potential.

It is fascinating to see the number of people designing breweries and brewing equipment who have never commercially brewed beer or studied brewing sciences. This is comparable to people who have never sold anything instructing others on how to sell, or someone who has never run a business explaining how to run the microbrewery.

When designing equipment, performance should address engineering as well as specific technical brewing considerations. These are not necessarily compatible. Oftentimes an engineer's focus does not take into account desired technical specifications. There are a number of different manufacturing steps with brewing, and desired or undesired chemical profiles are determined by the production conditions and techniques as well as the materials used. If a design is too skewed for a particular intent, the resulting implementation of the design can very easily affect beer quality. Microbreweries can be overengineered and underengineered.

However, a brewer's perspective might also be insufficient. Many capable brewers can work within a given brewery setting, but they are lost when it comes to engineering. For any brewpub, microbrewery, or large brewery that manufacturers a consistently good product efficiently, there had to have been a considerable amount of engineering thinking that went into the design and operation. There is no other way. The need for adequate engineering input is so recognized that within the beverage industry there is a saying that farmers make wine, and engineers make beer.

A well-engineered system is both efficient and capable of the necessary production levels required. Efficiency translates into ease of production. There is a cohesiveness of the manufacturing program. Additionally, worker input levels should not be too cumbersome. If workers are too involved with having to constantly deal with incidental tasks, or if the brewery is too physically demanding, areas such as quality control and laboratory support tend to decline. Plant capacity is reduced, and operating expenses are increased with an inefficient operation. For aggressive projections it is imperative to have a highly efficient brewing system.

Feasibility assumes a product which is competitive within the market. Can the brewery supply the product that is correct for the market? Does the brewing system satisfy the technical issues? Shortcomings of the production system will result in inefficiencies and/or a less marketable product by creating a technically flawed product.

Technical issues include thermodynamics, material handling, process monitoring, reproducibility, raw materials, laboratory support, fermentation, fluid dynamics, filtration, packaging, and chemistry. Undesirable results within any one of these areas will adversely affect production efficiency and product quality. A few of the many common shortcomings that may seem insignificant but adversely affect beer quality include:

1. Failure of the brewhouse to achieve correct temperatures and heat exchange
2. Excessive oxygen pickup in the brewhouse, conditioning, and packaging areas
3. Extended hot wort manufacturing and handling times
4. Insufficient cold wort aeration or oxygenation
5. Excessive trub carry-over during vessel transfers
6. Incorrect read out of monitoring instruments
7. Fermentation and aging temperatures not properly controlled
8. Insufficient refrigeration (especially during the summer)
9. Chemical make-up of brewing liquor not properly addressed
10. Yeast deficiencies (viability, concentration, handling, storage, nutrients, etc.)
11. Reoccurring equipment failure

Some of these problems may ultimately lead to more serious situations whereby the product is not marketable. Such product is not salvageable if this point is reached. The problem is compounded much further if the flawed product reaches the consumer. Besides the obvious loss of revenue, the future of the microbrewery is severely cast in doubt when these instances arise. There are examples of large well-established breweries going out of business when this occurred.

To be a strong and successful microbrewery the three main areas of business, sales, and production all need to be working in harmony. All weak links related to those operations need to be recognized and remedied. With the increasing number of micros, it is even more important that planning be done with foresight, adequate financing secured, and reasonable feasibility studies conducted.

Chapter 3
Building a Brewpub

by Jack Streich
Brewery Consultant

As I hold my empty pint glass up to the gleaming copper kettle, Irish lace comes to mind. A faint white ring marks the progression of each sip taken. Between the rings is a fine web of dried foam. To some this is a dirty beer glass, but to an experienced brewer this is a sign of excellence. As the bartender replaces the glass with another pint, the analysis starts afresh. Just like the one before, this beer is crystal clear with three-quarters of an inch of dense foam, a rich, malty flavor which gives way to a refreshing bitter bite, and a color which rivals the spotless brewing vessel beyond it.

The brewer who crafted this pint of beer analyzed the raw materials on hand, the capabilities and limitations of his brewing equipment, and with the end result in mind, determined how to best manipulate them in order to deliver the finest product to the customer.

The word "craft" is often misused in our industry. Crafting a beer involves much more than just following a recipe. It requires complete focus on the part of the craftsman. Constant recall of past experiences and education are part of the "crafting," decision-making process. It is often difficult for a craftsman to simply explain his decisions because they can derive from a complex lattice of information.

In 1994 I took a short-term position at a traditional German-style lager brewery. My prior experience producing English ales differed in many ways from the production of German lagers. In order to prepare myself for

the task at hand, I compiled a collection of personal notes, magazine articles, notes from telephone interviews with several colleagues, and a number of technical books on the subject of brewing lager beer. Drawing from my experience and my resources, I formed a detailed, but not rigid, plan for operating the brewery *before* I went to work. When I arrived at the site, I discovered that many of my hypotheses held true, but some of my ideas needed to be modified to fit the actual operation of the brewery.

The important thing was that I wasn't surprised by anything I encountered. I had prepared myself for the project, and was ready to confront any number of circumstances.

Producing lager beers came quickly to me because I had an intuitive, internalized idea of what the finished products should look and taste like. I also had an organized, but flexible plan for how to begin crafting a quality lager beer.

Just as I planned to craft a lager beer for the first time, so should an entrepreneur prepare for the complex task of building a brewpub. Instead of crafting a beer, business management guru Henry Mintzberg speaks of "crafting a strategy." A company draws from the experiences in which its constituents are strong and employs outside resources to lend expertise to areas where the company is less confident.

Throughout the planning process, the company *evolves*. The entrepreneur(s) has an intuitive feel for where the company will go, but there must be flexibility. They should look upon changes in the company's landscape as opportunities.

The advantage of "crafting" your company strategy, as compared to conventional business planning, is that the company has a common "feel" or identity for where it is headed, and developmental decisions can be made based on this identity. The focal point to which the organization must always return is quality beer. Every future step will be taken toward the end of developing a company whose identity is synonymous with quality beer. The size of the restaurant, the dining room layout, the menu, the location, etc. can change as long as the changes enhance the central theme of quality beer.

In the next several paragraphs I'll discuss the four components of the brewpub — the brewery, the kitchen, the dining area, and the office — and tie in planning strategies to help develop each area effectively.

The Brewery

The hub around which your business will be built is the brewery. Since your primary focus is on excellent beer, great care must be taken to create a brewery to be proud of.

If your company doesn't have an experienced brewer on board from the outset, then one must be found. There are several equipment manufacturers who will vie for your business. An experienced professional should analyze and compare bids from the various suppliers.

During the planning stage, make some fundamental decisions. In order for your brewer/consultant to properly solicit bids for brewing equipment, you must determine the styles of beer to be produced (different styles require different equipment), and how much beer of each kind is to be produced. These are critical decisions, and an experienced brewer should address them. Solicit as many bids from as many manufacturers as possible. Obviously, the size of the restaurant will determine the volume and style of beer to be produced, but there are other considerations to take into account as well.

Based on the size and layout of the building, projections can be made of approximate gross beer sales. However, other factors to look at, depending upon local and state laws, are:

1. Can you sell beer for takeout?
2. Can you sell kegs of beer to other retailers?
3. Can you sell bottles of beer to other retailers?
4. Can your dining room/bar area expand?

These are factors that will affect your annual production. Even if you don't plan to exploit these options initially, plan to be able to do so if you want to or need to in the future. Leave room for additional vessels if possible. Plan on having a small bottling line in the building eventually. Build in *flexibility*. The market may change over time, and you should be prepared to adapt to changes.

The Kitchen

The explosive growth of the brewpub sector of the brewing industry has shown us many successful formats for operating a brewpub kitchen. We've seen everything from sandwiches and chips, to four-star dining. Go with your strengths, but don't stray from your central focus of quality beer. The selected menu should complement your beer, not overshadow it. A friend recently dined at a brewpub with a high-priced fine dining room. "They brought me a twenty-dollar salmon steak with a Christmas tree of tarragon growing out of it and suggested a wine to go with it!" he blurted. "I forgot I was in a brewpub!"

The brewpubs most successful at connecting the kitchen and brewery are the ones with a healthy relationship between the chef and the head brewer. Without a relationship of mutual respect and *open lines of communication*, the customer will be slighted. A good brewer can develop a beer to complement a seasonal dish, just as a good chef can develop a dish to complement a seasonal beer.

Furthermore, a brewpub kitchen should not be an afterthought. A professional should plan the menu and purchase the equipment. Even if the restaurant will serve sandwiches and chips, consult a professional. Just as the brewery was sized and designed with the style of beer and the projected volume to be sold, so should the kitchen be planned.

The chef/restaurant consultant's agenda should be to:

1. develop a menu which complements the types of beer to be served with assistance from the president and the brewmaster.
2. maximize the use of space in the designated kitchen area.
3. set up efficient, manageable work stations which will minimize labor costs and preparation time.
4. purchase equipment which matches the selected menu and size it according to the projected number of meals to be served per day.
5. establish regularly scheduled meetings with the brewmaster to further the complementary relationship between the food and the beer.

The Dining Room/Bar

The dining room and bar of your brewpub are the face of your company. Customers do not judge their visit to the brewpub based simply on how good the beer or food was, but on their *entire* experience. Their experience generally doesn't include a tour of the kitchen or the brewery. (While I highly recommend offering tours, you'll find that a minute percentage of customers participate.) The dining and bar areas are where your customers will spend virtually all of their time. They are the sales floor, and every effort should be put forth to enhance your company's ability to sell products.

Designing and operating a successful bar and dining room are crucial components of your business. Again, do not take these tasks lightly and have a professional handle them. A restaurant and bar manager needs to work with the brewer and chef to bring the carefully prepared products to the customer in a tasteful, efficient presentation. This requires careful planning of the room(s)' layout, training of service staff, and diligent focus on the customers' needs.

While a tastefully decorated dining room is an important facet of your business, the decor is only part of what makes a well-run dining room and bar. When planning the layout, your restaurant manager or consultant should have several considerations in mind:

1. Customer comfort: Adequately space the tables so servers can move around them without disrupting the diners' enjoyable experience. Have the music system set up so that the manager can readily adjust it to suit the time of day and number of customers in the restaurant. Lay out the bar area so that servers do not disrupt drinkers when picking up and delivering drinks. Have the temperature of the dining area readily adjustable by the manager.
2. Easy flow of products to and from customers: Do not have the servers travel through congested bar or waiting areas with food and beverages. Carefully place the beer taps. Bartenders should not be queued up waiting for access to taps. Do not have bartenders travel back and forth to deliver large orders of drinks to wait staff. Situate service stations so that servers can quickly bring customers condiments, utensils, water, etc.
3. Cleanliness: The restaurant should remain spotless at all times; your staff should *never* be too busy to clean up a spill. Design the dining area so that it can be cleaned easily and thoroughly. Place mop and sponge stations where staff can readily access them in emergencies. Restrooms, restrooms, restrooms! Monitor, clean, and restock them *at least hourly*.
4. Server training: Your host staff, wait staff, and bar staff are probably the only people who will come in contact with your customers. Therefore, you count on these people to represent you, the owner. Train your staff to treat each customer as you

would treat them yourself. The server is a salesperson. Virtually all of the company's revenue derives from their efforts to encourage the customer to spend money in a pleasant, positive manner. There are a number of good training texts which one can refer to, and all of them reiterate the same theme: *Constant retraining of staff is a must.*

In the highly competitive restaurant industry, a knowledgeable staff is crucial. They should enthusiastically convey your positive message to the customer and have learned responses to commonly asked questions. A good server knows the components of each dish on the menu and can give a thorough description of each beer with several key words which the owner and brewer determine to convey to the customer.

Last, it is important to constantly remind the server that his or her job is the one which brings in virtually all of the revenue to the company. His or her appearance, disposition, preparedness to educate and serve the customer, and his or her drive to sell your products are what make the company successful.

The Office

A well-planned, well-run brewpub cannot be successful without an organized office. I regard the staff accountant as the anchor of a well-run office. The staff accountant is a watchdog for all of the department heads. The brewer, chef, restaurant manager, and maintenance director should look to the staff accountant as an ally, helping to cut costs and losses, and not as a censor.

Expedience is extremely important in the operation of a brewpub office. Department heads should inspect and sign off on invoices and then submit them to the staff accountant for processing (accounts payable, receivable, etc.). A good staff accountant will carefully inspect incoming bills, identify irregularities, and query department heads for explanations. Late payment penalties, interest, and overpay-

ment of bills can undermine all of a company's cost-cutting measures. Closely monitor payroll, employee benefits, tax payments, and account balances.

Like any other area of the brewpub, set up the office with efficiency in mind. Wherever possible, minimize paperwork. When selecting a computer system for restaurant operations, try to choose one that interfaces with your accounting software. Many dining-room computer systems cannot be downloaded into a personal computer and require time-consuming data entry.

Keep organized files of each vendor. Meticulously document tax payments and data, and file for audits by the company's accounting firm and government agencies.

A professional should operate the office, just like any other area of the brewpub. A good staff accountant will save you enough money to justify a good salary.

The Feasibility Study/ Appropriate Financing

Will this work? Can this venture generate enough money to pay your vendors, your taxes, your payroll, your insurance, your bank, your investors, and yourself? In short, is it feasible? There is no foolproof formula for opening a successful brewpub, but there are ways to predict costs, market trends in the area, and tendencies of potential customers.

The feasibility study is your way of showing investors that you have planned to use their money wisely and will show them a return on their investment. The sample business plan included in chapter 22 of this book will help you address the major points necessary to secure financing and will help you to create a budget for your project.

There are a number of questions which banks and investors will want answered. You must ask yourself these questions and come up with responses which will assure success to financiers. The ultimate question is, will this work? Demographic studies are an excellent tool for determining this.

Your local chamber of commerce and real estate broker have a tool they use called a demographic study. These studies are readily available at little or no charge. A demographic study is a listing of a specific area and some data about its population. Examples of useful data for a proposed site are the number of cars passing the site, average income of the residents, and breakdown of ages and races of constituents. The number of restaurants in the area, the degree of success they enjoy, the types of popular food, and the average cost of meals and drinks are also determining factors. You need to convince the investor that you know what the customers want and that you are prepared to supply it to them.

Another issue to address is the actual building in which you will build your brewpub. If it was a restaurant, why is it available and was it closed because of poor management, poor location, or other factors? Your business plan must reflect your response to this question.

While you compile information for the business plan, prepare a spreadsheet with projected costs of goods and services necessary to open the brewpub. This is your start-up budget. A certain amount of capital must be set aside for paying salaries, vendors, insurance, and rent before there is cash coming in and in the event of a slow start to your venture. This is working capital. The reason why so much importance has been placed on hiring experienced professionals during the planning stage of the start-up is that they can project costs accurately and can save money by avoiding expensive mistakes. In the planning stage of your business, develop a strong relationship with an accountant. A good accounting firm can take the information you have compiled with the help of your departmental experts and see to it that the numbers work to make the venture profitable.

Another necessary ally is a good lawyer. Set up a corporation complete with a partnership agreement. You will sign a number of contracts which your attorney needs to inspect.

A brewpub is a multifaceted business. There are several different departments that need to be set up properly. Crafting a strategy for opening and developing your business requires the cooperation of several professionals. The benefits provided by their expertise will offset the cost of consultants in the short run.

Bibliography

Mintzberg, Henry. *Mintzberg on Management: Inside Our Strange World of Organizations.* New York: The Free Press, 1989.

Suggested Reading

Sullivan, Jim, and Phil Roberts. *Service That Sells.* Denver: Pencom Incorporated, 1991.

Chapter 4
Tips for Starting a Microbrewery

by Marcy Larson
Managing General Partner of the Alaskan Brewery

A popular slogan up here is, "Alaska: land of the individual and other endangered species." I've often thought that statement had a lot in common with the microbrewery movement and its distinctively flavorful beers. Beers with unique character, full of taste, and something to say were very nearly snuffed out by the bland beers of an automated modern America. Then along came people like Jack McAuliffe and Fritz Maytag who let their individual personalities shine through in their beers. A pioneer spirit was awakened in the individual brewer, an identity quite different from the company brewer. To me, the strength of the microbrewery industry has always been its personality. And, it is upon the personality and individuality of its beers that a brewing business should be based.

Having said all that, it is up to you to use the following information accordingly. Everybody is different, and what works for one potential brewer may meet with disaster for another. This is not a "how to" essay, it is merely a "what worked for us" guide. Here are ten tips that helped us out.

The Written Word

Information is the single greatest resource available to a new venture. We subscribed to every brewing and beer publication we could get our hands on. It's rather overwhelming to discover how much is written about one subject. We started collecting books, magazines, and articles concerning the beer business seven years before we started our brewery. It cost a small fortune, but it was the best investment we made. We still subscribe to many of the periodicals, and every now and again I go back and reread our collection of old issues. It can be very enlightening.

Historical Lessons

Another area of information that radically impacted our business was the historical section in our local library. Our Alaskan Amber Beer originated in the Alaska State archives. It was pure luck, but I was able to find detailed records on one of the breweries that flourished here prior to Prohibition. We discovered methods of brewing that made a lot of sense to our specific location. Until that point, we had been reading about breweries in the Lower Forty-eight and had formulated our plans according to what was working for them. The archives discovery was really an eye opener, and it gave our beers that much more local character. We also learned about other ventures in the area that had not survived and tried to avoid the mistakes they had made. It would have been all too easy to have wandered down the same path.

School

I realized early on in our endeavors exactly where the priorities were. Two days after we were married, my husband, Geoff, flew off to Chicago to attend the Siebel Institute of Technology. We did go on a honeymoon after he got back, but in the meantime I continued working to pay for his education. And, what an education! He must have put on twenty pounds before he returned home. Seriously though, the folks at Siebel were really great. The instructors there provided our fledgling plans with a great base of knowledge. For us, they were not only good educators but also our first connection to the industry.

The Industry

We were impressed with people in the brewing industry right from the start. We all are in pursuit of better beer. Not everyone wants to produce distinctively different beers, as in the case of the company brewer, but we all are striving to improve whatever beer we brew. It is an ongoing art with many forms of expression. You can learn a lot from other brewers and suppliers if you are careful to not insult them. They worked hard for the insight and information they acquired. It is a slap in the face to expect them to hand it over to you. Some freely give and some are extremely reserved, but they have earned that right. If you can gain their respect, you will be able to tap into the real world of brewing.

Apprenticeships

Nothing beats working in a brewery prior to starting your own. If you can get paid to do it, all the better. But if you can't land a job in one, then sign up for an apprenticeship. Several small breweries are offering them. From my own point of view, the diverse impact a bunch of neophytes add to a streamlined operation isn't worth the money. We should know. We were neophytes at the Millstream Brewing Company six years ago, and I think that was the last time they offered an apprenticeship.

We pestered them with a thousand questions as we inefficiently "worked" at the brewery. Yes, there is a learning curve even if you've been to school and know how to homebrew. They were really nice to us and never lost patience, but I'm sure there was a collective sigh of relief when we finally left.

Paper and Balsa Wood

Ideas don't become plans until they are on paper. Once they are there they can suddenly look really awful. While the business plan is a great tool, it is also something most brewers dread. A business plan can help you avoid a bunch of mistakes in the start-up and can also create a working reference for the next five years. In the roller-coaster ride of our first few years of operation, we found ourselves digging out the business plan every few months as we made countless decisions on a rapid-fire schedule. What was amazing to us was how much we had actually thought of prior to getting underway. The other great tool was our balsa wood model. Geoff built the brewery to scale in model form first and made sure he could add things for growth. It's much easier to push around balsa wood tanks than the real thing.

Market Research

A subtext of the business plan is the marketing plan. To put together our marketing plan, we looked at demographics, shipping routes, state gallonage figures, margins, distributors, and then we went out and talked to our future customers. We have an interesting marketplace because Alaska is so spread out. As a comparison, just one county in the Seattle area has three times the population of the entire state of Alaska! Our beer has to travel over five hundred miles just to get to the next biggest town. With this kind of market, we knew we had to look at packaging constraints right from the beginning.

Rules and Regulations

The laws controlling alcohol are always changing. Make sure you get current copies of regulations when planning and then stay abreast of any updates. You have the Federal law, the state laws, and the local laws to contend with. We have found most administrators to be really reasonable if you are up front with them. They hate surprises. They also hate having to rush things through. So be sure to leave enough time to have all paper work and permits in order before sending out the invitations for your grand opening.

Personnel

Don't make the mistake of thinking you can do everything yourself, or you will die young. For us there was a tendency to schedule ourselves for twelve-hour days since we knew we could handle it. However, it is much better to plan for normal working schedules and let the overages happen than to plan on being superhuman. There are many hats to wear in a brewery: choose the ones you want to wear and hire out the rest. I'm not sure how we got so lucky, but we have a dynamite crew that has stayed with us from the start. We consider our staff to be our strongest asset.

Equipment and Supplies

As micros become more abundant, it gets easier and easier to find exactly what you need. We make it a policy to get three quotes before placing our initial order for any one item. It's surprising the variance you find if you look around. In planning your equipment needs, remember not to lock yourself in to any one size if at all possible. We've always tried to leave the door open for easy growth. JV Northwest did a fine job supplying us with custom-designed brewing equipment for our plant. And there are numerous used equipment suppliers as well.

When we were first starting, one old-timer showed us the time, work, and money triangle. It looks like this:

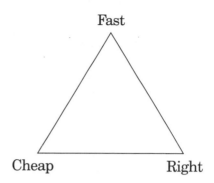

They are all connected, but you can only have two of them at the same time. For example: You can do it fast and right, but it'll cost you. Or you can do it cheap and right, but it'll take you forever. Or you can do it cheap and fast, but it won't be right. We found this useful in deciding what was important to save, and what we could look forward to giving up.

Most of what has been mentioned is plain common sense, but that's what worked for us. As I said before, I don't think there is a wrong way and a right way, there is just *your* way. After all, it's your beer! It should have your personality written all over it. So, *say something* and wake up another complacent consumer to good beer! Happy brewing!

Chapter 5
Contract Brewing

by Ted Marti
President and Brewmaster of August Schell Brewing Company

With the tremendous growth in demand for specialty beers during the past decade has come an equally impressive rekindling of the romantic spirit of brewing. Mash that in along with the lure of a tidy profit, and you have created today's craft-brewing movement. This movement, which came on the heels of some difficult times for small, old regional brewers, was able to benefit from regional brewers' ample, unused brewing capacity. The craft-brewing opportunity still exists for those with ideas and marketing expertise to create and build beer brands and styles, but who have neither the capital nor the desire to manage the brick and mortar of a brewing facility. This opportunity, however, is not as open as it once was. At smaller brewing facilities, where you generally have more flexibility and an easier entry into the beer business, unused capacity is filling up. Capacity at larger facilities is not as limited; however, their brew sizes are larger and present a slightly different set of problems for the potential contract brewer.

As a contract brewer, you need to be aware of two fairly elementary, but important, things. First, you need to either have an existing beer you want brewed or have a good idea of the type and style of beer you want and the sincere desire to develop it. It is important to remember that we are also brewers and are continually developing our own new brands and styles. It would be unusual for a commercial brewer to create and develop a new beer and then turn it over to a contract brewer.

Unfortunately, we as bigger brewers have a more limited opportunity to do the types of experimenting with different styles and ingredients that some of the smaller-scale operations may have. Nonetheless, the experience we have with our own brands as well as past and present contractors gives you, as a potential contract brewer, a valuable asset when you need to develop a beer from scratch.

Second, it is important that you know as much about the beer business as possible. Know what's involved in beer production, including how and where it gets sold — simple things, but things that we as brewers don't particularly want to teach a potential customer.

Something we at August Schell Brewing Company, a contract brewery, look at is the primary geographic sales area. Although the country is getting smaller from a marketing and distribution standpoint, we make an effort to spread our contracts out. We do this to help avoid any marketing conflicts that may or may not arise.

Next we look at the style of beer. Does it have unique qualities, customer appeal, a different flavor, and a potential market? With the proliferation of new products in the market and also with the number of products we produce personally, we value uniqueness because it offers us a challenge as a brewer and a potentially successful relationship with our customers, too. These considerations are just that — considerations — they are also dependent on the commercial brewer's situation and excess capacity, among other things.

Tying in with the uniqueness of the product is its marketability. An existing successful brand is certainly a plus, but a strong marketing plan is equally important. I am not suggesting that you should share your unique marketing plans beyond convincing the commercial brewer that the beer you are asking him or her to produce is marketable. In fact, we prefer to remain somewhat ignorant to a contractor's marketing and sales, provided they are legally and tastefully done.

Next we consider the management/ownership team. What is their level of knowledge and experience in the industry? Do they possess experience in related fields or areas which might help them market their products? Do they have access to distribution and the ability to deal with the distribution side of the business? Again, experience is not essential, but it is helpful.

Another thing we consider is if the product or products fit into our production system. Ingredients are generally not a problem; however, procuring them effectively and in a timely manner can be. Do the brewing methods desired match what we are able to provide? Do times frames fit well into our existing schedules? We try to remain as flexible as possible within the capabilities of our equipment, but we do have limitations.

Yeast, yeast, yeast. Because of the difficulties in maintaining one or more clean strains of yeast within the same brewery, we are not always able to accommodate every contract's desire for a particular yeast. To do so can become a major challenge from the production side. If at all possible, try to utilize the brewer's existing strains.

Along the same lines, we look at the beer — ale or lager — and whether we have fermenting capacity for each.

Cellar times are important, and I don't mean to question or discourage any particular requirements. How do they fit within our capacity, and do they allow us to maximize the use of our existing equipment? Other issues we initially consider are filtration needs, and bottling and packaging requirements. Do they fit within our existing equipment, and if not, can we reasonably make the necessary changes?

Another important item we measure is the distribution needs of the contract brewer. Who will distribute and sell the product? Who will bill the product out? Although we can assist with those issues, we do not necessarily want to assume those duties.

In addition, we consider initial production requests and the growth potential. We look at the number of beers desired and the time frame for their release. Be realistic in your estimates for production.

Finally, we consider the financial wherewithal of the contract brewer. Do they have the ability to get their product off the ground? Are they able to consistently supply packaging needs? Can they support their marketing effort and their brand extensions? Typically, most contracts start out on a cash-in-advance basis. After a certain length of time, they often move into a line-of-credit situation. Your ability to build and maintain a level of financial comfort between yourself and your brewer will go a long way toward maintaining a successful relationship. Remember that your financial demands don't end with the initial purchase of packaging and beer. The second wave of beer and packaging oftentimes needs to be purchased before the initial order leaves the brewery. Compound that with the length of terms you give your distributors and the inevitable past due or bad accounts, and you have a cash-flow problem. Don't short yourself — for it is bad news to start distributors on your products, and then allow the shelves to go empty because you aren't able to purchase beer or packaging.

When you begin contract brewing, expect to do one or more test brews. Depending on the brewery, the size of the test brews and its ultimate repeatability on a large scale are important factors. This process is time consuming, so be prepared. Depending on how busy your brewer is, brews must be scheduled well in advance. Along with that, yeast availability must be considered as well as ingredient procurement. As mentioned earlier, ingredients are generally not a problem. They do, however, take time to order and get shipped.

Then there is packaging. For the most part, a contract brewer should be well along in the design process of their packaging, including labels, when they decide on a brewer. Label production, six-pack production, crown production, and case production all have time frames that vary for a number of reasons. In general, lead times become greater in late spring and early summer due to heavy demands by major brewers and soft drink companies. Don't underestimate the time it takes to get the things you really want quickly.

Getting packaging in a timely fashion is probably the greatest source of stress in a contract relationship. Make sure you utilize the experience of your brewer relative with their packaging specs and equipment. This is particularly true of labels. If you do prefer to use your own suppliers, talk to your brewer first. Dull and unimportant details like right-handed and left-handed opening knockdown cartons make a big difference in running a smooth and efficient operation. The wrong packaging specs can also mean wasted packaging as well as poorly packaged products — neither of which make for a successful relationship.

Storage of empty packaging as well as finished goods is a big challenge to the contract brewer. It is something that needs to be addressed early in a relationship. How much is the brewer willing or able to store and for how long? The same relates to full products.

I touched on distribution earlier. A good, reliable distribution system means the product moves through our system efficiently. It means our warehouse doesn't back up with product to the point of shutting down production. It means maintaining a fresh product, which is important to our next issue, quality control.

Beer is best with age when it can be brewed with what it is supposed to made with, aged the proper length of time, packaged when it should be, and placed in distribution in a timely manner. The challenge to the brewer, as well as the contract brewer, is to make sure that all the ingredients are in place all the time to allow this process to happen.

Finally, there are Brewer's Notices to file, and assumed names and label approvals to get. This means time, time, and more time. If the process should take two weeks, allow four weeks. Then when you finally get your approvals, it's onto the states! Fifty states and myriad forms including, but not limited to, contracts with distributors, territory assignments, etc. Again, the point is it takes time to accomplish all these things with a limited brewery staff and in the necessary sequential order.

To maintain that successful relationship means constant attention to details on both sides. Remember to be open and honest when communicating with the commercial brewer. If your packaging won't be on time, say so! Likewise, expect to be told your brewer cannot meet expectations. Be flexible with time frames and schedules. Always plan ahead. It goes a long way towards establishing a smooth relationship. And finally, be patient. We don't like delays and problems any more than the next person.

Hopefully this information sheds some light on this grand industry, and how to make your entry into it a bit smoother. *Prosit!*

Chapter 6
Tips for Opening a Brewpub

by Scott Smith
Founder and President of CooperSmith's Brewery

There are a number of things to consider when opening a brewpub. Please realize that each tip outlined here is exactly that, a tip, as in "tip of the iceberg." Each one will take additional time, effort, and study on your part but will at least start you in the right direction towards opening a successful brewpub.

Tip 1: Commitment

Make sure you know what you're getting into and that you are the right person for the job. The brewpub is a combination of the restaurant business (yes, you must like people) and the brewery business (yes, you must be mechanically inclined, hard working, and process oriented). Both sides of the business require a distinctive set of characteristics that either you or your partners must have. Make sure that before you commit to opening a brewpub you are in a position to quit your day job and go months without a paycheck while developing your concept, securing your financing, and building your facility.

Tip 2: Concept

Is the brewpub a brewery with a restaurant, a restaurant with a brewery, or a unique combination of both? While most people prefer to treat it as the latter, there are successful brewpubs in each of these categories. Develop your concept according to your philosophy. Realize that microbrewed beer is no longer a novelty in most parts of the country. To be successful, a brewpub must have quality food, beer, service, and ambiance and must do a good job of controlling costs and managing finances. Resist the temptation to open a chain of brewpubs. Open one, master the aforementioned key ingredients, and only then think about a second location. Remember it's called *micro*brewing.

Tip 3: Site Feasibility

When searching for your brewpub answer these questions: Is the location appropriate? Does it have the necessary parking, exposure, foot traffic, and synergy with other businesses to generate the number of customers, and therefore sufficient revenue? Is it zoned correctly, ADA (Americans with Disabilities Act) accessible, and will the fire department and health department approve the facility? Are the utilities and ceiling height adequate? Is the roof in good shape and will it bear the weight of additional equipment? What will it cost to upgrade any deficiencies in the items listed above and is there room in your budget to do so? Answering these questions before you begin negotiations to lease or purchase the building will save time and may determine the success of your project.

Tip 4: Key Players

There are four key areas of the brewpub that must be managed by different individuals:

1. The floor
2. The kitchen
3. The brewery
4. Administration and bookkeeping (payroll, payable accounts, cost of goods, and profit and loss statements)

Of the four key areas, only administration and bookkeeping can be subcontracted and handled off-site. If this is done, make sure this person has restaurant accounting experience. The other positions are vital to the success of the operation and must be held by people working day-to-day in the operation. Hopefully you will be filling one of these positions. Fill the others with the best people you can afford. When hiring, make sure these individuals have the same goals, philosophies, and work ethic as you. Do more than look at résumés and check references. Long serious talks over several beers are in order. When you have found the right person, pay them well, institute a bonus program, and allow them to earn an equity in your company. Get them involved in your project as soon as your budget allows.

Tip 5: Consultants and Other Professionals

It takes a large assortment of expertise and talented individuals to put a brewpub together. You and your partners may have some expertise; the rest will have to be hired. Some of those people are professionals you will retain for the life of your brewpub (CPA and attorney), others for the construction phase (architect, general contractor, and real estate broker), and others will only be involved in the start-up (restaurant, brewery, and marketing and graphic design consultants). Hire the best you can afford, but only after qualifying these individuals. Make sure they are locally successful, have appropriate experience, are politically connected, and most importantly, understand *your* concept and *your* budget. Money spent to buy the expertise lacking in your partnership will pay

for itself many times over during the life of your brewpub.

Tip 6: Design

There are three simple words to remember when considering the design of your brewpub: form follows function. While aesthetics are important, the functioning of this manufacturing facility is even more important to the success of the operation. Involve your brewer, kitchen manager, and floor manager in the design of their departments. There are many beautiful but impractical breweries and kitchens designed by architects and interior designers for aesthetics alone. Listen to the people who will work in them for input on how the flow of these areas will work and how they interact with the other areas. A plethora of ideas will be offered on how your brewpub should look. Remember it is *your* place, and *you* must remember your budget. If possible, allow room for expansion. This may mean taking an option on space above, below, or beside your facility. A well-run brewpub will most likely need additional space within three years of opening.

Tip 7: Equipment Purchasing

Suddenly there are many brewery manufacturers, all promising many different things. Get recommendations from existing brewpubs. Meet the purveyors at the annual Institute for Brewing Studies' National Craft-Brewers Conference and Trade Show. Get references, not only the ones they give you but find out who their last five customers are. Talk to those people and the brewers who operate those breweries. Find out what is and isn't included in the equipment package, and how much the "extras" will cost. Allow yourself enough time to make a well-informed, educated decision, and allow the brewery manufacturer enough time to fit you into their schedule. Avoid basing your choice of companies to buy from on who promises the fastest delivery. Kitchen equipment can be a mix of new and used equipment, but always buy new refrigeration and ice machines. An unwritten rule of the restaurant business is that a good point-of-sale (POS) system will lower your controllable costs by 2 to 5 percent. A POS system is a computerized cash register and cost-tracking system. Although a substantial investment (approximately $30,000), this is money well spent. Research this equipment purchase as you would the brewery and talk to the restaurants that currently use the systems you are considering. Make sure to evaluate hardware and software requirements, training, expansion capabilities, and most importantly, service and support. Open with the best one you can afford.

Tip 8: Capital

Your project will cost more and take longer than you plan. Every dollar you borrow, you must pay back. Every dollar you spend in excess of what you raised will haunt you. If your project costs more than you have, you must borrow more. The greater your debt service, the more sales must increase to meet your original profit projections. These points may seem obvious, but are often forgotten, overlooked, or ignored. Remind yourself of them often.

Not every dollar spent must be borrowed from the bank or investors. Pursue economic development grants, city incentives, equipment leasing, energy conservation loans, and tenant-finish contributions from your landlord. Ask everyone associated with your project if they know of other sources of capital.

Tip 9: Financial Controls

Have a bookkeeping system in place from the time you write your first check. Your first system may start as a simple manual ledger, evolve into a computerized spreadsheet, and end up in the hands of a professional bookkeeper, but make sure there is a system in place. A shoebox full of receipts is not sufficient.

Use the "Standard Chart of Accounts" for restaurants. This is available through the National Restaurant Association or your CPA. Break your budget into specific categories, such as brewery equipment, restaurant equipment, furnishings and fixtures, legal, etc. Keep track of your actual dollars spent versus your budget for each category. If the category is over budget, where will the money come from?

Tip 10: Acknowledge Weaknesses

To start a brewpub you must have access to capital, restaurant experience, brewery experience, and a variety of other talents and expertise. Nobody knows it all. Hire the professionals discussed in tip 5, but educate yourself about the industry. Read trade magazines, attend trade shows, attend the Institute for Brewing Studies' National Craft-Brewers Conference, read books published for and by the industry, and take classes. Finally, assemble a management team that possesses the knowledge and skill you may lack.

Chapter 7
The Hot Pursuit of Capital

by John Hickenlooper
President of the Wynkoop Brewing Company

Raising money is worse than kissing your sister through a screen door with storm windows. The banking fandango which ravaged the eighties has left most public and private sources of capital bruised and depleted. Capital is scarce.

Still, there are brewpubs and microbreweries to be built. Money must be raised. Even in perilous times such as these there are basic guidelines for rounding up capital. This chapter will provide an overview of how to prepare to ask for money and which groups and individuals to ask.

Thorough preparation not only increases your chances with each potential funding source, but also protects you, the fundraiser, from suffering excess "rejection dejection." At best only a fraction of the people initially interested will ultimately invest in your project. That means lots of people saying no. Often the biggest obstacle becomes your own mood. You need the strength of mind to persevere.

The Plan

The first step in asking for money is to have a great business plan. You don't have to spend a lot of money, but it should read well and look good. No matter how smooth your patter, a few days after your presentation the potential investor will likely remember only isolated fragments. A good business plan becomes your agent in cajoling the investor, by reminding him or her to consider your project more seriously.

There are whole books on the construction of business plans. Check at your local bookstore. A good business plan must not only dramatize the wonderfulness of your intentions, but also convey your ability to realize the vision and make it a commercial success.

It will center around a simple and clear description of your business. With a brewpub, everything from the decor to the cuisine, from the service to the floor plan must be described in detail. Plans for micros obviously need less space to describe the environment but still must be very detailed. Estimates of capital costs, such as construction and purchase of equipment, should be as extensive as possible. You should include the terms of your lease if possible or at least what you anticipate those terms will be.

Your business plan should evaluate existing competition and show why your business will be superior. The marketing section should be extensive, explaining in detail how the public will learn of your superior product and how they will be enticed to flock to your establishment. What will your advertising budget be, and how will it be used? Think of a variety of promotions and how you would implement them. A well-conceived marketing plan becomes a blueprint to refer back to once you are open and too crazed for much creative thinking.

A savvy investor will turn immediately to your pro formas, perhaps the heart of any business plan. Making accurate financial projections is part business and part magic, with the emphasis on the latter. The food service aspect of brewpubs creates a whole different dimension. If you don't have a strong restaurant background yourself, you need to avail yourself of someone in your area who does. Even without a brewery, a restaurant is a complex business. You have to convey to investors a mastery of that complexity. With or without food service, most investors expect a minimum of three years of financial projections.

Finally, all this intellectual fermentation must be distilled into an executive summary. Investor-types tend to be very busy, and many will read no farther than the summary. Make it good. Touch all your highlights, but keep it to a page, a page-and-a-half at most. Abstract only the essentials from the pro formas.

Terms of Investment

So now you have a glorious business plan. Its value will be amplified by its versatility. Not just investors, but everyone from bankers to government officials to insurance agents will listen longer and closer if you have a solid business plan. Hopefully while writing it you have been deciding what kind of deal you are going to offer your investors.

A new business is usually some combination of debt and equity. Limited liability companies, limited partnerships, or "subchapter S" corporations seem to be the vehicles of choice, and each can be used to blend an individual investment into debt and equity. Consult a lawyer as to which structure would be best for your project.

Some of these structures are limited to thirty-five investors, so you need to make sure your "units" are large enough to raise all the capital you'll need, but not so large that people feel they're unaffordable. Obviously, the larger the unit of investment, the fewer the investors, which equals less hassles.

Each deal will be different. If you're a brewpubber, you might find a large restaurant that is available in a good location — perhaps with an adjacent storefront empty and aching for a brewery — and you will need to raise far less capital than someone starting from scratch in an old warehouse. A space that is already finished could be equally important in starting a micro. You will most likely have a much higher rent each month, but the lesser capital requirement should allow you to keep more of the equity and still offer investors an attractive return for their risk.

To exactly define an acceptable return and be able to exactly measure risk is what allows certain pretentious windbags to refer to dealmaking as an art. Most investors in speculative ventures (such as brewpubs and microbreweries) expect to see at least a 30 to 50 percent annual return if everything works. This is why the pro formas in the business plan are so important. You must document as best you can that your projections are conservative enough to be achievable, but at the same time they must be optimistic enough to convince investors that the return is worth the risk.

One simple structure that is aggressive but seems to work well is to divide profits 50/50 between the investors and yourself and your partners, but only after the investors have gotten all their initial investment back at a fair rate of interest. In a limited partnership, this would be done with a provision that would allocate all proceeds be distributed 90/10 in favor of the investors until they have gotten back their investment with, say, 10 percent interest. At that point, with their "risk" removed, the investors would receive only 50 percent of future profit distributions. It is important to let investors know how long it will be before you intend to begin paying them back and to express your priorities should there not be sufficient cash flow for everything. (There seldom is.)

In a "subchapter S" corporation, each investment would be divided into shares of stock (equity) and some debt instrument, such as a subordinated debenture. A debenture is simply a corporate form of a loan, similar to a promissory note. By being subordinated, it means that a bank or other institution can loan the company money, and if problems arise, the bank will always be paid before the investors. Without this "subordination" no bank would lend to you. They probably won't anyway, but more on that later.

Using this method, roughly 10 to 20 percent of each individual investment would go towards purchasing shares of stock. The total of all the shares of stock purchased by all the investors would equal half the total issued by the company. You and your partners would purchase the other half of the shares at a greatly reduced rate. The other 80 to 90 percent of each individual investment would purchase a debenture, say at 12 percent. One would offer the higher interest because the investor is receiving it only on 80 to 90 percent of his investment, unlike the limited partnership. The debenture would be for a fixed period of time, perhaps four to eight years. Like a home mortgage, each payment would contain principal and interest, until the whole amount was repaid.

Such a structure works better for a brewpub than a microbrewery. A brewpub is more likely to generate sooner the positive cash flow necessary to begin repaying the note. In the case of a microbrewery, most cash flow is reinvested in order to "grow the business." Repayments of debt would have to be flexible so as not to cripple the new company's growth potential.

Clearly any of these options can become quite complex, and a lawyer's assistance is a necessity. It is valuable to remember that lawyers charge by the hour and are seldom benevolent to their clients. By planning out the essential structure of the deal you want to offer your investors ahead of time, you will likely save yourself vast sums in legal bills.

The project and the terms of the investment are generally described in a separate document, usually in a private offering circular or private placement memorandum. If your lawyer or a friend can provide you with a sample from another start-up business, you can adapt the basic structure to the particulars for your enterprise, and eventually present your lawyer with a rough draft ready for his or her revision. Your savings will be significant.

Finding Mullets

So now you are armed with a business plan and some explanation of the terms of investment. Ideally you believe that you are offering investors a good deal — an opportunity to help create something unique, have a lot of fun, and make a sound investment at the same time. Who do you ask?

Start by asking everyone you know. Spare no one. Ask old friends, family, even business acquaintances. If you feel awkward you can pose a request humorously or just talk about your plans without directly asking for an investment. Be enthusiastic, but don't make it difficult for them to say "no." You need allies. Those with insufficient means or cautious dispositions might have friends more affluent or speculatively inclined. Their friends will have friends of their own. This is why it is so important to keep your spirits up even after a long string of rejections. Being a homebrewer is a great help in this phase.

If you can consistently keep a positive attitude, you will find that today's rejection often leads to tomorrow's investment. Don't judge yourself by the frequency of success, but rather by how often you ask. Babe Ruth set the record for striking out the same year he hit sixty home runs.

Primary Initial Target

Aside from yourself, one of your best potential supporters is your landlord or landlady, who has a lot to gain if you are successful and will still have a renovated building even if you fail. He or she is more likely to be motivated if you are lucky enough to find an underappreciated building considered a nuisance by its owner.

It is best to negotiate a low-base rental rate (now there's some sage advice), but often if you are willing to include a percentage of the gross sales in the equation, a landlord/lady will be willing to grant a longer lease or option terms to extend the initial lease. This allows him or her to participate to a limited extent if you prove to be wildly successful (especially deserved if you convince him or her to invest $100,000 or $200,000 into your tenant finish).

Some landlords/ladies, if they really get involved emotionally in the project, become direct investors as well. This is usually a good idea, when possible, as it will increase the probability of cordial relations.

Most of your potential investors will likely want to invest $25,000 or less. Sometimes much less. There are investors out there with the capability to make larger investments, but they are harder to find. Many cities have venture capital clubs — groups of investors and entrepreneurs who meet monthly or quarterly to discuss various projects. Often you can get yourself placed on their program and have five or ten minutes to present your proposal. Most of these larger scale investors are very skeptical of restaurant-related deals, unless the operating partners have extensive experience.

You should probably expect to raise at least 75 percent of your capital from private individuals. Endeavor to get commitments for 125 percent, because up to 40 percent of the people who tell you they are definitely going to invest will fail to do so. This is a law of nature.

Once you have gotten some firm commitments from private investors, you are ready to talk to banks. This phase is usually where the real frustration begins.

Banks and Other Institutions

Bankers are generally a strange breed. Most of what you may have heard about them is true. They get paid a great deal of money to avoid any semblance of risk. Ironically this is almost the reverse of the typical brewpub entrepreneur, who takes on incredible risk, often with scant compensation.

A common truism is that bankers only like lending to people so wealthy they don't need to borrow. For the rest of us mortals, bankers are addicted to the term "collateral." You must own real property, such as cars, houses, stocks, and bonds, worth at least 25

to 50 percent more than the value of your loan. You pledge this real property, which usually is the core of your life, to the bank in case the business is unable to pay its loans. Welcome to the world of collateral. Banks also like to see that the individuals seeking loans personally invest in the project as much as possible, although this is not a necessity.

Even with ample collateral and significant personal investment, banks are unreliable participants in start-up ventures. Perhaps their best potential is for a small loan in a larger package that is centered around some other institutional financing.

Many cities have revolving loan funds set up to encourage development in certain designated parts of the city. Some of these loan funds are for "blighted" areas, others perhaps for historic districts. The latter are usually good places to look for a home for a brewing facility. Municipally controlled loan funds also require collateral, but are more willing to accept equipment to be owned by the business for that collateral.

Most Federal loan programs, such as the Small Business Administration, are impossible to secure for start-up restaurants and are equally difficult for start-up microbreweries. Other local loans such as those mentioned above are not always so restrictive. Ask around to see if there is a pro-downtown development group which could provide information of such loan programs in your city.

Another source for capital, also very difficult for start-ups, is leasing companies. Even a modest full-grain brewing system runs well over $100,000. The right leasing company, if they have faith in the overall project, might be willing to lease back up to 75 percent of that cost. Certainly "point-of-sale" cash register systems are commonly leased throughout the restaurant business, as well as dishwashing machines and some other kitchen equipment. Micros might find a leasing company for bottling lines or distribution trucks. Leases commonly are 2 to 3 percent higher than bank loans, but they are willing to accept more risk.

A Final Note

Perhaps the easiest way to raise capital is to need less of it. If financing is a problem, try to do as many tasks yourself as you possibly can. Work on the design yourself long before you talk to an architect. Keep legal, accounting, and other consulting services to a minimum.

And shop wisely. Used brewing or bottling equipment can often be rehabilitated for a fraction of the cost of new equipment. Restaurant auctions are an excellent way to learn the business as well as affording the opportunity of saving tens of thousands of dollars. Local craftsmen and tradesmen can sometimes seem like small potatoes, but the total carpenter's bill on a large brewpub can easily get into the $50,000 range.

Raising capital is usually the hardest task in the entire process of starting a microbrewery or brewpub. But perhaps because of that, it is also one of the most satisfying once you have succeeded. Especially if you can enjoy that satisfaction while drinking one of your own beers.

Chapter 8
Handling Local Regulatory Authorities

by Peter Egelston
Co-owner of the Northhampton Brewery

The reason I was asked to write this chapter is because I have a lot of amusing horror stories to tell about opening our brewery. My purpose, however, is to prevent you from having such horror stories.

We opened Northampton Brewery in August 1987, after about a year of planning and construction. The first step we took in organizing our project was to visit other brewpubs. In 1986 there weren't many brewpubs, and none on the East Coast, which meant that we had to go to the West Coast to do our basic research. Then we took a proposal to the planning board of the city of Northampton for initial approval, which we received pending further information. In December 1986 we acquired a site, went back to the planning board for a formal hearing, and secured approval for the project. We extensively renovated our building and installed our brewery between January and August 1987, when we opened. This all sounds very easy, but there were a few stumbling blocks and pitfalls along the way. You will likely encounter some of the areas of regulations that we ran up against.

One important point I want to emphasize is education. Most of the problems you will encounter in dealing with regulatory bodies come from misconceptions about what you are supposed to be doing. Most people's familiarity with a brewery consists of their tour of Busch Gardens or the Heineken plant. To some people, a brewery is a huge industrial plant belching out noxious fumes and other pollutants. Your job is to educate them. One way to do this is to put together a press packet. There is a lot of material in the mainstream press about the micro- and pubbrewery movement. Cut clippings from *Newsweek, Time,* and *USA Today.* Virtually every newspaper in every metropolitan area has carried articles on small breweries, so add them as well. Get photographs of operating brewpubs and microbreweries. Your role first and foremost is educating people to prevent problems rooted in misconceptions.

One of the first questions you'll encounter will be about zoning. Zoning is an important issue for brewpubs, especially because they are usually located in a commercial district zoned for retail business and restaurants as opposed to an industrial district. On the other hand, microbreweries producing a strictly wholesale product are usually located in an industrial district, since there is no sense paying the high rent charged in a commercial district for an industrial operation.

The main problem in dealing with the planning board or zoning commission is how to convince them to let you set up a business perceived by almost everyone as industrial in a commercial setting where industrial uses are prohibited. The tactic that a number of brewpubs employ is the analogy of a restaurant with an on-premise bakery. This is a very useful analogy to draw, and it holds true for the most part. Many restaurants operate their own bakeries, and their raw materials are similar to those used in breweries. Likewise, bakeries' waste products are not unlike the waste products produced in breweries.

After zoning, the second issue most likely to cause problems is waste — solid and liquid. In July 1987 I had just gotten the brewery on-line and was running my first test batches. I thought I was home free. Everything had been taken care of, I thought. Midway through my brewing, a large man with a red face came storming into the brewery waving sheets of paper under my nose, telling me my operation was illegal. He was the manager of the municipal wastewater treatment plant, who had been notified by a friend that a brewery was opening in downtown Northampton. Before the manager came in, however, he had called the manager of the wastewater treatment plant in Merrimack, New Hampshire, where Anheuser-Busch operates a 3.5-million-barrel-a-year brewery. So our local treatment plant manager came to our 1,000-barrel-a-year brewery expecting to find an operation similar to Anheuser-Busch. He had in hand applications for industrial wastewater discharge permits and told me that I would have to test my own wastewater four times a month at my expense, send the results to the municipal plant for approval, and dig a manhole over the sewer outlet at an estimated cost of $3,000 so he could install an electronic testing device to test the effluent at the point of entry into the sewer. This would have been fine if I was opening a Coca-Cola bottling plant, but in our case it was rather ridiculous.

Once he looked around the brewery, he realized what he required of us was overdone. But he had painted himself into a corner. He had notified the city authorities, and there was no easy way for him to back down. Finally, we went to the mayor, fortunately a great fan of our beer and a supporter of our project, and he arranged a compromise whereby the wastewater treatment facility sent an engineer to the brewery to watch me clean the mash tun. She took samples of our effluent and reached the conclusion we had told them all along: "Yes, our wastewater is of a very high potency, but the volume we put down the drain is a minuscule quantity and is not any way significant to the wastewater problems of the city." They let us off the hook. However, we were lucky to have a friend in city hall, or we could have been in grave trouble.

When starting your project, keep constant contact with the people in charge of treating wastewater. At our original zoning hearing, the head of the zoning board was responsible for inviting every person with an interest in the project (i.e., electrical and building inspectors, the city attorney, etc.), but he had neglected to invite the superintendent of the wastewater treatment facility. The superintendent regarded it as a personal slight, and it became our problem. So seek out these people. The element of surprise does not work in your favor. People in charge of regulating your brewery do not like surprises.

Wastewater treatment is an important issue. People who deal with wastewater have a real problem. Most of our public waterways are in great danger and many of them are open sewers. There has been a lot of improvement in cleaning waterways, but it is an on-going problem and continues to increase. So despite the problems I had with the wastewater supervisor, I have a lot of sympathy for his situation. In dealing with wastewaster treatment people, get to know the initials TSS, for total suspended solids. That is the amount of organic material that goes down the drain. Most brewery solids coming out in the wastewater are dissolved in the water and cannot settle out in the sludge ponds of the treatment plant. Only about 10 to 15 percent of the brewery solids going down the drain can be settled out and removed as sludge.

Treating wastewater is somewhat similar to brewing. It is a microbiological process in which microbes in the treatment plant break down organic matter of all types and render it harmless and able to be discharged into the receiving water.

This brings us to biological oxygen demand (BOD) — the amount of dissolved oxygen it takes microbes at the wastewater treatment plant to break down the organic waste in the water. If the oxygen is depleted (if there is an excess of organic materials going into the wastewater), the microbes will die, the waste will not be converted into harmless material, and dangerous waste may go into our public waterways. For this reason the plant management will be very interested in the BOD count of your wastewater, which for breweries is very high. To give you some comparative figures, the acceptable maximum BOD rate of our plant in Northampton is 300 milligrams per liter of wastewater. A soft drink plant pays a surcharge for any excess beyond that maximum, and its waste averages between 900 to 2,000 milligrams per liter. Household waste averages about 200 milligrams per liter. Pure beer averages about 200,000 milligrams per liter. That's an incredibly high figure, but you rarely put pure beer down the drain. Usually it is very dilute and is flushed in small quantities.

Along with the strength of the waste, the major wastewater concern is containing spills. If you make a batch of beer you have to ditch, you need to notify a number of people. You have to call the Bureau of Alcohol, Tobacco, and Firearms because you don't want to pay taxes on beer you put down the drain. You have to notify the state authorities. But most importantly, notify the wastewater treatment plant manager. He or she wants to be certain from the outset that you have some type of procedure for containing spills or putting large quantities of waste or beer down the drain. Chances are they'll want you to put it down the drain in small quantities over a long period of time in order to keep the wastewater plant from being slammed with a tremendous amount of high-potency waste at one time.

Another concern is the pH of your wastewater. Caustic soda alters the pH of the wastewater, as do acids.

Ideally you'll be able to convince the wastewater people that you put such small amounts of waste down the drain that you won't need constant testing. But they will question you, so do your homework. Get in touch with other operating microbreweries. There is very little printed information on this topic, and most of it applies to large industrial breweries and is not applicable to a microbrewery or brewpub.

Regarding building codes, expect to be dealing with a number of inspectors, whether you're renovating an existing structure or building something new. Although most municipalities have adopted a uniform code, inspectors have a certain amount of latitude in interpreting that code. With respect to building codes, your first task is to educate yourself. You do not need to be an expert; just be familiar to the point where you can identify unreasonable requests. *Inspectors are not always right.* There will be times when some negotiation is required. Here's a tip: do not let your contractor serve as your proxy in negotiating with your local code enforcers because your contractor's interest may not always coincide with your interest. He or she is bound to think first and foremost of preserving a good working relationship with city hall and will be more than happy to spend your money accommodating the building inspector, rather than fighting for your rights. Our electrical inspector required that all of our brewery wiring be in hard conduit as opposed to PVC flexible wiring. All the junction and switch boxes had to be rated for high-moisture, wash-down areas and were extremely expensive. Also, because we run a brewpub, our code has a very high standard. But this is an area where we didn't want to cut corners.

Let me reiterate the word "education." Unless you are in an area that already has a brewpub or microbrewery, your local inspectors probably don't know what to expect from your establishment. This is true for both electrical wiring and plumbing.

Fire regulations are another area of concern. Are the entrances and exits adequate? Is there a sprinkler system? This is generally dictated by code. Is there handicap access? Your contractor should be familiar with local building codes and know the specific requirements for these.

Beyond building codes there is a parcel of miscellaneous issues that may or may not apply to your operation. Grain dust is one. At our original zoning hearing, one member of the zoning board had read an article about a grain silo that exploded and was worried about grain dust explosions. Finally, in order to satisfy this person, we offered to purchase pre-ground malt or mill the malt off-premise. He was happy, and we left it at that. By the time we opened, we showed him our wash-down procedure, and he relented. Consequently, we mill our own grain on-premise and don't have any problems with the city.

Noise is another public concern. When appling for your initial zoning, you may have a public hearing, and your neighbors may ask about noise. Get information about noise from other operating brewpubs. As far as I know, noise hasn't been a problem with a brewpub beyond that of a typical bar or restaurant.

People will also ask about odors. I was asked recently to write a letter for a brewpub opening in another city attesting that no one has complained about odors from our brewery. People have a perception of a brewery as a large industrial operation with foul odors. This is certainly not the case with microbreweries.

Volatiles such as steam coming out of the kettle may be a problem. Greg Noonan, owner and brewmaster at the Vermont Pub and Brewery in Burlington, Vermont, had to bend over backwards to address that issue when people questioned the volatiles coming out of his kettle. What Greg did was to reroute the steam coming out of the kettle into the kitchen so it could be released through the hood over the stove and grill. Consequently, he has the cleanest hood of any restaurant in the state, maybe in the country.

Health codes vary in different localities. Your health inspector may be very interested in what you do or may be totally mystified by it. In our case, the health inspector is very interested in our kitchen. He comes in with a white glove and thermometer and checks out the kitchen temperatures. Then he walks into the brewery, looks around, scratches his head, and leaves. But you may not have the same experience, so be prepared to address health issues. Brewing pretty much monitors itself from the health standpoint. You're not likely to poison anyone when you're making beer. If your sanitation procedures aren't up to snuff, your beer won't sell.

To recap and also give you my suggestions for dealing with individual inspectors, let me point out again that you must educate people. Don't wait until misconceptions have already been formed. Most regulators have an alarm signal that goes off when they hear the word brewery. For example, Greg Noonan had leased his site but hadn't received his zoning approval when he ordered his brewery tanks from England. He had no place to put them when they arrived so he stored them in the space he had rented. The superintendent of the planning commission just happened to drive by, see brewery tanks in the window, and get into a snit because no one had consulted him. As a result, he forbade having a brewery in downtown Burlington. That was the point that Greg had to start from, and he ran into stumbling blocks every step of the way. To give you an idea of what he went through, he had to put a sprinkler system inside his walk-in refrigerator.

Do your homework. Don't be caught by surprise because you don't know enough about something. Depending on how far along you are, a surprise could be very inconvenient or costly.

Don't depend exclusively on someone else's knowledge of codes and regulations. For example, don't depend solely on your contractor's knowledge of the codes. Remember, contractors are not spending their own money. Get to know the codes yourself.

Also, get to know the people who have the control over regulations affecting your brewery: inspectors and decision-makers. Northampton is a small city with one electrical inspector, one building inspector, and one health inspector.

This is both an advantage and a disadvantage. It might be better to be in a very large city where you're dealing with a large, faceless bureaucracy, rather than individuals.

Let all the concerned parties know about your project from the very beginning. You want to create good will. Do this by telling people what to expect. You sometimes have to play politics but do so carefully. Many inspectors and regulators operate autonomously. They have their own little fiefdoms and they don't like to be told what to do. Remember that what your building inspector approves may not be approved by your electrical inspector. Get to know the jurisdiction of each inspector. A colleague of mine says that his philosophy is "We don't ask for permission — we beg for forgiveness." While that may work in some cases, in general, I think it is a risky way to conduct business.

Learn who influences whom. As a last resort, you may have to go over people's heads. We've had to do that sometimes, but it doesn't create good will. In two situations, we've had to run straight to the mayor and say, "You'll have to fix this if you want any more beer."

Understand your regulator's point of view. A fire marshal has opinions about what is safe and what isn't — ditto for the electrical inspector and the wastewater treatment people. Think about why they want you to do something; often there is a good reason for it.

Try to avoid adversarial positions. This brings me to the point of whether or not to hire an attorney. I recommend having a good lawyer in the wings. But I've found that most of the time, I'm better off talking to the regulators myself. I've been in front of the Alcohol Beverage Commission more times than I care to think about, both with lawyers and without. I usually get what I want when I talk to them person to person. Lawyers can be helpful; they can also create an adversarial situation just by their presence. Use the services of an attorney with some common sense.

Accept compromise. You may not get everything you want and you may have to spend some money. If it is a choice between paying extra money and jumping through hoops to get your project done or being stubborn and not, then the answer is obvious.

Finally, be ready for anything. Sometimes even after you have done everything right, things come up. In the very last stage of our project when we were ready to open, we hired a sign maker to design a nice sign for Northampton Brewery. The city has very strict sign codes, and the city attorney refused to let us use the word "brewery" in our signs or advertisements. To get approval to operate our brewpub in a commercially zoned district, we had to convince the city that the brewery was an accessory use to the restaurant, much as a bakery would be. On the other hand, in order to satisfy the state liquor authorities, because we still have a strict three-tier system in Massachusetts and there is no brewpub law yet, we had to establish two separate corporations, each with separate ownership. One is the bar and restaurant, the other is the brewery. We were playing both sides of the fence, and it caught up with us.

The city attorney's rationale was if we were going to operate a bar and restaurant where the brewery would only be an accessory, then we wouldn't be able to promote ourselves as a brewery because people would complain about an industrial use in a commercial district. It came down to the fact that the attorney didn't want people calling her office and complaining about our zoning.

We went to the mayor and explained the problem, but he wouldn't overrule the city attorney. Instead, he suggested a compromise wherein we would call our company the Northampton Brewery at the Brewster Court Bar and Grill. Now everyone simply calls it "The Brewery."

Even after you have done everything right in planning your brewery, something is likely to come up. You have to retain a sense of humor about it or you won't be able to tell these amusing horror stories in the future.

This chapter is based on a presentation I gave at the Institute for Brewing Studies'

Microbrewers Conference in 1989. As I review what I have written, seven years and two brewery openings later, it seems to have held up pretty well, even with the enormous changes that have taken place in the craft-brewing industry since 1989. In some respects, things are easier today than in the past, mostly because there is so much more information to draw from. One point that I will add now, with more than seven additional years of hindsight, is to prepare for growth and all of its ramifications. A brewpub that was originally designed for nine hundred barrels of annual production may someday evolve into a three-thousand-barrel facility. This may require some reassessment of the issues covered in this chapter, especially disposal of wastewater. This is exactly the case for us in Northampton, where we are in the process of making some very expensive changes to accommodate the growth we have undergone.

Chapter 9
The Microbrewing Industry and Industrial Wastewater

by Michael J. Pronold
Environmental Specialist for the Bureau of Environmental Services, Portland, Oregon

The wastewater generated from brewing and cleaning operations by microbreweries must be discharged to a wastewater treatment plant, thus subjecting it to the restrictions and/or regulations of the local sewerage district through local ordinances or a pretreatment program. The purpose of these restrictions and programs is to control discharges of harmful pollutants from industrial and commercial sources which interfere with the wastewater treatment plant, collection system, and sludge disposal operations. The program also protects worker safety, the public, and the local environment. Brewery wastewater is a concern because of the pH of the wastewater (cleaning solutions, beer wastes) and high total suspended solids (TSS) and bio*chemical* oxygen demand (BOD) which may interfere with the wastewater treatment plant's ability to adequately treat wastewater.

Control Programs

Programs that a local sewerage district may implement to restrict the wastewater discharge from a microbrewery can vary. These types of programs include: (1) a rigid permitting program; (2) a discharge authorization; (3) informal agreements; and (4) a surcharge program.

Pretreatment permit. A microbrewery may be required to obtain a wastewater discharge permit from the control authority and be subject to the same discharge limitations and permit requirements that regulate other industries in the sewerage district. If the wastewater discharge is 25,000 gallons per day or more, the microbrewery is required by Federal regulations to obtain a wastewater discharge permit. A permit may include any or all of the following:

1. Applying for a permit and paying an appropriate permit fee. The permit application generally requires schematics of all sewer lines, sewer connections, and floor drains on the site, water usage, facility layout, production records, chemical storage areas, and general information.
2. Installation of a sampling manhole so the control authority has access to take random samples of the wastewater from the facility.
3. Monitoring and reporting requirements where the facility must sample the wastewater, have the samples analyzed, and report results to the control authority.
4. Creation of an accidental spill prevention plan that must be approved by the control authority.
5. Allowing on-site inspections of the facility by the control authority.
6. Meeting discharge limitations set forth in the permit.

Violations of any of the permit requirements can subject the microbrewery to enforcement that can include compliance orders, requirements for the installation of pretreatment equipment, additional monitoring and reporting requirements, and fines.

Discharge authorization. A discharge authorization program may include a formal written agreement between the sewerage agency and the microbrewery. These are generally less stringent and have fewer requirements than a pretreatment program permit. Actions required of the microbrewery could include a plan to keep spent grain out of the sewer, control the rate of discharge, and other best management practices (BMPs) to limit the impact of the wastewater on the sewer system.

Informal agreements. If the microbrewery's wastewater discharge is deemed to have a minimal impact on the sewer system, the sewerage agency may only request that certain BMPs be implemented. These may be in the form of requests, directives, or educational brochures which are given to the establishment.

Surcharge program. A surcharge program is a vehicle used by sewerage agencies for recovering the cost of treating wastewater that has high TSS and/or BOD. Whereas the treatment plant is designed to treat biological wastes, it costs the facility more money to treat high-strength wastes. This is due to the increased solids that must be handled or disposed of and the increase in operating costs for things such as blowers that supply oxygen to the bacteria that feed on the high-strength wastes. This fee may be referred to as an extra-strength sewer charge. These charges can be in addition to the permitting programs described above.

The costs are based on the poundage of TSS and BOD calculated using the amount of flow and the "strength" of the waste (concentration of TSS and BOD) in excess of the level of ordinary domestic wastewater. Sometimes a chemical oxygen demand (COD) test is substituted for a BOD test. This substitution is made because a COD test only takes two hours, whereas a BOD test takes five days to perform. For samples from a specific source, a COD can be empirically related to a BOD. These costs can be

significant and should be evaluated when starting a microbrewery.

The type of program implemented by the local sewerage agency depends on the perceived impact of the microbrewery on the sewer system. Microbreweries with a greater impact will be subject to more controls. The impact is site specific and will depend on many factors. The closer the microbrewery is to the treatment plant, the greater the impact will be on the sewer system. In addition, the impact of a microbrewery will be more significant on a smaller wastewater treatment plant.

Sources and Characteristics of Wastewater

The sources of wastewater in a microbrewery come from two different general operations. One source is from production operations, which includes spent grain and yeast; filtering media; and the heels of fermenters, conditioners, brew kettles, and whirlpools. There are also small amounts of spilt beer in the bottling and kegging operations, and spent beer in returned kegs. At times there may even be a need to dispose of a bad batch of beer. These wastewaters from the production process contain product or by-product at some stage in the brewing process. Wastewaters generated from these operations are generally very high in TSS and/or BOD, with a low pH. The suspended solids from heels of brewing vessels can be well over 1,000 milligrams per liter (depending on the amount of yeast and trub). BOD of finished beer is approximately 80,000 milligrams per liter, and the pH of finished beer generally runs around 4.2. In comparison, wastewater from households has TSS and BOD in the 150 to 300 milligrams per liter range with a neutral pH (6.0 to 8.0).

The other source of wastewater comes from the cleaning of production equipment. This includes washing of tanks, kegs, bottles, and other equipment with a caustic cleaning solution. Wastewater generated from cleaning is reflective of the high caustic solution used to clean the equipment. These cleaning solutions by themselves are generally low in TSS and BOD but may be high depending on the amount of product in the wash water. They are also very high in pH (10.5 to 13.5). If captured, this caustic solution may be reused until the pH drops to approximately 10.0 to 10.5 or becomes unusable due to contamination by other materials. It is then generally discharged to the sewer. Acidic sanitizers used to disinfect equipment is often made up of phosphoric acid and iodine. This wastewater is low in TSS and BOD and has a low pH (3.9). Acidic cleaning solutions are used for bright tanks and are a combination of phosphoric and nitric acid.

Table 1

Wastewater Characteristics from Several Microbreweries

	TSS (mg/L)	BOD (mg/L)	pH
Range	45–3,460	690–7,580	4.8–11.2
Average	1,024	3,323	7.1

TSS and BOD are twenty-four-hour composite samples, and pH is grab samples. Averages are based on thirty-six samples for TSS and BOD, and thirty-four samples for pH.

Table 1 lists the results of wastewater sampling at several microbreweries. Even though the samples are twenty-four-hour composites, the range in TSS and BOD is very large due to microbreweries conducting different operations on different days. Monitoring for pH showed three violations for the limits of 5.5 to 11.5 in thirty-four discrete samples. This is due to the aggressive pH control measures that microbreweries have implemented. In addition, microbreweries have implemented BMPs for the control of TSS and BOD.

Wastewater pH

The pH of wastewater is regulated by the sewerage district and has limits that vary from locale to locale. Typical limits are 5.5 to 11.5, but could be as restrictive as 6.0 to 9.0. These limits are set to protect the wastewater treatment plant and the collection system. Wastewater at the treatment plant is treated biologically by microorganisms which thrive in a neutral pH range. Wastewater with a low pH may be corrosive to the sewage-collection system and be a worker health and safety concern. In fact, wastewater with a pH less than 5.0 is a prohibited discharge by federal regulations. The wastewater generated by the brewing process and cleaning operations can fall outside the acceptable pH range if discharged by themselves without pretreatment. The possibility of this happening is common in microbreweries. Larger breweries may have cleaning and brewing operations occurring simultaneously which may dampen the pH range of the wastewaters as the low pH brewing wastes combine with the high pH cleaning wastes. Nevertheless, it may be necessary to install pretreatment or BMPs for the control of wastewater pH.

pH Controls

One option for controlling of pH is to collect the various wastewaters into a collection vessel and adjust the pH if necessary. The low pH of beer wastes, sanitizing solutions, and acidic cleaners and the high pH of the caustic cleaner waste may result in a pH that is within the permitted range. The collection vessel would need to be sized according to the volume of wastewater, and this may present space constraints for some facilities. Space constraints may necessitate that a facility install a continuous collection/treatment system with a smaller capacity.

Also, supplemental pH control may be necessary to adjust the pH to an acceptable range. This would require adding an acidifier (sulfuric acid, CO_2) or a caustic (spent caustic solution, lime product) either manually or automatically to a batch system or through an automated pH control system that continuously monitors and adjusts the wastewater pH. Operation and maintenance of the system and the cost of chemicals incur additional expenses. Also, hazardous materials (acids, caustics) on-site must be stored and handled accordingly.

Another pH control mechanism is to control the pH of the wastewater at the source. Prior to discharging the heel of a brewing vessel, caustic (used on-site for cleaning) can be added to raise the pH to the acceptable range. Practical experience or bench testing can determine the appropriate amount of caustic to add.

Control of caustic wastewater can be made cost effective for the brewery by installing cleaning-in-place (CIP) units. These units are made up of a receptacle for the caustic solution used in cleaning vessels. The solution is pumped to the vessel and used in cleaning and returned to the CIP unit. The solution can be used numerous times until the pH falls to below 11.0. The solution then needs to be disposed of; but, the pH may now be in the acceptable range.

Care must be taken when combining waste streams in an effort to achieve a pH in the allowable range. If chlorinated caustic cleaners are used, neutralizing with a strong acid will liberate chlorine gas. If iodine solutions (acidic sanitizers) are made too alkaline, the iodine can plate out, in effect scaling the tank.

Wastewater TSS and BOD

TSS and BOD may or may not be regulated by the sewerage district. If the brewery represents a significant amount of the TSS and BOD loading at the wastewater treatment plant, or poses a threat due to a slug load, the district may put limits on the amount that the brewery can discharge. Whereas the treatment plant is designed to treat biological wastes, it can become overburdened with high-strength wastes. Wastewater that is inadequately treated by the wastewater treatment plant may be discharged to the receiving stream, resulting in the treatment plant violating its discharge permit. This concern rises as the wastewater treatment facility decreases in size and the strength and amount of brewery wastewater discharge increases. In addition, if the microbrewery is located near the treatment plant, it may pose a threat due to slug loads. Microbreweries located further from the treatment plant may have their flows diluted from other wastewater in the collection system and reduce this concern. If the strength of the waste is high enough, local conditions may necessitate that a microbrewery install pretreatment for the control of TSS and BOD.

TSS and BOD Controls

The control of TSS and BOD can be accomplished through pretreatment and/or source control. Pretreatment can be accomplished in several ways, including centrifuges, filters, screens, settling basins, or an activated sludge system. The first four methods are designed to remove settleable solids from the waste stream. An activated sludge system is similar to a wastewater treatment plant where biological treatment is used to reduce the TSS and BOD. The result is a sludge which must be handled and disposed of in some manner. An activated sludge system can reduce TSS and BOD significantly, but are expensive to install and operate and are not very common except in large breweries. However, as more microbreweries start up operations and existing ones grow, it is inevitable that some will be required to install these systems. It may also be cost effective to install a treatment system to reduce the surcharges that a microbrewery may incur.

Source control through good housekeeping is a very effective way for a microbrewery to control TSS/BOD and the associated higher sewer bills. Spent yeast can be killed by cooking, and when added to grain it can be given away as feed. Killing the yeast is necessary to maintain the health of the animals consuming the spent grain. Waste beer from returned kegs can also be heated and disposed of in the grain or separately in a tank for transporting liquids. Filtering media and the associated yeast can be cleaned "dry" and disposed of as a solid waste. If it is removed with water, the solids may be able to be removed through settling and the liquid discharged to the sewer. A large portion of the extra-strength charge is generated from dissolved BOD (i.e., dissolved sugars and carbohydrates). Removal of solids will not reduce this source of BOD.

Summary

Wastewaters generated from microbreweries can be a concern to the sewerage district that the brewery is located in because of the pH, TSS, and BOD of the wastewater. The brewery may need to be permitted and also possibly implement controls for pH, TSS, and BOD. The permit requirements and control measures may add significant costs for the brewery through higher operation costs and/or sewer fees. The requirements will vary depending on the local sewerage district. These issues should be addressed prior to starting any brewing operation by contacting the sewerage district you will be located in.

Glossary

BOD (biochemical oxygen demand). The quantity of oxygen utilized in the biochemical oxidation of organic matter over a period of five days at a temperature of 68 degrees F (20 degrees C) and usually expressed in milligrams per liter.

COD (chemical oxygen demand). COD is a measure of the oxygen equivalent of the sample's organic content that is susceptible to oxidation by a strong chemical oxidant.

pH. A measure of the acidity or alkalinity of a solution on a scale of 1.0 to 14.0, decreasing with increasing acidity and increasing with increasing alkalinity.

TSS (total suspended solids). Solids that are suspended or floating in a liquid and measured by removal through a specified filter size and usually expressed in milligrams per liter.

Chapter 10
Filtration: Types and Techniques

by Tom Anders
Vice President of Sales for Scott Labs

During the infancy of the modern microbrewery industry, it may have been sufficient for brewers to produce beers without filtration or with relatively simple filtration devices. With ongoing concerns relative to improvement and consistency of quality, longer storage and shelf life, and colloidal and microbiological stability, brewers have recognized the need for a well-managed filtration program.

While filtration does give clarity and brilliance to a beer, its main function is to provide microbiological, colloidal, and flavor stability. As a result, a beer with greater clarity is produced. During the filtration process, suspended particles in the beer, namely yeast and agglomerated proteins, are separated from the liquid beer by passing the unfiltered beer through a semipermeable media. The beer passes through the filtration media, and the suspended particles are retained on — or ideally within — the media. The clarity of the filtered beer depends on factors such as the type of filtration media used, particle size of beer-suspended solids, rate of filtration, and so on.

Owing to the practical experiences gained by many established craft breweries and knowledgeable filtration-equipment and filtration-media suppliers, a practical and manageable filtration program can be selected. Still there are choices for each brewery program and brewer. Take caution not to make the choice of a filtration program solely on price, as minimally sized or poorly designed filtration equipment usually results in long working hours for brewers and has adverse effects on the beer.

Filtration Media

Beer filtration operations in the brewery can be grouped into two types. The first is bright beer filtration for serving tanks and for kegs and bottles with cold storage and limited shelf life. The second group is microbiologically stable beer filtration for bottled beers (ambient storage) and keg beers (cold storage) for extended shelf life.

The type of filtration media selected may be the primary criteria for choosing a brewery's filtration program. Filtration media from which to pick normally include diatomaceous earth, perlite, cellulose fiber filteraids; depth filter sheets; and membrane cartridge filters. When choosing which filtration media to use, the decision is generally based on beer quality and the most economical method for achieving the desired result. The selection of a filtration media then leads to the selection of the required filtration equipment needed for that particular type of filtration.

Diatomaceous earth (DE) or diatomite filteraid is the skeletal remains of single-celled prehistoric plants called diatoms. This powdery material consists of a variety of shapes which, when collected on a septum interlace, form a filter cake that is 85 to 90 percent voids and open spaces and is not readily compacted or compressed by the exertion of pressure. The voids and open spaces are microscopically fine openings which allow beer to pass through while mechanically trapping the unwanted suspended particles.

DE filteraids are produced in various grades. The term *grade* generally refers to the physical size distribution of the filteraid particles. The choice of a fine or smaller particle grade results in a *bright beer* filtration, while the choice of a coarse or larger particle grade results in a *clear beer* filtration, which might not visibly show bright clarity. Generally, the medium to finer grades are used for beer filtration. The brewer can blend DE filter grades at the time of use by in the filter system to achieve the degree of clarity desired.

Perlite filteraids are a silicate of volcanic rock origin. This material is mined and milled to a sand. These sand granules contain some moisture, and with heating to near 2,400 degrees F (1,315.55 degrees C), the sand, now a molten glass, expands rapidly to form multicellular structures approximately twenty times greater in size. This expanded material is then milled to obtain particle sizes for a range of filteraid grades.

Filtration fibers such as cellulose or cellulose-cotton mixtures are used with precoat filteraid filters. These fibers are normally used in the formation of an initial precoat layer on the woven stainless steel screen septum of pressure leaf filters. This precoat layer forms a porous bridging mat or paperlike layer on the woven filter screen to assure retention of the subsequent filteraid (DE or perlite) layer and to aid in easy removal of the final accumulated filter cakes. The term "cakes" is used to describe the accumulated mixture of filteraid and beer-suspended solids which looks like a uniform coarse cheesecake layer on the filter screens.

Table Summary of Commonly Used Diatomaceous Earth Filteraid and Grades*

Manville Celite	Eagle Pitcher Celatom	Grefco Dicalite	Whitco Kenite	Harborlite Perlite
Filter Cel	——	Superaid	100	——
577	FP-2	UF	101	——
Std. Super Cel	FP-4	Speedflow	200	200
Hyflo Super Cel	FW-12	Speed Plus	700	635
535	FW-40	Speedex	1000	——

Chart does not show all grades produced by these manufacturers.

Filteraid filtration is generally regarded as providing the most economical form of filtration. The cost of the filteraids is quite low, and long filtration cycles at high filtration flow rates are possible. Filteraid filtrations are performed with the use of pressure leaf filters, candle filters, or with a plate-and-frame filter equipped with deep frames. It is important to consider the use of this method of filtration for beers with considerable haze, such as short-aged beers or beers that do not settle suspended particles well, either through natural settling or with the use of a settling aid such as isinglass. Certainly, if large quantities of beer are to be filtered, it is advantageous to use a filtration system that incorporates the use of filteraids such as DE, perlite, and cellulose fibers.

The factors affecting the natural settling of beer-suspended solids can include:

1. Temperature. The fermented beer should remain in the temperature range of 31 degrees F to 35 degrees F (-0.5 degree C to plus 1.7 degrees C) for a minimum of four days.
2. Yeast strain used. Some beer yeast strains have characteristic flocculations/cold-settling ability, while others are known to be nonflocculating or to have moderate flocculation characteristics.
3. Beer viscosity. Heavy-bodied beers with even a slightly greater viscosity can have a reduced natural settling.
4. Protein content. A greater concentration of suspended and colloidal proteins in the fermented beer can have a significant effect on natural clarification. The malts used, brew-house practices, and wort clarification can all influence the beer's protein content.

Filter Sheet Filtration

Filter sheets are a formulated depth filter media usually consisting of a blend of cellulose (paper) fibers and diatomaceous earth. Sometimes perlite is also incorporated. These materials, along with approved synthetic resins for bonding and hardening, are mixed into a uniform slurry and made into a depth filter media using sophisticated paper-forming equipment. Formulation and food-grade-approved materials used and control of formation are proprietary with the manufacturers. Series of media grades for specific applications provide a range of depth filter sheets with nominal, not absolute, retention ratings. Absolute retention ratings generally apply to filter media with a 1.0 micron rating or less but can also apply to certain filter media with larger micron retention ratings. A beta rating is used to further describe the term "absolute." Generally a beta ratio of 5,000 to 1 or greater (i.e., ratios of 10,000 to 1 or 20,000 to 1 which apply to absolute membrane filters) is called absolute. For example, a filter media said to be 0.5 micron absolute (beta 5,000) should retain 5,000 suspended particles of 0.5 micron or larger while allowing no more than one particle of 0.5 micron or larger to pass through. The beta ratio is established with standardized testing procedures. Depth-filter-sheet media falls into a beta ratio below the range considered absolute and is referred to as having a "nominal" retention rating. The range of retention ratings generally used for beer filtrations is 10 microns to 0.4 micron.

When placed in a plate-and-frame (or plate-to-plate) filter each incremental portion of beer passes only through one depth of a filter sheet. The flow entry side of a filter sheet generally has a slightly rough appearance and is a little more porous than the actual micron retention rating of the sheet. The increasingly tighter structure provides void space for retention of beer-suspended particles while allowing the clear beer to flow out the exit-smooth surface of the sheet. As with filteraid filtration, filter sheet filtration is a depth media filtration. Factors influencing the filtration results with filter sheets include: turbidity of incoming beer, filtration flow rate, retention grade of filter sheet used, and particle size of beer-suspended solids.

The size of the filter sheet used is dependent upon the filter equipment. The most common sizes found in or chosen by craft breweries are 40-by-40-centimeter, 60-by-60-centimeter, and 1-by-1-meter (commonly purchased as 1-by-2-meter) foldover sheets.

Summary of Depth Filter Media[*]

Depth Filter Media	Nominal Retention (microns)	Recommended Uses for Beer Filtration
Seitz-EK	0.4	Microbiologically stable beer, sterile bottling filtrations, premembrane filtrations
Seitz-KS50	0.5	Microbiologically stable beer, sterile bottling filtrations, premembrane filtrations
Seitz-K280 Celite 577	0.8	Yeast-free beer, brilliant clarity, premembrane predepth cartridge filtration
Seitz-K250 Celite Standard	2.5/3.0	Bright-clear beer filtrations — generally used for light- to amber-colored beers, predepth cartridge filtrations
Seitz-K300 Celite 512	3.0/4.0	Bright-clear beer filtrations — generally used for light- to amber-colored beers
Seitz-K700 Celite Hyflo	5.0/6.0	Clear beer filtrations — generally used for amber/brown to dark beers
Seitz-K1000 Celite 535	10.0/12.0	Clear to slightly hazy filtrations — generally used for dark beers and beers where a slight residual haze is preferred

Notes: (1) Filter sheet performance for microbiologically stable beer or yeast-free beer require beer previously filtered to bright beer clarity. (2) Nominal ratings for DE filteraids are based on a filtration precoat depth of 3 to 3.5 millimeters, 2.5 to 3 pounds/square meter of filtration surface. (3) Performance of depth filtration media is based on the operation of filter at filter-media manufacturers' recommended beer flow rate/square meter of filtration surface.

[*]Celite-DE, Harborlite-Perlite, Seitz-Filter Sheets are shown in this chart. Similar items are available from other manufacturers.

Filtration Equipment

The filtration equipment most commonly used in breweries include pressure leaf filteraid filters; plate-and-frame filters, plate-to-plate filters; and cartridge housing filters. *Pressure leaf filtration* systems, usually referred to as DE filters, consist of the following components:

1. A high-pressure centrifugal pump with a throttling flow control valve on the outlet side.
2. A pressure chamber with filter elements. These filter elements, commonly called screens or leaves (or candles in a candle filter), are positioned in either a vertical or horizontal orientation with uniform spacing between the filter elements. Each filter screen consists of an outer tightly woven stainless steel cloth and an internal open structure drain screen. Vertically oriented filter leaves have a woven screen on both sides. Horizontally oriented leaves are made with a top cloth screen and a bottom dish plate of stainless steel. Both types have internal drain screens.
3. A tank with a slow to moderate speed mixer for preparation of filteraid slurries. Associated with this slurry tank is a positive displacement adjustable rate of delivery dosing pump for the constant feeding of filteraid into the unfiltered beer flow entering the filter chamber. Some small pressure leaf filters use a flow-dilution method for dosing of the filteraid slurry. On these filters the slurry tank is a closed vessel positioned just downstream from the filter pump. Adjustment of small entry and exit valves allows for some unfiltered beer to enter this vessel and exit with a portion of the filteraid slurry into the main beer flow stream.
4. Connecting piping, valves, sight glasses, pressures gauges, and electrical control components (most filters available to craft breweries are complete monobloc, mobile, or stationary systems which include all

these.) Usually only compatible inlet and outlet fittings and an electrical plug (or hard wiring) need to be installed to make the filter system ready for operation.

The filtration principle involved in a pressure leaf filtration system is *depth filtration*. The initial depth layer is the precoat. This can consist of two individual layers: a bridging precoat layer and a filtration precoat layer. A single thicker layer can be applied for bridging the woven screens and providing the initial depth filtration layer. It is necessary to bridge the openings of the woven mesh-cloth screen. Filter screens are made with different size openings in the woven stainless steel cloth, generally ranging from 60 to 130 microns. A set of screens in any one filter has all the same screen material, and the choice of precoat materials to bridge the screen remains uniform for any particular filter. The secondary purpose of the bridging precoat layer is to retain subsequent layers of filteraid.

After completely filling the filter chamber, manifold piping, and the precoat slurry vessel to a convenient mixing level, a precoat slurry is made. The liquid used for precoating should be clear. While it is convenient to use the beer to be filtered, use water if the beer is very cloudy. Special practices can be used when using beer with CO_2 for the precoat liquid. The first precoat layer can be a layer of cellulose fiber or a layer of DE. Generally it requires less cellulose fiber to bridge the screens.

Cellulose fiber is precoated in the amount of 1.3 ounces/square foot to 2 ounces/square foot on all common filter screens. If only DE is utilized, use a medium to coarse grade. The minimum amount that will bridge the screens differs depending on the size of the screen's openings. For 60- to 80-micron screens, a precoat amount of 1.9 ounces/square foot to 2.3 ounces/square foot is sufficient, while for filter screens in the 120- to 130-micron opening range size, an amount of 2.6 ounces/square foot to 3.3 ounces/square foot is necessary.

The second precoat layer consists of DE or perlite and can be made with a single grade or mixture of grades. There are two schools of thought on the purpose and use of this clean precoat layer of filteraid. If a relatively thin layer is made (about 2 ounces/square foot), it functions primarily as a retaining layer for subsequent body-feed filteraids. It thereby serves as a mechanical or retaining layer and should consist of the same grade, or mixture of grades, as the body-feed (dosing slurry) filteraid. If a thicker layer is made (approximately 5 ounces/square foot), it serves as a bridging layer and also as a depth filtration layer for collecting beer-suspended particles that may not be retained in the body-feed layer. The thicker layer should consist of the same grade or mixture of grades as the body feed but it can be made using a slightly tighter grade or combination of tighter grades of filteraids. This clean thicker layer thereby is used as a final filtration layer, as the beer first passes through the accumulating body-feed layer and then through this filtration precoat layer. The desired filtration clarity must be achieved in a single pass of the beer through the filter. The previous chart showing nominal retention values should be helpful in selecting the correct filteraids. However, it is important to note that it is not a usual practice to use both diatomaceous earth and perlite filteraids in the same filter setup.

For most filtration systems, conduct precoating at a high flow rate. After the precoat layer is applied, allow the filtration system to recirculate for a number of minutes at the highest rate of flow to achieve maximum compaction of the precoat. While the filtration system is in this recirculation mode, the body-feed slurry can be prepared. This slurry is metered into the beer flow stream between the beer pump and the filter chamber.

The concentration of the dosing slurry and metered amount is determined through experience. The ideal filtration cycle is one in which the filter's cake volume capacity is achieved along with a pressure reading near the normal maximum recommended for the filtration systems or the volume of beer scheduled to be filtered is completed. For most pressure leaf filtration systems, the maximum cake capacity is 1.2 to 1.4 pounds/square foot, and depending on the filter system being used, the maximum pressure is 75 psi, 90 psi, or 100 psi. In brewpubs the total capacity of the pressure leaf system is oftentimes not required. The ideal filtration, in this case, is one in which a predicted amount of body-feed slurry is used in the completion of a beer filtration system, and perhaps the actual pressure is somewhat less than the maximum gauge reading.

The normal maximum recommended flow for vertical and horizontal screen pressure leaf filters used in the microbrewery can be as high as 45 to 50 gallons/square foot/hour. The overall average flow rate may be 50 to 70 percent of the maximum rate or approximately 25 to 35 gallons/square foot/hour. For rough or polishing filtrations, these filtration flow rates should provide satisfactory beer clarity. It is recommended that a flow rate no greater than 25 to 35 gallons/square foot/hour for most pressure leaf filters or a maximum rate no greater than 70 percent of the precoat flow rate be used for consistent bright beer clarity.

The filtered beer's clarity may determine the actual flow rate possible. If the desired clarity is not observed in the filtered beer, a satisfactory clarity may be achieved by reducing the flow rate. At a reduced flow rate, the filter cake is more capable of retaining the suspended particles, thus setting the maximum flow rate possible for this particular filtration cycle. If proper selection of precoat and body-feed filteraids has been made and is part of the brewer's regular program for each type of beer produced, the filtration results should remain consistent and predictable. When a satisfactory result is achieved at the beginning of the filtration cycle in a pressure leaf filtration, a slight increase in the clarity usually occurs as the filtration cycle continues. The explanation is that as the cycle continues, a thicker filter cake is formed, and the differential pressure increases, causing additional compaction of the filter cake. Because a high-pressure centrifugal pump is commonly used, the flow rate decreases as the downstream pressure increases. These three factors result in increased particle retention capability.

Single filtrations using a pressure leaf filter are used in the brewery for bright beer filtrations for: serving tanks or kegs in a brewpub; keg beer for a microbrewery or regional brewery, bottled beer for refrigerated storage, or with flash or tunnel pasteurization for ambient storage and a longer microbiological shelf life; and initial filtration clarity of beer to be filtered with tight retentive depth sheet and/or depth cartridge and membrane cartridge filters.

Generally the size of the filter system required is a ratio of one meter squared of filtration surface for each ten barrels of beer to be filtered. This figure is based on the filtration of ales. Lagers require about one-half to one-third the filtration surface per barrel.

Plate-and-frame filters can contain filter elements for filteraid filtrations or for filter-sheet-only filtrations. These filters, which are designed for use as filteraid filters, typically consist of the following components:

1. A beer pump with a constant and nonpulsating flow which can be a centrifugal pump or a positive displacement pump.
2. A DE slurry dosing system positioned for dosing of the filteraid slurry into the unfiltered beer stream between the beer pump and the plate-and-frame filter.
3. A stainless steel plate-and-frame filter having a stainless steel filter chassis with inlet and discharge piping, valves, sight glasses, pressure gauges, and flow rate indicator, as well as 1.5-inch or similar depth filter frame elements alternating with 0.5-inch or similar thickness filter plate elements.

The filtration principle involved in the use of a plate-and-frame filter with filteraid is also a depth filtration. The arrangement in the filter chassis consists of the deep open frames alternating with the narrower plates. The plates have a smooth support surface, usually of a perforated stainless steel sheet for plates made with stainless steel or with a uniformly grooved surface for plastic plates. A manufactured support sheet of cellulose or similar media is placed against each of the plates. This porous support sheet is the holding septum for the filteraid and the eventual accumulated filter cake. It also serves to form a seal for the outer edge of the frames and plates. The support sheet usually has a high flow rate capability with a particle retention capability sufficient to retain filteraids (18 to 25 microns), but not to retain the suspended particles from the beer being filtered. It is possible, however, to choose a retention-rated filter sheet as the support septum. The choice should be a filter sheet with the same, or only very slightly tighter, particle retention rating than the filteraid being used for precoating.

Operation of a plate-and-frame filter system requires the placement of a slurry doser inline after the beer pump and the filter. A thin precoat layer can be formed on the support sheet with water or a relatively clear beer by setting the dose at a higher rate of dosing for a number of minutes or by recirculating with a slurry tank. The precoat amount should be approximately 3 to 3.5 ounces/square foot of sheet surface. The flow rate for precoating should be about twice the regular beer filtration flow rate. When satisfactory beer clarity has been obtained or water has been "pushed out" of the filter, the beer flow is directed to the bright beer tank through the use of a filter outlet "tee." It also is advisable to set the slurry dosing pump at a higher rate during the beginning of the filtration cycle and then later to reduce the dosing rate to a level based on experience for the beer being filtered.

It is not possible to operate a plate-and-frame filter for filteraid filtrations at as high a filtration flow rate as that of a pressure leaf filter. This is a function of the liquid flow pattern in each style of filter. The beer flow enters the inlet piping of the plate-and-frame filter and the external tube formed along the top and bottom of the filter elements. A portion of the unfiltered beer with added filteraid enters each deep frame. The filteraid, along with beer-suspended particles, is retained on the support sheet. The filtered beer is collected in or on the plate elements and collected in the outlet flow tube formed on the opposite side of the filter. The normal maximum recommended filtration flow rate for this type of filtration is 12 gallons/square foot/hour, and a normal maximum pressure is 60 to 70 psi. At too high an internal pressure, there may be excessive dripping of beer from the outer edges of the cellulose sheet septums.

Although the plate-and-frame style of filter is found in many established European breweries, it usually is not a current choice in the North American brewing industry. The equipment cost to achieve a desired filtration flow rate and total volume capacity is higher than a pressure leaf filter. The operation and cleaning can be more difficult, operating cost can be higher, and the floor space required is generally greater for the plate-and-frame filter/slurry tank arrangement.

Regularly use plate-and-frame filters for plate-to-plate sheet filtration. Many breweries regularly use these filters, which are easy to set up, operate, and clean, are used for single-filtration bright beer filtrations in many brewpubs or for sterile sheet filtration of prefiltered beers in many micro and regional breweries. A plate-and-frame filter for filter sheet filtrations consists of a filter chassis as described previously, but in this case it contains only filter plate elements, no open frames. Filter plates are of stainless steel or plastic and only depth filter sheets are used as the filtration media.

The use of a plate-and-frame filter for sheet filtration only is best suited for the filtration of beers with a minimum of suspended particles, as no filteraid use is possible. In this style of filter, there is no collection space for a filter cake. The filtration is accomplished with a depth filter sheet, and only the 3.5- to 4.2-millimeter depth and void space are available to collect, adsorb, and retain beer-suspended particles and microorganisms.

When operating a sheet filter, it is important to monitor the sheet-filter manufacturer's recommended maximum filtration flow rates and gauge pressure between the inlet flow (differential pressure). The filter sheet collects suspended particles in a network of small porous pathways in the defined depth of the filter sheet. These are usually made with a slightly looser matrix on the entry side of the filter sheet and an increasingly tighter matrix through the depth of the filter sheet. If too great a flow rate is used, this liquid flow lessens the performance of the filter sheet. If the pressure difference between the entry side and exit side of the filter sheet is too great, some particles already retained may be forced through the filter sheet and into the filtered beer stream.

In general, the guidelines for beer filtration flow rates used by filter-sheet manufacturers are as follows:

Filtration	Filtration Flow Rate in Gallons/Ft²/Hour	Maximum differential pressure in PSI
Rough *(if necessary)*	3 to 25	30 to 40
Polishing	3 to 14	25 to 30
Sterile	3 to 6.5	18 to 20

To assure satisfactory performance of a filter sheet, it is necessary to choose the correct filter sheet for specific uses. For instance, it is not practical to use a tight-grade or sterilizing-grade filter sheet for a beer with a high level of suspended particles and yeast. For these filtrations the beer must initially be prefiltered with filteraids or with looser grade filter sheets to remove the larger particles within the matrix of the filter cake or filter sheet. Larger particles may deposit only on the surface of the tighter grades and form a nonporous layer. Too great a quantity of suspended particles in the incoming beer stream can diminish the optimum performance of the tight or sterilizing grade even at the recommended flow rates.

The plate-and-frame filter also can be equipped with a flow diversion chamber. This facilitates the use of the filter as a two-stage filter for a single-filtration operation. The beer is initially prefiltered in the first section of the filter, then passed through the flow-diversion chamber and into the second or final section of the filter where final polishing or sterile sheet filtration is accomplished. The filter chassis for two-stage filtrations can be equipped only with filter plates in both sections, thereby a looser filter sheet is used in the initial section, and a tighter grade filter sheet is used in the final section. If filteraids such as DE are not used, this filter setup prolongs the filtration cycle for beer with moderately high suspended solids.

However, the most versatile arrangement for two-stage filtrations is one equipped with deep frames, support sheets, and plates in the first section, and with filter plates holding only filter sheets in the final section. This provides the greatest flexibility for the filtration of beers with variable levels of suspended solids and assures a final filtration result equivalent to the rated performance of the filter sheet used in the final section of the filter.

In sizing a particular filter for a two-stage operation with a filteraid or looser grade filter sheet in the first stage and a tight or sterile filter sheet in the second stage, it is important to remember that the overall filtration flow rate desired be based on the recommended maximum flow rate of the final filter sheet. The first-stage prefiltration section should provide sufficient surface area or filter cake capacity so that most of the suspended particles in the beer are removed in this section. Use a filter sheet with a medium retention rating or a medium polishing grade of DE. The prefiltered beer now entering the final or sterile filtration section will contain only a slight haze of submicron-sized particles to be removed in the final-stage filter sheets. The choice of many new breweries is to use a monobloc pressure leaf filter for the first-stage prefiltration and to pass the outlet prefiltered flow directly through a plate-to-plate sheet-filter. Only the beer pump incorporated with the pressure leaf monobloc is used to push the beer through both filters.

Choosing a Filter for Bright Beer Filtrations
Pressure Leaf Filter (DE Filter)
Recommended for:
- all microbreweries with a fermenter size of 10 barrels or greater as preparing, operating, and cleaning a DE filter for lesser quantities is not very practical. All regional-sized breweries.
- the filtration of beers which remain quite hazy prior to filtration. This could be due to factors such as, short aging time, minimum temperature possible for cold settling, and yeast strain used.
- breweries equipped with unitanks or aging tanks with only a bottom outlet (without internal stand pipe).
- breweries where there is a regular filter operator and not a sequence of employees where constant training may be necessary. In such a brewery a plate-and-frame filter is recommended.
- brewpubs where 30 to 40 barrels of ales, 60 to 80 barrels of lagers (if a lager-beer-only brewery), or greater quantities are to be filtered per filter run.
- prebottling filtrations for limited shelf life (cold storage).

Plate-and-Frame Filter (Plate-to-Plate Filter Sheet Filter)
Recommended for:
- most brewpubs with fermenter size up to 40 barrels, or 80 barrels if brewing lagers only (based on cost/barrel considerations).
- the filtration of well-settled beers where an easy-to-operate filter is preferred. Unfiltered beer tanks should be equipped with either a racking valve, a racking valve with racking arm and sight glass, or a stand pipe.
- practical and economical use with up to 40-barrel quantities of ales, 80- to 100-barrel quantities of lager beers.
- breweries where floor space is minimal for operating and cleaning a beer filter and where the disposal of wet paper sheets is more convenient than the disposal of filter cake materials.
- prebottling filtrations for limited or extended shelf life.

Generally the size for a plate-and-frame filter used for single-filtration bright beer filtrations, as in many brewpubs, requires a ratio of from one to two medium-grade filter sheets, size 40 by 40 centimeters, for each barrel of beer to be filtered. This sizing is based on the filtration of ales. Lager beers normally require about one-third to one-half the number of sheets per barrel to be filtered.

Construct filtration equipment to facilitate sterilization with steam, hot water, or chemicals. Cleaning procedures following each use of the filter should include rinsing away all organic materials followed by sterilization. Periodic cleaning with warm alkaline or caustic solution is recommended. This is done in a plate-and-frame filter by leaving an exhausted set of filter sheets in the filter and then discarding them after chemical cleaning, acid-neutralizing, and rinsing. Sanitizing chemical solutions compatible with the filter-constructed components can remain in the filter between uses.

Beer microbiological stability achieved by filtration is important for the microbrewer producing bottled beers or keg beers for distribution with uncertain storage practices. There are a number of methods of filtration in use for this purpose:

1. Sterilizing filter sheet filtration using a plate-to-plate sheet filter
2. Sterilizing filter sheet filtration followed by a membrane cartridge filter using cartridge filter-using filter(s)
3. Depth cartridge filter followed by a membrane cartridge filter, a depth cartridge filter, or a depth-mass filter cake filter

Sterilizing filter sheet filtrations have been performed for many years for the purpose of sterilization filtration of beer. This method is widely used throughout Europe. The critical factors to note here are the importance of the all-sanitary design of the filtration equipment; good sanitation practices; well-prefiltered beer; use of a smooth, constant pump; and a filtration flow rate not exceeding 6.5 gallons/square feet/hour (0.21 barrels/square foot/hour); and a maximum allowable differential pressure of 20 psi.

The advantage of this method is that it requires no secondary filter equipment or materials. The disadvantage is that it uses a depth filter medium rather than an absolute *beta* ratio of five-thousand-to-one or greater particle-size-rated filter media. A large filtration surface is required for filtrations at higher flow volume as low flow rates per square foot of filter media are required. *Beta* ratios refer to standardized testing method for particle size retention. A *beta* ratio of five thousand to one for a filtration media stated to be 0.5 micron absolute means that for particle sizes of 0.5 micron or larger, one in five thousand particles of 0.5 micron or larger may pass through the media even under normal use conditions.

Sterile sheet filtration followed by *membrane cartridge filtration* provides the additional assurance of the membrane filter for microbiological stability as well as longer life for the more expensive membrane filter media by using the sheet filter as a secondary prefilter. The usual production process is to first filter the beer through the sheet filter into a bottling-government cellar tank or into a surge tank. Immediately, as with a surge tank, or within one to three days storage at a low temperature, the beer is filtered through the membrane filter which is located just prior to the bottle (or keg) filler. The membrane filter offers several advantages over sterile sheet filtration only. This filter media has micron ratings such as 0.45 micron, 0.65 micron, 1.0 micron, and 0.65 micron. This is an absolute rating with most manufacturers providing a *beta* ratio of ten thousand to one or greater and giving retention assurances of 99.995. Most membrane filtration units can be "integrity tested" to determine the ongoing integrity of the membrane media. This is commonly done before and after each use of the production cartridge housing containing the membrane filter element(s).

It should also be noted that a great number of the capillaries within the membrane media have constructions of much less than the rated maximum pore size. It is these small openings that rapidly plug and require membrane regeneration and eventual replacement. Membrane filters may possibly remove important taste constituents from specialty beers.

Filteraid filtration may be followed by sterile sheet filtration or by premembrane depth filtration followed by a membrane. With the use of the finest, tightest grades of DE, submicron filtrations can be accomplished in a pressure leaf filter or a plate-and-frame filter. The pressure leaf filter is precoated with a cellulose fiber followed by a thick layer (6.5 ounces/square foot) of the tightest grade of DE. The body-feed slurry used is also of this tight grade. The filtration flow rate is adjusted from the start of the filtration cycle to no greater than 15 gallons/square foot/hour. The filtration cycle can continue up to the maximum normal operating pressure of the particular filtration equipment used. If DE is used in a plate-and-frame filter, the filtration is also performed with a tight retention grade of DE. The filtration flow rate recommended is up to 12 gallons/square foot/hour, and maximum pressure is 45 psi. It is more practical to use the plate-and-frame filter in the two-stage method, as described previously, if sterile sheet filtration in a single-filtration operation is desired. The prefiltration is accomplished with a tighter grade, not necessarily the tightest grade of DE, and the final filtration is done with a filter sheet. It is also possible and practical to use the pressure leaf filter inline with a plate-to-plate sheet filter to perform a two-stage filtration in a single operation.

Some pleated depth cartridge filters with absolute retention ratings or depth-mass filters may be used just prior to the beer-filling machine with or without an accompanying downstream absolute-rated membrane cartridge housing filter. If the only prefiltration of beer for this method is with a pressure leaf filter, this filtration must be with a tight-retentive filteraid, such as Celite 577 or an equivalent. The operation of the pressure leaf filter must be used at reduced flow rates.

These depth cartridge filters may have absolute retention ratings, as *beta* five thousand to one. Depth filter cartridges and perhaps depth-mass filters can have a good *beta* ratio, as five thousand to one, but these cannot be integrity tested. It is important to note that all methods for sterile/microbiological beer require excellent clarification or a tight polishing filtration prior to the sterilization filtration to assure the expected microbiological and colloidal particle retention.

The brewer has a choice of well-proven filtration methods and should choose the filtration method that best fits the needs of the brewery.

Suggested Readings

Manville. "Filtration & Minerals," *Celite Filter Aids* (1989).

Grefco, Inc. *Dicalite Filtration Bulletin B-16*, (1979).

Thilert, Tom. "Beer Filtration," **The New Brewer**, vol. 4, no. 2 (1988): 1, 16–23.

Chapter 11
Insurance for the Brewery

by Peter Whalen
President of Goggins and Whalen Insurance Agency Inc.

Like any other business decision you will make, when purchasing insurance it's best to know what you need before you buy into a plan so you can make an informed decision. The following information outlines specific tips and coverages which are meant to supplement basic property and liability policies. While this information will not make you an insurance expert, it will prepare you to obtain an adequate property and liability insurance program for your business venture.

Property Insurance

This section includes coverages for hard assets as well as cash and lost income opportunities. Two general rules to follow are to always purchase *replacement cost coverage* and to always *insure to value*.

Replacement cost coverage insures that at the time of a loss you will be paid enough to replace the damaged property. Other contracts deduct for depreciation, which can leave you short of the cash you need to get back in business quickly.

Insuring to value means you have chosen an amount of coverage (limit) which accurately reflects the total figure needed to replace all of your property, including building, contents, and loss of income. If insurance costs get too expensive, you should look to save money by increasing your deductible rather than scimping on the upper limit of coverage.

Another reason to insure to value is that most insurance policies require you to do so.

If they determine that you cheated, they will apply a penalty when paying a partial loss. This might also jeopardize their interest in renewing your policy.

The following are short definitions and discussions on certain property and liability coverages you need as a business, and particularly as a craft brewer.

Loss of income (a.k.a. business interruption). This is probably the most "important but ignored" coverage available. It provides you with the funds to pay bills during the period you are shut down after a loss. After the fire, bills do not stop, particularly debt service and key salaries. In addition, you still need an income to maintain your lifestyle while you are rebuilding. Loss of income coverage is there for you to pay any ongoing bills and profits that would have been earned if you were open. You should definitely purchase a sufficient amount of this coverage.

Boiler and machinery. It is important for breweries to have boiler and machinery coverage because it protects you from losses due to machinery breakdowns, including your equipment and your HVAC systems. If you cannot produce or distribute your beer because your equipment malfunctions, the consequences could be severe, especially if it triggers a spoilage problem. Make sure when you purchase this type of insurance policy that it includes off-premise power failure and loss of income.

Employee dishonesty and money and securities. Both of these coverages protect you against the loss of cash or its equivalent. Unless you write (and sign) all checks yourself and no other employee handles cash, you need employee dishonesty. Money and securities covers you if someone else other than an employee steals money. Since it is often difficult to determine just who did the crime, it is preferable to have both coverages so as to avoid any possibility of a denial of the claim.

Selling price endorsement. This is an addition to your policy which can make a big difference to microbrewers. It simply changes the language of the policy so that you receive the full selling price, rather than just your investment, for your finished product on-site at the time of a claim. This is another way of protecting your profit.

Liability Insurance

It is important that you buy enough liability insurance. I suggest a minimum of $1 million for smaller operations with additional layers of coverage for larger breweries.

Non-owned automobile. Most businesses occasionally ask an employee to run an errand, whether it be on their way to or from work or during normal working hours. If the employee is driving their personal automobile at the time of an accident, you, the employer, could be sued. Although your employee's personal auto policy would pay, they may be carrying very low liability limits and any lawyer would be swift to include you in the suit upon discovery that the employee was doing something on your behalf. Unless you have a non-owned auto policy, you would have no coverage for this exposure. The good news is that obtaining this type of policy is usually uncomplicated and quite inexpensive.

Product recall. This coverage is appropriate to a craft brewery with any outside sales. If you were to find out that there was something wrong with the beer you provided to either retail liquor stores or restaurants, you would have to react immediately. The beer industry is known for having a very high standard of quality control. However, there is a chance that your product could leave your premises providing some threat to the public. For instance, a contaminant could infiltrate your beer or perhaps your bottling machine malfunctioned leaving tiny pieces of glass in the bottles. The cost of recalling your product could be severe, but you would have no choice. Product recall would reimburse you for the expense related to such an operation.

Liquor liability. This presents a separate and distinct exposure from general liability. The need for this coverage is obvious to brewpubs who are serving alcohol daily, but micros need it as well. Manufacturers often are named in lawsuits as a matter of routine. If someone was in an accident after consuming your product, there is little question that you would be involved in any subsequent legal preceding. Additionally, most craft brewers participate in beer festivals and/or occasionally donate beer to charitable or promotional causes. Regardless of how ridiculous the circumstances may be, thousands of dollars in legal fees could easily be spent proving just that point. Of course, make sure legal expenses would be covered by your liquor liability policy.

The information here is in no way intended to be complete. Every business is unique and deserves individual analysis to determine all that is required to accomplish comprehensive insurance protection. However, this information will allow you to approach the insurance marketplace from an educated position.

The reason automobile and workers' compensation insurance is omitted here is because these coverages, although usually less complex than property and liability policies, can vary dramatically depending on the state in which the brewery is located.

When choosing an insurance company, consider the company's financial strength. Unless nothing else is available, never elect to do business with a company less than an A.M. Best rating of A-. You buy insurance to feel secure. The last thing you need to worry about is the inability of the insurance company to pay your claim in the unfortunate event that one occurs.

Chapter 12
Product Development

by Jim Koch
Founder of the Boston Beer Company

The first time I went to the Institute for Brewing Studies' National Microbrewers Conference was 1983. There were only twenty of us microbrewers, and we were vastly outnumbered by the hundreds of homebrewers in attendance. In 1987, there were 120 people at the conference. We were all amazed at how many of us there were. I noted that in the intervening four years in North America, there had been a small brewery started for each and every one of those 120 people. Now, almost ten years later, I am amazed that there were only 120 people at the conference. Since then, there have been half a dozen breweries started for every individual at that conference. We did not know what the future held then and we still do not know. The future may continue to surprise us in its hospitality for more breweries. I offer this as a word of encouragement and welcome.

I want to discuss product development in a little broader sense than just a "beer," and maybe in a little narrower sense than what you may think. What I don't really feel any need or desire to write about is what small breweries have sometimes worried about during the last forty years: things like marketing, finding a niche, targeting the consumer, and segmenting the market. My words of advice on that are: forget about that stuff. It is probably the least useful thing that will enter your head. It has been my opinion that the emphasis on marketing has been one of the worst things that has ever happened to American business. That shouldn't sound surprising. After all, you are

all consumers. How many of you want to buy a better *marketed* product? How many of you want to buy a better *made* product? I think the answer is pretty obvious. This is something I want to stress.

Another thing I want to emphasize is the importance of what we do and who we are — the importance of selling ourselves as the brewer and the individual, while we sell our product, even if it means going from bar to bar selling our beer. Those of you who enter this business will learn that selling is one of the most important concepts. In fact, the quality of our beer also depends directly on how well it sells. If it doesn't sell, it goes bad sitting in the wholesaler's warehouse or on the retailer's shelf. You will realize that your livelihood every day depends on going out and selling. No amount of marketing will sell your beer for you. I emphasize that. People often talk about marketing, but they forget to talk about selling.

The analogy I use is this. I tell people that the difference between marketing and selling is very much akin to the difference between masturbation and sex. One of them is something that you can do by yourself in a dark room and feel like you're accomplishing something. The other requires the complexity, joy, and sometimes the anguish of human contact. Remember that when you start up a small brewery. The selling is very important; the marketing you can forget about. We become our beer in the minds of our customers, and sometimes in our own minds as well.

You will find that when you are selling your beer, you are also selling yourself and your own integrity. The product that we as brewers sell is first and foremost what is in the bottle. In addition to that, to be successful in any business you also must have a very clear idea of what constitutes your own notion of integrity. For instance, ask yourself why you are doing this and what your objectives are. Determine the way in which you make the hard choices in defining and developing your product, and notice what you are selling.

Making those hard choices defines your product. Let me give you an example. There is a brewpub out west that has a two-vessel system and brews from grain. One day, the drive on the mash/lauter tun broke and couldn't be fixed. The brewpub was out of beer. To get going, the owners called a supplier of malt extract. Some people think malt extract is terrible, while others don't mind it at all. The owners got the malt extract and made their beer with it. It turned out that the beer was a lot better with the extract. Anybody who has worked with a brewhouse with such a small mash/lauter tun, and who knows its limitations and quality, will understand why it can very well be possible to make better beer with malt extract than with grain. Ask yourself what you would do in this case. Would you continue to make a beer that is a better beer, a beer that people like better because it tastes better, although you are using someone else's extract? Or would you continue to be a whole-grain brewer and perhaps produce a less desirable product? I submit that there are many ways of being in this business, and they can all have their own integrity. That choice struck me as being very compelling. There are no right answers. One way emphasizes the quality of the beer. The other emphasizes the nature of the brewery. Both are right.

Product development is fundamentally about what you are trying to accomplish by entering this industry. Look at existing craft breweries, and you will find that there are three main variations from which people have chosen. There is the traditional microbrewery,

there is the brewpub, and there is the contract brewer. I can talk about these choices since Boston Beer Company makes beer all three ways: in our brewery in Boston, as a contract brewer in several breweries, and in a Samuel Adams Brewpub in Philadelphia.

When you are in the restaurant business, brewing is important, but often less important than running the restaurant portion well. If you want to be in the restaurant business, start a brewpub. Or you can instead choose to be a contract brewer or an owner brewer. Then it is distribution that you must worry about. With the brewpub, you must start by getting people to walk in the door of your establishment. As a contract brewer, or as an owner brewer, you have a whole different set of considerations. You have to sell to the bar owner and you have to sell to the distributor. I leave it up to you to try to figure out which one is the bigger hassle. Is it the guy who walks into the restaurant and wants a light beer? Or is it the bar manager you are trying to persuade to take off the Amstel tap and put on your own beer? I don't know who can be the bigger problem. They both have their own levels of difficulty, and you must make a choice.

Being a contract brewer has its own set of compromises and its own set of methods for improving what you do. One thing you should consider is that being only a contract brewer can be less satisfying than having your own brewery. I say this because your beer and your brewing becomes your life — in fact, they eat your life. It is nice to have something tangible you can look at and feel is yours. It's kind of an "edifice complex." I raise this as a very important point. In 1988, I built a brewery in Boston. It cost about $2.5 million. It's a great brewery for small production and particularly for developing new beers or perfecting existing ones. But from a business point of view, there was really no good business reason to spend that money, as my investors have reminded me repeatedly. Luckily, I still own the company and can spend the money any way I please. I'd guess that to build a decent lager brewery with a bottling line in a major city with a big market, it costs $2 to $4 million. That is a lot of money. Those of you who are familiar with the experiences at Old New York Beer Company know how difficult it can be. That company had almost $4 million and vaporized it. It is all gone — $4 million. The brewery was sold in pieces, and the owners wrote off the money. That is frightening. Having your own brewery is not going to make the beer better, it is not going to be any cheaper, and there is a lot of risk in it. But as a contract brewer, you will probably dream of your own brewery. You can't help it.

The other thing you should consider as a contract brewer is that you are locked into brewing a beer that fits the equipment choices of the brewery that makes your beer unless you have millions of dollars to spend on changes. We spend several million dollars a year making changes but we're lucky to be able to spend that kind of money. If you want to brew with two-row barley and the brewery has only one malt silo, forget it. You are going to have to use six-row. You can select the hops you want to use, but how your beer is stabilized depends on the brewery's system. You may end up with a tunnel pasteurizer when you would have preferred something else. You may have to compromise and use their yeast. You may have to limit the kind of mash program and therefore certain characteristics of the finished beer. Kraeusening with an all-malt brew may be impossible since you probably won't get your volume up to one brew a week. These are hard choices.

How you choose to stabilize your beer is an interesting choice. Unless you bottle condition, you have to do something — either sterile filter or pasteurize (or you could just let bugs grow in the beer!). Pasteurizing is expensive, and it creates a big marketing problem. "Unpasteurized" sounds a lot better to the consumer. Micro-filtering the beer not only costs less, but allows brewers to exploit the ignorance of the "sophisticated" beer drinker by telling him how their beers aren't pasteurized. Even Miller has seen the marketing value here with the micro-filtered Genuine

Draft. I say "exploit the ignorance" here for a reason many of us find surprising: pasteurization, unless it is done wrong, does not noticeably affect the flavor of beer, whereas micro-filtration does. Micro-filtration robs the beer of the subtler, more delicate flavors that pasteurization leaves in.

I once did an experiment. I asked twenty brewers, or those with good palates, to evaluate three versions of Samuel Adams, all bottled two days ago from the same tank. One was pasteurized (at about 15 PUs), one was micro-filtered (at 0.5 microns, the size you need to be assured of filtering out bacteria), and the third was totally fresh, neither pasteurized nor filtered. I asked the twenty brewers to pick the beer, either pasteurized or filtered, that tasted most like the totally fresh sample. This experiment was to show whether pasteurization or filtration affects the flavor more. I was a little surprised when the people from the Association of Brewers gave me the results: of the twenty tasters, fourteen felt that the pasteurized beer tasted most like the totally fresh beer. Only six picked the filtered beer. I did the same test recently with the taste panel at the brewery, and everyone picked the pasteurized beer. As an interesting sidelight, a majority of the twenty tasters also picked the pasteurized beer as the one they liked best.

I did this experiment to make a point about hard choices. Pasteurization seems to give you better beer, but it is more expensive, and it is a big marketing disadvantage. One of the most respected craft brewers in the United States pasteurizes not only its bottled beer, but also its draft beer. It just doesn't make an issue of telling people. Filtration will degrade the beer, but it is cheaper, and it allows the marketing high ground. And for many, selling an unpasteurized beer feels better. No choice is right or wrong.

There are also hard choices for the owner of a traditional microbrewery to make. One is whether to brew an ale or a lager. As any homebrewer knows, ale is much easier to make than lager, and problems with ale are not immediately obvious to the drinker. With lager, brewery deficiencies stand out like a sore thumb. Ale also is financially much easier. As a rough idea, it costs twice as much in capital costs to make lager as ale. Roughly, you can turn your tanks over every ten days with an ale. With a lager, it may be once every forty days. As you can see, you can make roughly three or four times as much ale as lager in the same brewery.

Then there is the decision whether to bottle or keg. Draft causes fewer problems, while a bottling line is a very expensive contraption to buy and run, and to bottle right is even more expensive. One of the things you worry about is air. When beer goes stale, it does so largely as a function of light, heat, and air in the beer during storage. In 1987, I tested eleven micro-brewed beers from the Northwest, and the average air in those beers was *three* milliliters. Big breweries would probably throw out a bottling of beer if the average air were *one* milliliter. These milliliters of air translate into about four weeks of shelf life. A lot, maybe most, craft beer doesn't make it from the brewery through the distributors to the retailer to the customer and into his mouth in four weeks. The fact is, a lot of craft brewers are selling stale beer much of the time because of the quality limitations of their equipment. Hard choices.

Small brewers sometimes make compromises and put out a beer that does not meet our highest quality standards. To have the kind of bottling line that meets high standards, where you can get a three- or four-month shelf life in beer, can cost $400,000, or something close to that. If you can't afford that, you are not going to get that kind of quality. That is a compromise you may have to make. The customer won't know that the beer is stale unless you are willing to mark the bottles with a freshness date. Currently, less than 20 percent of craft brewers are willing to share that information with consumers.

Distributing beer is a big problem for everyone. Freshness, and therefore quality, is at risk from the day the beer leaves the brewery. Getting the beer right at the brewery eliminates perhaps a third of the bad beer that the consumer gets. From my experience, two-thirds of the bad beer that reaches consumers comes from deterioration *after* the beer leaves the brewery. Preserving actual quality rather than perceived quality is a very difficult problem. You have to watch wholesalers' inventories, ship in small quantities, and absorb higher freight costs.

I have done something that may backfire, but I think it is a risk worth taking. I hope others also will take the risk in order to guarantee fresh beer to the consumer. It is something that German brewers do. I mark each bottle of Samuel Adams with a freshness code that consumers can read. Every bottle of Samuel Adams now says on the side, "Enjoy before month so and so." I think that Redhook also has adopted this system, and I applaud them for that. It takes guts to do it. Virtually every brewer does, in fact, date the beer in some way or another, but it is in a secret code that the consumer — and usually the retailer and wholesaler — can't read. Hopefully, we as small brewers can upgrade the quality of specialty beers in this country and let the consumer know how fresh our beer is. But we have to walk the walk, not just talk the talk. It is a choice you have to make. Are you willing to take the chance that if your beer is not fresh the consumer will know it? This, again, is a hard choice, and you must ask yourself once more what you got into this business to do. Do you mind selling stale beer to unsuspecting consumers?

Another question you will face regardless of whether you are a contract brewer or brewery owner is, where do you sell your beer? You will find that every small brewer has wholesalers calling him from outside his area wanting to buy his beer. You may think that is a great problem to have. But it isn't. It is not only a big problem; it is a great temptation. A guy calls you from Dallas, Texas, wanting to order one thousand cases of your beer. Do you sell it to him? The answer probably should be no if it is going to take him three months or more to sell one thousand cases of your beer. And it is going to take the package stores another three months. After all, who in Dallas, Texas, has heard of your beer? You are going to be responsible for putting a lot of stale beer on the market unless you turn down that order.

How you respond to that kind of temptation defines the original integrity of your idea. In going back to my original thought, it is important to remember that what you are going to be selling everyday is yourself, your beer, and your own integrity. It is very important to have a clear idea of what that integrity means to you. There are a lot of people in the small brewery business. They handle their businesses differently, and they all have their own clear sense of what they are doing, why they are doing it, and the integrity behind it. I think we all will find it much more comfortable to go out there and sell our beer if we do have a clear sense of what it is that we are all about and believe in the rightness of the choices we make.

Chapter 13
What Have They Learned?

by Jim Dorsch
Editor of *American Brewer* and *Beer, the magazine*

Everyone makes mistakes, and everyone makes decisions based on predictions of the future that may not prove accurate. What decisions would brewers make differently if they could make them again? What did they learn from hard experience? What made them winners?

No one will ever run a business without making decisions they regret. It may not seem so at the time, but bad decisions can lead to important learning experiences. How can you guide your decision-making to minimize the number of bad decisions you make? How can you drive your business with positive decisions? Each brewer has a unique vision. You will make different decisions than another brewer would because you have a different vision of yourself and your business. Only you have the intimate knowledge of what you really want as a brewer and businessperson.

Paul Shipman, president of Redhook Ale Brewery, Seattle, Washington, has a vision of a company that grows and moves from stage to stage, always expanding its scope. Redhook operates several breweries and sees the United States as its target market.

Jerry Bailey, president of Old Dominion Brewing Company, Ashburn, Virginia, has entered the ranks of regional specialty brewers and plans to keep it that way. Jerry wants, first and foremost, to be a local brewer.

Paul Shipman and Jerry Bailey are very different as individuals and as businessmen, but each knows what he wants to accomplish. Each has a concept of his business that acts as an anchor, pulling his efforts back to the master plan if he makes a decision that steers him off course.

The Strategist

Jim Koch, president of Boston Beer Company, calls Paul Shipman "a master strategist, the best strategist in the business." Since 1982, Shipman has grown the Redhook Ale Brewery from a tiny neighborhood microbrewery to a national player with multiple breweries and distribution through one of its major investors, Anheuser-Busch.

"We had a rough start on product quality. We're lucky we were one of the first in the Northwest," says Shipman. He takes credit for launching the industry in the Northwest region, saying, "Competent homebrewers figured they could do better than us in their basements." It was during this rocky time that quality became Shipman's mantra: "We began to see quality as a basis for survival. It's deeply imbedded in our corporate memory."

Keeping your financial structure simple in the beginning, says Shipman, is important as well: "You should really think about your corporate and financial structure, so there's nothing to unwind or correct in terms of becoming a public company. Keep the financial structure simple; try to stick to a single class of stock."

If he could do it over again, Shipman feels he would plan better for growth: "I focused more than necessary on the risks, and not enough on the upside and the potential for success." While Redhook selected wholesalers carefully, Shipman says he would have been even more careful if he did it again: "We would have exercised even greater control and care in setting up our wholesaler relationships, anticipating what happens in success as well as stress. You need to anticipate evolution in relationships. Wholesaler relationships should be contractual in nature because," as Shipman points out, "it's a lot more practical to negotiate at the beginning."

Shipman and his partner, Gordon Bowker, tried to formulate a clear vision of the playing field and how they would enter the game. They made some wrong assumptions, but their vision never faded. "We saw the business in big terms," he says. "We saw brewery closures as a great opportunity for specialty products to compete with imports. I see domestic specialty producers as destined to replace the imports."

When he was raising additional funds in 1987, Shipman already envisioned a public offering. "Investors asked me how they were going to get liquid. I told them we were going to go public," he says.

When a company starts to grow, adjustments need to be made quickly. Don't put off building a new facility when the time is right. "We expanded our first brewery, and moved out before the paint was dry," says Shipman. "I've determined an indicator of when it's time to go to the next step; it's whenever you're doing special engineering of equipment to make it fit in your building."

One of your first decisions should be whether it's a good time to start your business. Shipman thinks it might be too late for some players, saying, "The golden age was way back in the eighties in most areas. It's hard in our enthusiasm to recognize that the golden age is in the past. The task for an entrepreneur is to ferret out some opportunities."

Determining whether your skills and aspirations will take you where you want to go is essential to success. If your vision stops at a certain stage, progress may come to a screeching halt. "If your vision going in plays out, and you don't reinvent your approach and aspirations, you get stuck. Meanwhile, the business is still pulsing, waiting to go into another dimension," says Shipman.

Redhook has used consultants in virtually every aspect of its business. Shipman advises brewers to use consultants at critical steps, including an evaluation of the fitness of the chief executive to handle these transitions. "Companies that don't have a strong board or outside consultants run a real risk," he says.

Shipman learned early to evaluate his skills and delegate tasks he wasn't good at. Coming out of college, he had become an apprentice winemaker. "I realized I wasn't that good at it," he says. So when he started Redhook, he concentrated on the business, and hired someone else to brew the beer.

Around 1991 and 1992, Shipman surveyed the southern California market and wasn't comfortable with the distribution. "I decided I was not going to take another step before I found a way to do it better." Before long, he says, he went to St. Louis and pitched his company to Anheuser-Busch, resulting in A-B's taking an equity position, and Redhook's gaining access to national distribution.

Shipman and company aren't immune to mistakes, but they've groomed an awareness that helps them take advantage of the associated lessons: "We keep asking ourselves how we can take a better, more effective, higher quality approach for the next step." He talks a lot about steps, revealing a clear focus on his goal of taking his business to new levels, one step at a time. Shipman's vision, the result of hard work and mental discipline, is what keeps Redhook growing.

The Realist

Jim Koch learned a tough lesson in 1986, when he attempted to install a 250,000-barrel brewery in the old Haffenreffer plant in Boston, where he operates a small developmental brewery today. "My big mistake was trying to renovate an old brewery," he says.

The Haffenreffer facility had lain dormant for twenty years, and was on the National Register of Historic Places. Because of this, to install a new brew house would require Koch to essentially take the building apart, install a steel superstructure, and reassemble the building, exactly as he had found it, around the skeleton.

Koch had bought all the equipment for the brewery, which he anticipated would cost $8 million. When the bids came in, the tab was projected at almost twice that amount. Boston Beer Company took a $2.25 million bath.

The lesson: "Don't treat stainless steel as an aphrodisiac." The result: Koch is forever cured of what he calls his "edifice complex."

Like Shipman, Koch has a vision of where he wants to go. For him it boils down to one sentence: "I've always had a goal to build a national brand based on quality, and the key is to have a very clear focus," he says. "It's allowed us to make the right choices. It enables you to know when you're on the right track, and when you go too far off it."

The Survivor

In November 1991 Kirby Shyer founded the Zip City Brewing Company, the first brewpub to survive in a tough Manhattan market. Shyer's persistence carried him through a bumpy ride while raising funds and building his restaurant.

Shyer's first piece of advice: "Get fully funded before getting going." He found himself raising money during construction, giving leverage to his contractor. "Unless you hold the purse strings," he says, "the balance of power goes away from you. If you have money and hold it back, you have leverage. Our contractor never finished. He did what he thought was right. Construction would stop periodically. As I got farther along, it was easier to raise money, because people could walk around in the building. At first I was trying to raise funds, having nothing to show my potential investors."

A top-quality dispensing system is a necessary investment too. Pay attention to the chilling, and how the beer is poured. Shyer's system shares glycol with the brewery and doesn't always work to his satisfaction. He recommends hiring a specialist, independent of the brewery installer, to design and install the dispensing system.

Shyer advises operators to retain the business's name and trademarks. As a first-time operator, he wasn't able to obtain these rights. After several years in business, Shyer negotiated the right to use the Zip City trademark at other locations in exchange for royalty payments. If you are putting together your first project, consider retaining rights to the name, even if it costs you a percentage of the ownership. Then you have control.

Zip City has expanded its brewery, and Shyer recommends buying extra capacity at the outset if you can afford it. "You might need the extra beer on-premise, or other bars might buy it," he says.

Think of your brewpub as a cohesive unit: "From beer to food to menu design, from salt and pepper shakers to staff uniforms, every choice you make sends a message to the consumer. Some places are sending mixed messages," Shyer says.

In regards to restaurant staff, Shyer comments, "You cannot trust restaurant employees. Set up all your systems so it doesn't make it easy for people to rip you off. Restaurant employees don't have a long-term commitment to you or an interest in what you're doing. They're there for the money. If they're not working out, don't hesitate to fire them. Hire more people than you need in the beginning, so you can fire the ones that don't work out."

It's very important to show customers a quality experience after you open your doors. "Don't serve sub-par beer; it will hurt your reputation. Be willing to take back food. Be particularly aware of mishaps. Do what you have to do to make customers happy."

You must have a mix of all the skills required to run a restaurant. "Make sure you have a professional restaurant staff," says Shyer. "Get the expertise you need to run your business, whether from employees, partners, or consultants."

Always remember that a brewpub is a restaurant. "A brewpub is like any restaurant," says Shyer. "The higher volume in beer will help you stay in business, but you're still running a restaurant."

The Trailblazers

"I've never heard anyone say, 'I wish I hadn't raised so much money at the start,'" says Kurt Widmer, president of Widmer Bros. Brewing Company, Portland, Oregon. "We were woefully undercapitalized," he recalls. "Make sure you have more money than you think you'll need."

Widmer sees a less forgiving atmosphere today than in 1985, when he and brother Rob started their business: "We were able to get used dairy equipment. I don't think there's much of that around anymore. Costs have increased dramatically in the last ten years." Widmer believes the public won't accept marginal products today from microbreweries, as they might have done ten years ago.

The Widmers set out to sell Altbier, but the public didn't take to their bitter brew in great numbers. But their second product, weizen, took off, especially in its unfiltered form. How did the Widmers deal with the rejection of Widmer Alt and acceptance of Widmer Hefeweizen? "It took us by surprise. But we were flexible enough to go with what was working for us," says Kurt.

Widmer considers his biggest mistake to be underestimating growth demand. "We started with a 4,000-square-foot warehouse. A few years later we realized we really needed 40,000 square feet. We added 70,000 square feet this time," he says.

The question of how to maintain a happy, productive work force is a concern for all businesses, including Widmer's. "We have 150 people here. Keeping them happy and motivated is a continuous challenge," Widmer says. An employee stock-ownership plan gives workers a vested interest in the Widmer Bros. Brewing Company's success. Other than that, Widmer cites a need to determine what employees want from their work. "Some guys just love being in beermaking. Some are in it for the money," he says. You can't give them what they want if you don't know what it is.

Did it hurt Widmer Bros. to stick entirely to draft beer until 1996? "We probably could have grown faster by not sticking with that strategy for so long," says Widmer. But, is it necessary to grow as quickly as possible? "There's a lot of satisfaction in being number one. It's hard to keep [superstar employees] happy with number seven."

Widmer experimented briefly with production at Heileman's Val Blatz plant in Milwaukee, Wisconsin, but pulled out. How much did the experiment hurt? "It was an inexpensive learning experience. We learned that no one cares about the production of our beer more than our own people," says Kurt.

Some keys, according to Widmer: First, as you experience transition and growth, seek outside professional help sooner rather than later. "I've seen a lot of guys make bad business decisions." Secondly, he suggests bringing important functions in-house as soon as you can. And third, check your ego at the door. "It's a big mistake to let your ego get in the way of business decisions." At times, the Widmers have brought people into the business and paid them more than they pay themselves. "I don't have to be the highest paid person here," Kurt Widmer says.

The Lawyer

Andy Klein was a lawyer before becoming president of the Spring Street Brewing Company, New York City, a contract brewer of Belgian-inspired beers, in 1993.

Like Shipman and Widmer, Klein advises potential brewers to raise as much money as possible. "At the absolute top of my list is to raise as much money as you think you need, then get twice as much. It's easier to sell a dream than something that's half successful," he says.

Everything is more complicated than you think: "You get awfully excited about having enough money to start. So you start. Then you realize the things you need to do. Talk to people who have done it. I regret that I didn't take the time to understand how the beer business works. If you don't know what you're doing, you can get hurt. Things seem simple because you don't understand."

Contracting for beer doesn't imply passivity. "As a contract brewer, you're going to have to brew your beer. That takes an active role. It's been a struggle to maintain the quality we want to maintain. We taste every batch before it goes out. We didn't do that a year-and-a-half ago. In some sense, contract brewing presents more of a challenge. You have to be diplomatic. You don't have ownership."

In the end, it often comes back to basics, like character: "A lot of things can go wrong, but you've got to believe in what you're doing."

The Neophyte

The neophyte is a person, who we'll call Bob, that knew little about beer and brewing when he took over an existing operation. Here are Bob's observations after several years of running a draft-beer microbrewery and contracting for bottled beer.

On personnel: "In the beginning I would have hired an experienced brewmaster. The less you know, the more you need to surround yourself with people who do know. If you have a problem with an employee, get rid of the person as quickly as possible. Don't let him drag the organization down. In hiring, check references closely and investigate claims. You've got to have people with integrity. If they lie, they're more likely to be disloyal to you. There are people with the attitude that they can bring anyone in at $6 an hour. It's not that way."

On equipment: "When you buy used equipment, have an experienced person evaluate it."

On expertise: "We were naive. We got into it knowing only the rudimentary brewing process, like you learn on a tour. It's better to get people who know more than you rather than less. If you are a novice, try to get some training in some of the technical areas, so you know enough when talking to others. You've got to know enough to know what questions to ask."

On distributor relationships: "Be very, very careful about distributor relationships. Check out their reputation. People don't know how to write an agreement with a distributor. You need to write in standards for how they will service accounts, what level of service they will provide, whether they'll have a service technician in the market. You can get reports on a regular basis, and you can get customer lists. There must be strict rules regarding rotation of stock and quality control. Require them to do projections and goal-setting. How else are you able to track their progress?"

On growth: "It's hard to balance growth against cost. Growth can put you deep in the hole. We just spent $70,000 upgrading our building. If we move, it's all lost."

On contract brewing: "Find out the credentials of all the brewing staff, not just the head brewer. If the head brewer quits, who will take over? What quality control procedures do they have? Is the brewer doing the lab testing? He shouldn't be. Quality control is always an independent function. The lab person needs to report to the general manager, not the brewer. Find out who's in the lab, how much experience they have, and what their protocol is. If they can't answer these questions, there's a problem. You need to specify what you expect in terms of quality control. It's not unreasonable to have samples sent to you to taste before bottling. Have the beer independently analyzed."

On the microbrewer's life: "Starting a business, you have to realize how much you give up. You make sacrifices along the way. On the way home at night I ask myself if I should stop and see a few accounts. Sometimes I have to say, 'No, I'm dog tired. I want to see my child.'"

Closing Thoughts

So much can be learned from experience — your's and others'. We close with a few thoughts from brewers around the United States.

"A lot of things I did to begin with were luckily the right thing. Get a brewhouse bigger than you need. We didn't change ours until we reached 18,000 barrels. Get good packaging equipment. We've focused on draft beer. We bottle only as much as we have to. Sixty percent of our production is draft beer. Some on-premise accounts wanted us to sell them some bottles to try us out. We just wouldn't sell them the bottles," says Jerry Bailey, president, Old Dominion Brewing Company, Ashburn, Virginia.

"It would never hurt to do longer studies, to spend more time studying the market. We did a lot of traveling, and talked to as many people as we could. Make sure you spend enough time planning the building and dealing with the contractor. I would have kept closer contact with the Chamber of Commerce. They are there to help people. Every step must be thought out very carefully. Take your time. Don't make overnight decisions," says Peter Camps, head brewer, Celis Brewery Inc., Austin, Texas.

"We put a total of three years into planning. When we first applied for bank loans, we were turned down. That gave us more time to plan. When we started, it was just one year from demolition to the first brew," says James Emmerson, head brewer, Full Sail Brewing Company, Hood River, Oregon.

"What would I do differently? I'd put rakes in my lauter tun. Not including them was stupid on my part, but it improves my shoulder muscles. I came out of Siebel, and I had worked at Sieben's (later Berghoff's, now closed) in Chicago on weekends. I got to see a lot of what did and didn't work. We originally opened with two restaurant concepts under one roof. We phased out most of the upscale dining and expanded the casual. Mistakes? Taking on a building that should have been bulldozed instead of saved. Know restaurants or know someone who you can trust implicitly," says John Gilliam, proprietor and head brewer, Ozark Brewing Company, Fayetteville, Arkansas.

"One of the things about having no money is being creative. You need to make good beer from day one," says Ken Grossman, president, Sierra Nevada Brewing Company, Chico, California. "We've stayed focused on beer quality. We've spent a lot of money trying to improve every facet of our brewing. We choose our distributors very carefully. In the beginning we went with the only ones that would take us. Do a lot of investigation. Talk to local accounts. See what kind of service the distributor gives them. Keys to success? As Jack McAuliffe, founder of New Albion Brewing Company, Sonoma, California, told me, 'You can't have enough money.' You've got to have adequate funding. It takes a lot of work and dedication. I've always had an abiding love of beer. I've loved beer since I was fourteen years old."

Chapter 14
Strategic Approaches to Promotional Tastings

by Keith R. Dinehart
Director of Public Relations and Sales for Chicago Brewing Company

Once a brewery has established its name and gotten its share of press coverage, creative promotional events still need to continue. As time goes by it becomes harder to come up with a fresh approach to get the brewery's name out. But, it is a vital task if you want to sustain your share of the beer-drinking public's buying habits. Implementing promotional beer tastings is one avenue available to raise the profile of your brewery and maintain your place in the market.

The utmost goal of the following suggested tasting formats is to further position your business as a source of brewing expertise. No matter which format is used, it is important to focus attention on the brewery and its exceptional level of talent. Never pass up the opportunity to sharpen the brewery's image as enthusiastic, sophisticated, and innovative.

Using the following suggested formats, a brewery can implement vehicles of promotion which go beyond general brewery advertising and public relations. Entrepreneurial brewers need to be relentless in their pursuit of establishing themselves as a nationally recognized brewer of distinctive beers.

Brewmaster Dinners

A brewmaster dinner demonstrates a brewery's versatility and showcases its brands in a sophisticated light. By cooking and pairing meals with beer, a brewery broadens its appeal, reveals the adaptability and complexity of its brands, and highlights their unique styles.

Along with serving a fine meal accompanied by a distinctive beer, a brewmaster dinner creates an opportunity for the brewery to enhance relationships with customers. The dinner becomes a forum for the brewery to convey its story and impart knowledge and enthusiasm about its beer. Through one-on-one presentations, the brewery articulates its depth of understanding in the art and science of brewing as well as showcases its personality.

Press promotion. It is important to look at a brewmaster dinner as part of a larger promotional plan for the company. Position these dinners as events that should be covered by the local newspapers, in effect serving as vehicles for promotion. Incorporating media when promoting the dinner elevates the importance of the event and enhances the credibility of the brewery. Press coverage provides positive word-of-mouth about the company, which by its very nature is more telling, valid, and truthful to the consumer than advertising.

One of the news media's roles is to act as a third-party filter for information. As a resource for information, newspapers are believed to be critical of the stories they choose to cover. For many readers press coverage of a company is perceived to be an objective validation of that company's inherent and distinct qualities. By captivating the media's attention a brewery can further establish its image and thus enhance the growth of its sales.

Approach the media by writing the editor of the desired section, preferably features or food. Tell of the planned dinner in a personal letter which states the holiday angle of the meal, the creative dinner menu planned, and the format of the event. Conclude with a note that this subject has not been offered to others, and if they choose to run it, they can have exclusive coverage. Allow the newspaper enough time to plan for the story to fit into its editorial calendar by sending information on the event at least four weeks in advance.

A number of points need to be present in the letter. First, plan the tasting around a holiday and incorporate the holiday theme into the dinner menu if possible. By targeting a future holiday, you present the editor with a timely seasonal story. Second, choose recipes that represent contemporary and progressive food trends. Innovative recipes are interesting and usually have a better chance of making the newspaper because they catch the reader's eye. Third, include the recipes of each course with the letter. In giving the editor the recipes the newspaper can then offer its readers the opportunity to create the dinner at home. Fourth, provide a professional photograph of the completed meal. A compelling photo will often be used by the press because it is visually inviting and intriguing for readers. Some stories are chosen first because of interesting visuals and secondly for interesting content.

Location. A key factor in hosting a successful brewmaster dinner, along with providing a great meal, is establishing an exciting atmosphere. To achieve the desired atmosphere a number of steps need to be taken. First, select a location where you can further an existing relationship with an important account. Be mindful that the brewery's ability to bring a special event to a restaurant, showcasing a chef's abilities, is a rare opportunity. Second, hold this event at a restaurant that can enhance the brewery's image by affiliating itself with an establishment that has a strong reputation. Again, look for a restaurant that can create a menu which is trend oriented — not all places provide the talent to accomplish this. Third, look

for an establishment that has a clientele your brewery would like to attract. Planning a brewmaster dinner is time consuming, so make sure your goals are met by targeting a restaurant with customers who potentially fit the brewery's demographic. Fourth, look to establishments that have a separate room in the restaurant to conduct the dinner. It is important to foster a mood and control the flow of the dinner, and this is best achieved in a quiet and comfortable space.

Presentation. Format the presentation around the history of the beers served, the beer styles, and the recipes. You want customers to walk away feeling excited and fortunate to have participated in a special evening, so take steps to make it that way.

To created an eventlike atmosphere, the following steps should be considered. First, discuss the beer styles and recipes of each course when served. By presenting each beer separately, the dinner will evolve as a continuous flow of highlights which shape the meal into an event. This creates an atmosphere of excitement, providing a better chance of persuading those attending toward your views and brews. Second, information on why the beer was chosen, how the style was used in the recipe, and what interesting history surrounds the beer should precede each course. The goal is to provide rich information that is topical, easy to remember, and fun. Third, throughout the meal it is important to include anecdotes about the brewery and its beginnings. This helps personalize the brewery and the presentation. The brewery's growth from an idea to a business is the epitome of the American dream. Tell people your story, they will trumpet it far and wide.

By presenting a memorable and entertaining event, the brewery will gain enthusiastic and loyal supporters for its beers and keep them buying its brands for many years to come.

Menu creation. When creating a menu for your dinner, use distinctive recipes which are contemporary in style. Innovative meals offer a more alluring reason to attend and report on a brewmaster dinner.

To further increase attendance, include beer in interesting ways. The attraction of the menu becomes doubly interesting when beer is incorporated as an ingredient. For example, using weiss beer in a salad dressing, red ale as a barbecue sauce, bock beer as a marinade, poaching in lager, and porter in chocolate desserts makes the menu more exciting. Beer cookbooks are available for ideas. To establish a winning event, the strongest most creative effort possible needs to be put forth.

Mailing lists. In addition to reaching out to the press, tap into established promotion mechanisms already in place at the restaurant. Many have lists of key, regular clientele on mailing lists for the brewery to use. Sending information to people on the restaurant's mailing list is an excellent way to promote the dinner.

Also plan signs inside the restaurant to announce the upcoming event. Many entranceways stand empty waiting for an aggressive brewery to place signs about an upcoming event. With management support, it is also valuable to insert bulletins about the dinner in the everyday menus. Although it can be troublesome for some staff members, placing announcements in the menus broadens the appeal and awareness of the dinner.

It is important to send out as broad an announcement as possible for good attendance. Lastly, remember that all reservations for this dinner need to be made with a credit card to cover those who fail to show up.

Beer Tastings

Beer tastings offer another chance for the brewery to enlighten consumers on the diversity of the world's beer styles. Beer tastings are a great way to teach consumers about the fundamentals of style and how to appreciate the different flavor profiles of beer. As the host of a tasting, the brewery can showcase itself and demonstrate its talent.

Small Off-Premise Tastings

Small-format tastings enable a brewery to offer free samples of their full line of brands to customers at retail accounts. This format is designed to exclusively feature one brewery only. There are no pressures from a comparison tasting, and the flow of information is more relaxed and freely given. Moreover, a small-format tasting allows the brewery to sell directly to customers while providing them with background information on the brewery. Face to face interaction allows customers the chance to get acquainted with brewery personnel as they discuss the interworkings of brewing. Through customer contact there is an exchange of information, and thus the brewery begins to develop a new buying customer — a customer who now has a deeper appreciation of the brewery and its brands.

Scheduling. Saturday afternoon is the best time to schedule a tasting. There appears to be a psychological barrier for many to drink beer on a Sunday. Saturday offers three important opportunities: First, many people are more willing to sample when they do not have to work the next day. Trust me, even if it's two ounces this is an issue. Second, customers are in a more relaxed state of mind on Saturdays and thus more willing to sample a new beer from a complete stranger. Third, many people feel obligated to purchase a beer after sampling it, especially after you have told them the story of how the brewery began.

Accounts. Hold retail tastings at established high-volume accounts. Conducting these tastings is tiring and time consuming. It is important that the store you choose rewards your efforts with many customers to solicit. Many accounts will value the opportunity to have a brewery representative in their store interacting with shoppers. Remember, it is important to concentrate on the largest locations first.

Holidays and weather. When selecting a day to conduct your tasting, pay attention to the calendar and the weather. Most liquor stores are very busy just before a major holiday and offer some of the highest customer-volume days possible. Weather factors can affect the success of your tasting. Watch for good weather patterns developing to anticipate the potential amount of beer to serve and sell. If the brewery can time its tastings for when people are more physically active, much more beer will be sold. As obscure as this sounds, it is practical and easier than you think.

Hours. When planning a retail tasting, expect to work from noon to 5 p.m. Most customers will not take free samples of beer before noon and will be more willing to drink as the day goes by. There are numerous customer waves that flow in and out of a retail store throughout an afternoon. The longer you stay, the more beer you will sell.

Displays. When setting up, look at a location where a large display can be built. It is best to set up your display close to the beer cooler. People will head to the coolers first. Keep in mind that for some shoppers a large display is an indication of the viability of a brand and the store's willingness to push it. For many customers a large display with a sale price will lead to an impulse buy.

Relationships. When business in the store is slow, take the opportunity to interact with the staff and management. Many of the store's personnel are in positions to recommend a beer to customers and often are requested to do so. Do not pass up the chance to talk about how interesting the brewery is and what it has taken to get the company growing. Many in the industry would like to open their own brewery and enjoy hearing about others who have made this attempt. Befriending staff and management goes a long way in helping you sell beer.

On-Premise Tastings

Coordinating an on-premise beer tasting offers a brewery another vehicle for promotion. Beer tastings showcase the brewery's talent, especially when its beers are compared to other more famous and not so famous brands. As the host of a beer tasting the brewery is in a wonderful position to create a presentation articulating the brewery's vision, expertise, and personality.

Preparation. An on-premise tasting requires a good degree of planning and preparation. As the host for a tasting, the brewery will ultimately be given credit for the results of the event regardless of the quality. Letting others manage the event could lead to an unsuccessful outcome and damage the reputation of the brewery. Only the brewery, through its brewing knowledge, industry contacts, and personnel, can develop a professional on-premise tasting.

Style formats. There are a number of beer formats available for a tasting. The first possible format could be represented by major styles brewed by the most famous brewers of the world. This should be an inclusive sampling and cover styles such as Pilsener, lager, ale, porter, stout, weiss, lambic, etc. This is the most fundamental of all the tasting formats available. Its strength lies in the definitive brews represented, and its weakness lies in the fact that most of the brands have been enjoyed before and offer no novelty. A major advantage of this tasting is its safe format, which offers little risk for the beer novice.

A second tasting format might focus on a country of origin. In this setup, major brands from within a country would be represented and compared with one another. Most European countries have a rich brewing tradition, and needless to say, there are popular brewing cultures which could be represented at this tasting, such as Germany, Britain, or Belgium. The down side of this format is the lack of depth in the range of styles available. Most cultures simply do not brew the diversity of beer we have available here in the United States. This format is, however, great fun when coordinated around a European holiday.

A third option could be to present the different types of top-fermented or bottom-fermented beers. In this setup, the subtle and pronounced differences within a range of a style are magnified. It can be an eye-opening experience to compare the famous brands and their recipes to lesser-known, more-distinctive brews of the same style. Not nearly as dynamic as other formats available, this comparison is, however, one of the most critical and revealing. Most people do not compare brands within a style category, thus they learn a lot from this format. Although a more intriguing focus, this format is generally not as interesting to the novice.

A fourth option might be to focus on a specific region of the United States. Specifically, this format could get as definitive as representing the Pacific Northwest, New England, Mid-Atlantic, Rocky Mountain, West Coast, Great Lakes, and Midwest regions, for example. North American brewers, specifically micro- and craft brewers, differ greatly in the flavor profiles they emphasize in their brews. Some regions of the country have breweries that brew bold-flavored beers, yet others that brew balanced and smooth brews. This tasting format has to be the "hottest" and most exciting to present. For many, the beers featured in this format will be new and boldly flavorful.

Finally, a tasting format could focus on seasonal brews. Once again there are incredible varieties of beer available which are specifically brewed for just one season. As seasons change, so can the drinking habits of customers. Many different brands are available for the spring, summer, fall, and winter seasons. This format offers the chance to present an ongoing quarterly series of tastings centered around each season. Thematically, this is a nice way to continue a beer tasting with an established format. The most striking feature of this format is noticing how beers with the same seasonal label can still taste dramatically different.

No matter how you structure the format of the beer tasting, remember it is important that a depth of range and complexity of styles are represented. These tastings are designed to educate and strengthen the consumer's beer knowledge, creating a more literate and informed beer-drinking public. The more they learn about beer from your brewery, the better

the chance it will be *your* beer in their refrigerator and *not* your competitors.

A beer tasting, like a brewmaster dinner, is an ideal setting to showcase the brewery's talent. A tasting demands that the brewery discuss at length the history, details, and specific insights behind each beer. As the tasting evolves, the brewery's skill of understanding and their grasp of the technical are revealed, leaving participants with a strong impression of the company.

These tastings are entertainment for many who attend, and as such, a good dose of levity should be incorporated. When a professional presentation is combined with humor, charm, and personality, tastings go a long way in shaping participants into lifelong loyal buyers of the brewery's beers.

The following is a list of points that should be discussed throughout the evening: (1) history of brewing — a quick reference to the beginnings of beer; (2) background on ingredients — the varieties of barley, hops, and yeast used; (3) how beer is brewed — a step-by-step process and the different equipment used to make a beer; (4) history of your brewery — from idea to reality discuss how you did it; (5) regional brewing history — relay the brewing history of your area; (6) industry analysis — separate contract, craft, and microbrewers.

Tastings require a lot of undertaking and understanding. However, the positive outcome achieved as a result of conducting a tasting far outweighs any potential difficulties. Managed and presented with strength, the tasting will reflect positively on the brewery and enhance the company's reputation and future success.

Large Festival Tastings

Large festival tastings are generally very time consuming and need long methodical planning. These are best coordinated with financial co-sponsors and with teams of full-time staff members. When well planned, these events draw the largest response of media attention, word-of-mouth promotion, and consumer response. These large festival events have the ability, if handled successfully, to showcase the brewery in an extremely vibrant and exciting light.

Sponsorship. When obtaining sponsors, specifically call upon wholesalers and breweries which have a vested interest in their brands being represented at the event. Most companies will provide a reduced wholesale price in return for exposure. If they feel the need to attend the event, they may also draw on marketing funds from their respected brands, contributing to the success of the festival. Also look to nonindustry-related sponsors such as radio stations, food companies, and airlines. Many of these companies would gladly pay to be affiliated with an exciting and successful event that attracts patrons who demographically fit their target market.

Advertising. The foundation of success for this event will in large part be due to the broad reach of radio. In particular, radio advertising reaches the elusive "twenty-something" beer drinker who gets most of their news from radio. Tie in sponsorship of the event with a local rock radio station. As a sponsor, a radio station will run ads promoting its affiliation with the festival far more frequently and will be more willing to feature a brewer as a guest on their morning drive-time talk show. Although expensive, radio advertising is ideally targeted to the beer drinker.

Public relations. In addition to advertising, a full-time publicist is recommended. Having the ability to concentrate all efforts on getting press attention for the event will yield much more feature-oriented press coverage. Someone should be positioned to "spin" interesting stories about the event's participants out to the media at a continual level. Through talent and diligence these efforts will garner stories that will draw a larger crowd to the festival.

Experts. To further the serious nature of the event it is advisable to bring in industry experts. Authors, journalists, and brewers will lend credibility to the festival. Industry critics and professionals will further the festival's distinction as a noteworthy event. These experts could be used in a panel format at key tastings to conduct question-and-answer sessions for festival-goers. In exchange, the festival offers the opportunity for the expert to speak and promote their own work at a well-attended event.

Plan an opening night dinner for sponsors, experts, brewers, and media to kick off the event professionally. At this dinner prepare a meal with beer and match it with a select few brews. Consider featuring an invited expert as the guest of honor.

Space. The festival must be held at a sight that can accommodate crowds easily. Renting a large tent in case the weather is bad is a good idea, too. The space needs to be large enough to offer easy traffic flow so people can get around. A sure way to sustain a high level of patrons at the festival is to provide a comfortable setting in which to sample beer. A crowd is more likely to stay and enjoy themselves if they are comfortable.

Food. Because alcohol is being served, it is recommended that a good supply of food be on hand for festival-goers. Many local venders would value the opportunity to serve their creations to an enthusiastic and captive buying public. Most food companies would be willing to get involved if the demographics fit.

In conclusion, there are a number of possible tasting formats to use in promoting your company. The type of tasting the brewery decides to promote will depend on time, money, and expertise. The options are up to the brewery, and hopefully the variety of selections presented here will offer a brewery some versatility.

In this competitive industry, a brewery's identity needs to be strong, clear, and persuasive. The aforementioned tasting formats position the brewery to do just that. The brewery needs to send sophisticated messages that establish it as an authority — an authority that exhibits a strong array of talent, expertise, and creative approaches to brewing and marketing in the industry.

Chapter 15
Public Relations 101

by Sheri Winter
Marketing Director for the Association of Brewers

Public Relations Overview

The goal of public relations is to generate good will, enhance your brewing operation's reputation and credibility, and inform the public about your brewery and products. A good public relations program exposes the public to your messages.

Public relations is not advertising because, unlike advertising, public relations is almost always delivered in a news format. Advertising is a paid publicity campaign in which you control the message and the medium. For example, you design a newspaper ad and pay for it to appear in Friday's edition. Advertising is another part of your marketing plan.

However with public relations you are dependent on the media to convey your message and deliver it to your intended audience. You count on the media to treat your message as news, and luckily they are always looking for news.

Your public relations job is to make news. News equals exposure. Exposure equals increased visibility, better-informed consumers, more customers, and more attendees at your events. The following are some basic guidelines to help you get started on your quest for exposure.

Creating a Public Relations Plan

Complete a realistic *situation analysis:* Where are you now? Are you in the planning stages of your brewing operation or are you preparing for a fifth anniversary bash? Take a hard look at your current level of visibility, your sales, and your budget. (Yes, budget. PR is cost effective but it is not free.)

The first step to creating your public relations plan is to *establish objectives* based on your situation analysis. Objectives might include increasing name recognition, building brand awareness, or generating sales. Generally, it's best to limit yourself to three or four realistic objectives, giving you the opportunity to focus on only those objectives that are most important to your operation's success.

After you have established your objectives, the next planning step is to *identify your target audiences.* Who are you trying to reach in order to meet your objectives? You will likely have several target audiences — examples include beer press, local press, distributors or tavern owners, local beer drinkers, and restaurant patrons. By targeting the media you will reach your other audiences. However, you may want to include other specific tactics that reach an audience directly, such as publishing a brewery newsletter or speaking to the Rotary Club.

Further build on your plan by *identifying tactics* that support your objectives and reach your target audience. (A list of sample tactics follows.) Tactics are the nuts-and-bolts activities that make up your plan. Some tactics will reach multiple audiences and achieve more than one objective. For example, attending a regional beer festival helps increase name recognition, build brand awareness, and hopefully generate sales by reaching the local press, beer press, and consumers interested in craft-brewed beer. One tactic, three objectives, three targeted audiences. Always remember to set a tactics time line — map out when promotional tactics need to happen — and plan PR activities throughout the year to establish a continuous presence with your audiences.

Remember, public relations is an ongoing process. The best way to build an effective program is to build on positive awareness. In other words, good public relations creates more good public relations opportunities.

Public Relations Tactics

Use the following list of tried-and-true tactics when building your public relations plan:

Develop and maintain a press list. A good press list is key to acquiring any type of coverage. This list is your little black book of PR. First of all, do your homework and identify the editors and reporters who cover your brewery. This is the basis of your press list. Which newspaper reporters, TV personalities, radio disc jockeys talk about, write about, or seem interested in beer? If you have a brewpub, who writes the food columns or does the restaurant reviews? If you're planning an event, who writes about what to do on weekends? All these folks should be on your press list. Now go beyond your local scene. Are there regional papers or magazines that can help your cause? Add them. What about the beer periodicals? Add them. Now you have a good starting point. Your press list is an ever-changing list demanding constant attention and revision. It is your job to keep this list current. Pledge that you will review the list before all major announcements. (Check the mastheads, make a few calls.) Nothing annoys a reporter more than getting a press release or an invitation that is addressed to his or her predecessor. Don't let it happen to you.

Build relationships with key media personnel. This tactic is still the best way to receive ongoing coverage, and all it takes is a little hard work on your part. Dig out that press list and identify the folks who really count. These are the reporters who can have the greatest impact in helping you reach your target audiences. Get to know them. Introduce yourself by phone or call and ask if you can drop off a few samples of your latest seasonal brew and say hello. Invite them to tour your brewery or to your next special event. This is an ongoing relationship, so the introduction is literally just the beginning. Common courtesy will go a long way in building these key relationships. Call about special announcements or events but respect the reporter's time, especially if he or she is on deadline. Always ask if the reporter has time to talk, or if you should call back later. If a reporter calls you, return the call promptly. Always tell the truth and don't exaggerate no matter how tempting. Give the media VIP treatment at all your events. Go out of your way to say hello no matter how busy you may be. And, remember to say thank you and compliment a reporter after covering your operation or event. These simple guidelines will help you establish a strong rapport and become a resource for your key media.

Issue press releases. Make sure your releases are factual and to the point, but don't be afraid to go all out for a major announcement. Humor, gimmicks, controversy (careful with this one), or other unique approaches can be very effective in getting your release noticed. Good follow-up (especially with your key media) and supporting materials can take your release from the "news-in-brief" column to the feature section of your local newspaper. And remember, issue releases throughout the year to keep your name out there. (More on the importance of press releases and a good press kit will be discussed later.)

Write and place articles in the local papers and in beer publications. Publications are always looking for good authors, and beer is a hot topic. If you have the time and the talent, this is another way to get your name and brewery name in print. Write about what you know but don't be overly self-promoting.

Chances are an editor will reject a story that reads like one of your press releases and won't give you a second chance. Some ideas for articles are: how to have a beer dinner at home; beer and food; beer festivals; the business side of brewing; an overview of the brewing process; an overview of craft breweries in your city/region/state; and an overview of beers in a particular style category.

Speak at meetings and conferences. Again, if you have the time and talent, this is a great way to increase your visibility. Offer to speak at local club meetings (Chamber of Commerce, Lions, Sertoma, Rotary, women's clubs, you name it) and don't forget to bring samples, if appropriate. What better way to meet all the local businesspeople? Let your local newspaper know your speaking schedule — it may get you a brief mention. Explore speaking on a panel at a brewing conference and promote your participation to the local press.

Join community groups. Community involvement can be personally and financially rewarding. Join a few local groups you identify with. (Consider joining your local Chamber of Commerce even before you open your doors.) Not only is this a good way to network, but by joining community groups you will also establish yourself as a responsible businessperson and a good corporate citizen. Plus there are many ways your brewery can be an asset to the group, and the group can help your business. (Think fund-raiser.)

Attend beer festivals. More and more of these popular events are held across the nation each year. Investigate which festivals make sense for your brewery (go back and review your plan objectives) and promote your participation. What can you do to stand out from the crowd? Give away temporary tattoos? Introduce an unusual beer? Have a local celebrity in the booth pouring samples? Make media opportunities happen. Publicize your gimmick. Local radio stations or newspapers sponsor many festivals. Say hello, invite them to your booth, and give them a sample and an update.

Publish a brewery newsletter. If you don't already publish a newsletter, give this tactic some serious consideration. A newsletter can be a cost-effective way to stay in touch with existing customers, reach new customers (hand them out at festivals!), sell merchandise, promote brewery tours and special events, announce new products, promote your retail accounts, and even generate press coverage. A newsletter doesn't have to be expensive — many breweries create their own in-house newsletters on a PC or Macintosh. Once you've published the first issue, distribute it widely to customers, festival attendees, distributors, and beer bars and mail it to your press list for maximum exposure.

Sponsor or participate in a beer tasting. Many local establishments host beer tastings or beer dinners featuring local breweries. If not, start a tasting series and publicize it! (Is it the first? Is it unique? Who is your speaker?) These events are popular with the local food and drink crowd and give you the opportunity to sell to a qualified audience. Don't forget to invite the media to the actual tasting.

Sponsor a special event or local athletic team. Local events often look for sponsors, creating excellent public relations opportunities for you. Also, several breweries have struck out on their own and created special events and promotional opportunities, including festivals, concerts, barbecues, sporting events, and tastings. Not only do these events generate lots of community good will, they also generate media interest. It's news! Again, don't forget to include the media on your invite list. Other breweries have hit PR pay dirt by sponsoring local athletic teams. Is there an adult softball or baseball league in your hometown that could use a sponsor? Promote your sponsorship whenever and wherever possible. (Maybe name a seasonal beer after your team. Have the post-game parties at your brewpub. Be sure the team uniforms have your logo on them. And, publicize it all!)

Sponsor a homebrew club. Homebrewers are avid beer fans and can be great evangelists for your brew. You can also do some great promotional tie-ins with the club — host a beer competition at your brewery and handle the PR or host a party for National Homebrew Day.

The Press Kit

A good press kit can result in both more and better press coverage. The press kit is designed to offer the media a complete overview of your brewing operation and provide important background information. Your kit should accompany major press releases (such as a brewery opening or expansion) and any "pitch" letters you send to a media target. (For example: A food writer from *Bon Appetit* is covering restaurants in your city. You send a press kit along with a pitch letter explaining why he or she should include your brewpub in the article.) Also send a kit with a thank you letter after phone interviews and in response to media inquiries you receive. Remember to take a few press kits with you to beer festivals and special events that your brewery participates in — you never know when a great press opportunity may arise. (I know one brewery owner who keeps a supply of press kits in his car trunk. Now that's prepared!)

Here are the basic components of a well-stocked press kit:

Press release. Always include your most recent press release(s). Press release topics can include new brews, personnel changes, expansion or sales growth, a special promotion, distribution updates, event participation, and awards won — you get the idea. As a guideline, press releases over sixty days old have lost their newsworthiness and should no longer be included in the kit. If the information is still important, add it to a backgrounder or fact sheet. (Need help with the basics of writing a release? See exhibit D for step-by-step directions.)

Brewery backgrounder or fact sheet — the "story" of your brewery. Include information on the brewery's location, the date it was founded, production capacity, an equipment overview, distribution information, brief biographies of principals, and a description of the beers produced. Also include anything that sets your operation apart from others — unusual beers, a historical site, awards won, etc. You can present this basic information as one backgrounder (paragraph or story form) or as a separate fact sheet (bulleted items). (Not sure what we're talking about? See exhibit A for a sample backgrounder and fact sheet.)

Industry backgrounder or fact sheet. Since the media often likes to put articles in a larger context, make sure you provide them with current industry statistics. Also, consider adding information such as an overview of the brewing process, definitions of key brewing terms, and descriptions of the beer styles you produce. (The Institute for Brewing Studies (IBS) produces a quarterly *Industry Fact Sheet* containing the most current statistics which you may use in your press kit. See exhibit B for an example.)

Other background information. You may want to include additional fact sheets or backgrounders that are specific to your press release. For example, if you sponsor a special event, you will want to include a fact sheet outlining the event only (see exhibit C). Or, if you announce a new specialty beer, you may want to include a backgrounder describing the history and characteristics of that particular beer style.

Artwork. A picture really is worth a thousand words. Include a good-quality photo or 35-millimeter slide of your product, brewery, or special event; or you can send along camera-ready artwork of your brewery or product logo. Since publications often use artwork if it's available, this is a cost-effective way to draw added attention to your story. (Remember to include a caption with your photograph!) If you want to economize, add this line at the end of your press release: PHOTOGRAPH AVAILABLE UPON REQUEST. Make sure you can fulfill any requests immediately.

Newsletter. If you publish a newsletter, include your most recent edition. Reporters have been known to "lift" story ideas directly

EXHIBIT A — Sample Backgrounder and Fact Sheet

INSTITUTE FOR BREWING STUDIES
736 PEARL STREET
POST OFFICE BOX 1679
BOULDER, COLORADO 80306-1679 USA
FACSIMILE 303 447-2825
TELEPHONE 303 447-0816
A DIVISION OF THE ASSOCIATION OF BREWERS

EDITORIAL BACKGROUND

CONTACT
Sheri Winter
Marketing Director
(303) 447-0816

A BRIEF OVERVIEW OF BREWING IN AMERICA

Brewing has been a tradition in America since the Pilgrims first landed on Plymouth Rock. According to ship's logs, the dwindling beer supply aboard the Mayflower led the Pilgrims to land in order to brew more. Since then, beer has been a part of our culture and our history. As a matter of fact, when Founding Fathers Thomas Jefferson and George Washington weren't busy creating a nation, they were busy brewing.

At one time beer was an American staple on par with flour and salt. By 1873 more than 4,000 breweries operated across the United States. Every neighborhood, town and city had a brewery of its own producing a variety of beer styles. Prohibition brought America's brewing tradition to a halt. Even the Volstead Act of 1933, repealing Prohibition, could not mend the injuries of 13 years. Many of the 750 breweries still in existence failed under the bleak conditions of the following years.

After World War II, small-town breweries became an endangered species. Like other post-war industries, brewing became a mass-production enterprise driven by conglomeration, transportation, refrigeration and advances in communications including television and national advertising. Smaller breweries could no longer compete effectively with the new regional and national brewing powerhouses. Many local breweries were bought up by larger companies; others simply closed their doors. Three decades later, only 40 of the 750 post-Prohibition breweries survived.

The year 1980 proved to be a turning point for the brewing industry. For the first time in more than 50 years, more breweries opened than closed. American consumers were developing a more sophisticated taste for beer and were becoming interested in alternatives to the traditional American lagers. Beer drinkers rediscovered specialty beers brewed locally with natural ingredients. Demand for classic European and pre-Prohibition beer styles increased.

The craft-brewing revolution continued throughout the 1980s with the greatest rate of growth experienced in the Pacific Northwest. Consumers sought out the flavorful beers that were brewed in small batches and distributed locally. The demand for craft-brewed beer spread, and microbreweries and brewpubs opened across the country.

The brewing industry has continued to evolve and today provides consumers with a continually expanding selection of beers. As of April 1996, the Institute for Brewing Studies reported that there are more than 1,000 regional specialty breweries, microbreweries and brewpubs in North America — the largest number of operating breweries since immediately following Prohibition.

Although overall domestic beer sales have dropped slightly, the increase in craft-brew market share has continued to increase dramatically for the fourth year in a row. Year-end production figures for 1995 rose 51 percent over 1994. Market share for craft-brewed beers in the United States jumped to 2 percent, compared with 1.3 percent from the previous year. As new brewing operations continue to open across the nation at a rate of five per week, 1996 should be another banner year for craft brewing.

About the Institute for Brewing Studies
With more than 1,900 members, the Institute for Brewing Studies is the leading educational association for craft brewers. The IBS publishes ***The New Brewer,*** a bimonthly craft-brewing industry magazine, and organizes the annual National Craft-Brewers Conference and Trade Show.

EXHIBIT B — Industry Fact Sheet

INSTITUTE FOR BREWING STUDIES
736 PEARL STREET
POST OFFICE BOX 1679
BOULDER, COLORADO 80306-1679 USA
FACSIMILE 303 447-2825
TELEPHONE 303 447-0816
A DIVISION OF THE ASSOCIATION OF BREWERS

CRAFT-BREWING INDUSTRY FACT SHEET*
June 1996

- There are 1,034 microbreweries, brewpubs and regional specialty breweries in North America as of June 1996.

  Breakdown:

United States	**Canada**
Total: 927	Total: 107
25 Regional Specialty Breweries	11 Regional Specialty Breweries
349 Microbreweries	38 Microbreweries
553 Brewpubs	58 Brewpubs

- Total U.S. beer sales for 1995 including domestic, imports and exports were: 196,554,000 barrels (1 barrel equals 31 gallons), according to the Beer Institute.

  Breakdown:
  Domestic   176,930,000 barrels
  Imports   11,263,000 barrels
  Exports   8,361,000 barrels

- In 1995 domestic beer sales dropped 1.5 percent from 1994; in 1995 import-beer sales rose 7.4 percent from 1994; export-beer sales improved by 15.8 percent from 1994.

- In 1995 craft-brewed beer sales were approximately 3,779,993 barrels, reflecting growth of 51 percent over 1994 production.

- The market share of craft-brewed beer in the United States in 1995 was 2 percent, up from 1.3 percent in 1994.

- There were 122 contract-brewing companies in North America as of April 1996.

- Forty-eight states and Washington, D.C., have either partially or entirely legalized brewpubs as of April 15, 1996.

- Failure rates for the industry are:

U.S. Brewpubs	1 in 7
U.S. Microbreweries	1 in 8
Canadian Brewpubs	1 in 4
Canadian Microbreweries	1 in 3

- In the United States, 287 new breweries opened in 1995 (196 brewpubs, 91 microbreweries).

- The total U.S. craft-brewing industry annual dollar volume for 1995 was $2,028,000,000.

- U.S. domestic per-capita beer consumption has declined slightly over the past 10 years (22.7 gallons per person in 1985, 21.1 gallons in 1995).

- Total U.S. domestic beer sales have decreased over the past five years (181,541,766 barrels in 1990 versus 176,930,000 in 1995).

- Craft-brewing industry definitions:

  Microbrewery: A brewery that produces less than 15,000 barrels (17,600 hectoliters) of beer per year. Microbreweries sell to the public by one or more of the following methods: the traditional three-tier system (brewer to wholesaler to retailer to consumer); the two-tier system (brewer acting as wholesaler to retailer to consumer); and in some cases, directly to the consumer through carryouts, on-site tap-room, or brewery restaurant sales.

  Brewpub: A restaurant-brewery that sells the majority of its beer on-site. The beer is brewed for sale and consumption in the adjacent restaurant and/or bar. The beer is often dispensed directly from the brewery's storage tanks. Where allowed by law, brewpubs often sell beer "to go" and/or distribute to off-site accounts. Note: Brewpubs whose off-site beer sales grow to exceed 50 percent of total are recategorized as microbreweries.

  Contract Brewing Company: A business that hires another company to produce its beer. The contract brewing company handles marketing, sales and distribution of its beer, while generally leaving the brewing and packaging to its producer brewery (which, confusingly, is also sometimes referred to as a contract brewer).

  Regional Brewery: A brewery with a capacity to brew between 15,000 and 500,000 barrels (17,600 and 586,700 hectoliters). Although its distribution may, in fact, be regional in scope, for categorization purposes "regional" refers to the brewery's size only.

  Regional Specialty Brewery: A regional-scale brewery whose flagship (largest-selling) brand is positioned as a "micro" or specialty beer.

  Large Brewery: A company with sales of more than 500,000 barrels (586,700 hectoliters). Some large brewery companies operate a single brewing facility, while others may have more than a dozen.

*This fact sheet is updated quarterly. Please contact the Institute for Brewing Studies for the most recent industry statistics.

from brewery newsletters! Your newsletter can also let them know about happenings in your brewery which may not merit a press release and serve as a reminder about upcoming events.

Business card. Make it easy for the media to contact you in the future — include your business card for their Rolodex.

Folder. You may want to package the entire kit in a folder for a neat presentation and easy filing. Create a custom folder look for your kit by adding a brewery sticker or logo to plain folders.

Extras. For additional attention, include a low-cost souvenir as a constant reminder of your brewery. Coasters, bottle labels, and refrigerator magnets are all nice press-kit extras that won't break the bank. Some breweries will also send along a bottle or two of their latest brew to help quench the reporters thirst for news. (You may want to consult a shipping company regarding the legality of shipping beer in some states.) And why wait for a press-kit opportunity? Consider dropping off a few bottles or mailing your latest T-shirt to your favorite reporters from time to time just as a way to touch base and maybe generate a call to *you.*

Your press kit doesn't need to be expensively produced to be effective. It does, however, need to look professional, and the documents should be well written. If you don't have the resources in-house to produce the sort of kit your brewing operation deserves, consider hiring professional marketing help. There are a number of public relations and marketing firms out there, as well as consultants or freelance practitioners to help you get started; or you may want to contact the business department of a local college or university for assistance. Your brewery may make a great class project!

And finally, don't forget about your professional network. The Institute for Brewing Studies is here to assist you with all aspects of brewery operations — marketing included. The IBS acts as an information clearinghouse and responds to dozens of media inquiries on

a weekly basis — from local papers to major magazines and television networks. It also proactively promotes the craft-brewing industry to the national media.

The IBS can also help you with your marketing program. IBS resources include: the Brewery Public Relations/Media Kit; the IBS Brewers' Forum, a moderated e-mail news group; regular marketing features in *The New Brewer*, the bimonthly magazine published by the IBS; quarterly marketing updates in the *Alcohol Issues Alert* report; special "Brewers Alerts"; quarterly compilations of industry statistics; dedicated marketing sessions at the annual National Craft-Brewers Conference and Trade Show; and much more. Please contact (303) 447-0816, FAX (303) 447-2825, or ibs@aob.org for additional information on any of these programs or to join the Institute for Brewing Studies.

The Press Release

Okay, you're ready to create some exposure. Before you begin writing, think about the event or news item you plan to feature in the release. Who will you send the release to? Local media? Beer press? The nationals? Your target audience will help you determine the "hook" or the main point of your release. If you're addressing different audiences, you may want to tailor the release for each audience. For example, when the Institute for Brewing Studies holds the annual Craft-Brewers Conference and Trade Show, we send press releases to the beer press highlighting the speakers and exhibitors — what's important to the brewers who will read those publications. We also send press releases to the local media in the city where the conference will be held. The release for the local media features more general information about the industry and the event, highlights local people and breweries involved with the conference, and talks about the impact of the conference and brewing industry on the local economy.

EXHIBIT C — Sample Event Fact Sheet

INSTITUTE FOR BREWING STUDIES
736 PEARL STREET
POST OFFICE BOX 1679
BOULDER, COLORADO 80306-1679 USA
FACSIMILE 303 447-2825
TELEPHONE 303 447-0816
A DIVISION OF THE ASSOCIATION OF BREWERS

THE BOSTON BREW-IN: CHARTING THE COURSE

1996 NATIONAL CRAFT-BREWERS CONFERENCE AND TRADE SHOW FACT SHEET

WHEN: April 27 through 30, 1996

WHERE: Hynes Convention Center, Boston, Mass.

AUDIENCE: Craft brewers and brewing industry suppliers

KEYNOTE SPEAKERS: Charlie Papazian, Association of Brewers

David Geary, D. L. Geary Brewing Co.

Michael Jackson, noted author and beer expert

SESSIONS: 36 information-packed classes and seminars for beginning and advanced brewers, including forums on hops, malts and yeast

SELECTED PANELS:
"Financing Growth and Expansion," "Brewpubs 2000," "Nurturing Wholesaler Relationships," "Essentials of Yeast Handling for Brewpubs"

SELECTED PRESENTATIONS:
"Quality Control After the Beer Leaves the Brewery," "Street-Fighter Marketing for Craft Brewers," "Advice From the Domestic Wine Industry," "Building a Brewery on a Shoestring," "Better Yields With Biological Acidification," "Helpful Hints for New Micro- and Pubbrewers"

SELECTED SPEAKERS:
Jim Koch, Boston Beer Co.; Jeff Slutsky, author of *Streetfighting and How to Get Clients*; Paul Shipman, Redhook Ale Brewery; Robert Weinberg, R. S. Weinberg and Associates; Dr. Michael Lewis, American Brewers Guild; Greg Noonan, Vermont Pub and Brewery; Carol Stoudt, Stoudt Brewing Co.; and Dr. Graham Stewart, the International Centre for Brewing and Distilling, Heriot-Watt University

TRADE SHOW HIGHLIGHTS:
Trade Show Hours: Sunday, April 28, from noon to 5 p.m.
Monday, April 29, from 10 a.m. to 5 p.m.
Tuesday, April 30, from 9 a.m. to 2 p.m.
Number of Exhibitors: 189
Square Footage: 88,000
Exhibitors: Brewing equipment suppliers, bottling line suppliers, packaging companies, malt and hop suppliers, filter and valve companies, consultants, logo and accessories companies, and myriad others

SPONSORS:
The Catamount Brewing Co., Chrislan Ceramics, Sahm GmbH, Celis Brewery, Jacob Leinenkugel Brewing Co., Shipyard Brewery, Dorette Co., Chef John Zearfoss and the Culinary Insitute of America, JV Northwest, Schreier Malting Co., International Beverage, Boston Beer Co., United Liquor, S & S Traffic Management/Kegspediter, Glass Packaging Institute, Vitro Packaging Inc., the Boelter Companies, Polar Tap and International Specialty Products

Writing the Release

Now that you've thought about your angle, you're ready to begin writing. As you can see on the sample press release we've included, you'll need to (A) date your release and (B) include a press contact name with a phone number. While press release formats can differ greatly, make sure the date and contact information are always at the top of your release.

Next you'll need (C) a headline. We also add a subhead on our releases to give additional up-front information. Remember, editors are inundated with press announcements, and most of the time it's up to your headline to pique their interest so they'll read the rest of your release. Make your headline interesting yet still factual. If it's too vague or too cute, chances are your release will end up in the circular file.

Almost as important as a good headline is (D) a good lead. Your lead is the introduction to the body of your press release. The lead should be attention-grabbing and convey all the basic information you need the reporter to know. This includes the "who, what, where, when,

why" that you've no doubt heard about. In the case of our sample release, you'll notice we have the sponsor's name, event name, location, dates, and a brief event description in our first paragraph.

The supporting paragraphs, or (E) the body of the release, provides information that further explains and enhances our lead paragraph. Include facts and figures, background information, and maybe a quote or two from relevant spokespersons. How long should the body of your release be? While the length will vary from release to release, make a real effort not to exceed two pages. (Take some of that excess information and move it into a backgrounder!)

We're almost to the end! Use the last paragraph to remind the reader who you are. At the close of every release, we drop in (F) a standard "who we are" paragraph that tells the journalist a little about our organization and what we do. Some call this a "motherhood"; others call it the corporate blurb. Whatever you choose to call this paragraph, it's a good idea to include it in your releases.

EXHIBIT D — Sample Press Release and Step-by-Step Writing Tips on How to Get Started

INSTITUTE FOR BREWING STUDIES
736 PEARL STREET
POST OFFICE BOX 1679
BOULDER, COLORADO 80306-1679 USA
FACSIMILE 303 447-2825
TELEPHONE 303 447-0816
A DIVISION OF THE ASSOCIATION OF BREWERS

(A) **FOR IMMEDIATE RELEASE**
August 29, 1995

(B) **CONTACT**
Sheri Winter
Marketing Director
(303) 447-0816

(C) **BREWERS SET SAIL FOR THE 1996 NATIONAL CRAFT-BREWERS CONFERENCE AND TRADE SHOW**
The Institute for Brewing Studies Announces the Boston Brew-In

(D) BOULDER, Colo. — Anchors away! The Institute for Brewing Studies announces the 1996 National Craft-Brewers Conference and Trade Show will be held at the Hynes Convention Center in Boston, Mass., April 27 through 30. The theme, *The Boston Brew-In: Charting the Course*, reflects the central purpose of the Conference — to help the brewing community plan for the future in a rapidly changing and expanding industry.

(E) The National Craft-Brewers Conference and Trade Show is the industry's largest and most important event, providing attendees the opportunity to share information, make industry contacts and learn how best to continue the current success of the craft-brewing industry. Brewers and individuals considering entering the industry will be provided with the latest information on: distribution, legislative issues, marketing, brewery safety, advanced brewing, sales and business operations. The 1995 Conference sold out, boasting over 1,900 attendees and 110 exhibitors. More than 2,500 attendees and 150 exhibitors are expected at the 1996 Conference.

"The Boston Conference will help craft-brewers chart their own course for the future," said David Edgar, director of the Institute for Brewing Studies. "The industry is experiencing explosive growth and undergoing a number of changes. The Conference will help attendees understand those changes, how they will affect the industry and how to plan for continued success."

The Institute for Brewing Studies has hosted an annual craft-brewing conference for the past 13 years. This year, in order to better reflect the broad scope of the burgeoning craft-brewing industry, the IBS has changed the name of the Conference from the National Microbrewers and Pubbrewers Conference and Trade Show to the National Craft-Brewers Conference and Trade Show.

Massachusetts has played a significant role in the craft-brewing renaissance and provides an ideal location for the 1996 Conference. More than 20 microbreweries and brewpubs have already established themselves in the market, and additional brewing operations are in the planning stages. Boston's many award-winning breweries and brewpubs will provide attendees with a strong representative sampling of the diversity and quality of America's craft-brewed beers, from cask-conditioned English ales to traditional German-style lagers and wheat beers.

(F) "There is already a tremendous amount of interest from prospective attendees and exhibitors who are looking forward to an even bigger and better Conference in 1996," said Nancy Johnson, special events coordinator for the Association of Brewers. "We're expecting Boston to sell out even more quickly than last year's Conference, despite having more space."

About the Institute for Brewing Studies
With more than 1,700 members, the Institute for Brewing Studies is the leading educational association for craft brewers. The IBS publishes *The New Brewer*, a bimonthly craft-brewing industry magazine, and organizes the annual National Craft-Brewers Conference and Trade Show.

About the Association of Brewers
Founded in 1978, the Association of Brewers, is a nonprofit educational association dedicated to the collection and dissemination of information on beer and brewing. The Association of Brewers has four divisions — the Institute for Brewing Studies, the American Homebrewers Association®, Brewers Publications and the Great American Beer Festival®.

General Press Release Tips

- Press releases should be mailed on corporate letterhead.
- Select a plain, readable serif font. (Times, Roman, or Palatino are good choices.)
- Use a wide right margin so the journalist can take notes to the side.
- Never single space between lines! Space and a half or double space, please.
- Spell check and then have someone else proofread your release before mailing.
- Offer photos at the bottom of your release, if available.
- Double check your phone number at the top. Seriously.

Chapter 16
Beer Packaging and Point-of-Sale Design

by Jeff Ware
President of Dock Street Brewing Company

In January 1995, Dock Street asked the question, Is the quality of our product reflected in our packaging? We believed that our success demanded packaging upgrade. The challenge was to preserve brand equity and insure that our identity stood out from the sea of other microbreweries. In addition, we wanted to position ourselves alongside top-shelf European beers.

The goals were fivefold: (1) to reaffirm Dock Street's position in the marketplace; (2) to revitalize the brand identity and packaging; (3) to visually strengthen and heighten brand awareness; (4) to integrate the three varieties bottled by Dock Street under a unified graphic system; and (5) to communicate the message that Dock Street's beers complement the finest foods. The last goal — to change the public's perception that only wine is a beverage enjoyed with food — was developed as a slogan and as an integral part of all advertising and marketing efforts.

We wanted to incorporate this without sacrificing the support of Dock Street's loyal following. A critical part of design is for the designer to gather as much information about the company as possible. The design firm sat in on several meetings where Dock Street's goals and philosophy were discussed, sales people were interviewed, competitors' packaging was reviewed, and our current packaging was analyzed. Two key elements to Dock Street's identity were retained: the illustrations, as these had become the company's quality icons, and the oval surrounding the illustrations.

The design company's inspiration came from the beginnings of the company; the nautical theme suggested by the name Dock Street; and the illustrations — the springboard for concept development. The initial presentation included some twenty sketches of labels only. The range of solutions varied from historical to contemporary and explored a range of color palettes, sizes, and die-cutting options. During the process, an obvious system that visually united the three products Dock Street currently bottled became apparent.

During the first presentation, the collaborative nature between client and designer is critically important. No matter how detailed the research and information gathering may be, the designer receives the most significant input as a result of the first presentation review meeting. Remember that the designer is not the expert in the beer business, you are. Their job is to translate your input and develop a design that meets your needs. Our marketing director, and later, the sales staff and management reviewed design decisions.

Initially, the bottle labels were designed based on the idea of semaphore nautical flags, a diagonally divided square with a diamond in the middle. Three primary colors were chosen — red, blue, and yellow — which rotated within each label, signifying the three varieties of beer bottled by Dock Street. The diamond color would constantly relate to a beer type and be translated to all components: the bottle body label, neck label, crowns, six-pack carrier, cartons, and all advertising and marketing materials. Additional color combinations were selected for application to future products soon to be bottled by Dock Street.

The design refinement stage was quite detailed, exploring type-style variations and subtle color changes. Full-size prototypes were created for all the components. At this point, the design company had the foundation of Dock Street's new brand identity which could be applied to various other projects, billboards, coasters, banners, point-of-purchase materials, matches, shopping bags, etc. The final packaging, with its intensely saturated colors, introduced a new, bold look, unique to the beer and beverage industry.

The design company was also responsible for the production of the new packaging which required constant communication with Dock Street's bottling company. For instance, the label size had to conform to existing equipment; the labels had to be submitted to the government for final approval; printing estimates had to be obtained from a variety of suppliers; and final suppliers selected. The design company attended all press approvals to supervise print quality and consistency from supplier to supplier.

Dock Street had other concerns. The timing of the new packaging's release was critical. With a costly inventory of old packaging in stock, Dock Street had to forecast when this inventory would be depleted. Everyone wanted to avoid having both the new and the old packaging appearing together in stores. Costs were also a concern. Dock Street's old packaging featured twelve-color labels and two-color six-pack carriers and cartons. The new labels were four-color process, realizing significant savings. However, Dock Street wanted four-color printing for the new carriers and cartons, significantly increasing these production costs.

The consumer impact of the new design was immediate. Wholesalers, being conservative by nature, initially voiced their concerns when shown preliminary designs for the new packaging. However, now they are impressed unanimously with the bold, innovative look and the quality materials.

Now when Dock Street asks the question, Is the quality of our product reflected in our packaging? We can unreservedly answer yes.

Chapter 17
Working with Distributors

by Tom McCormick
Principle of McCormick Distribution and Marketing

Distribution has become one of the most important, yet commonly overlooked, components in the operation and success of a microbrewery. A common misconception by those entering the craft-beer industry is that once the beer is brewed, packaged, and shipped to a wholesaler, the brewer can essentially forget about it, leaving the sales, marketing, and promotion to the distributors. This is not the case since beer wholesalers are primarily a delivery mechanism; most do little actual selling and promoting of the smaller brands in their portfolio. Hence, it is imperative that the microbrewer knows and understands the second tier of the business — distribution — in order to ensure their products are adequately marketed and handled after leaving the caring hands of the brewer.

Self-Distribution

One avenue brewers have available to ensure good distribution is self-distribution. This practice is not allowed in some states and is only practical within the local market area. Self-distribution should be limited to within a one-hundred-mile radius of the brewery in order to maintain cost efficiencies. Your local market is both your most important market and also the easiest to gain recognition and retail placements because of the "local appeal." Self-distribution has the advantage of personal, hands-on selling that beer distributors cannot give to most products, given the extent of their product portfolios. The disadvantages

are the time and resources involved in running a company within a company. Some small brewers have initiated self-distribution for the first few years to gain good product representation and placement, and then turned the distribution over to a beer wholesaler to further penetrate the marketplace.

Selecting the Right Distributor

Eventually it is necessary for the microbrewer to select and secure distributors. In any given market there are a number of distributors to choose from. Normally, each market will contain three "major brand" houses (distributors are often referred to as a "house"), one each for Anheuser-Busch, Miller, and Coors. Rarely will these three brands be found in the same house. Major brand houses are the largest, most dominant beer distributors within the territory. They have very high levels of service, are in all retail licensed accounts, and are aggressively competitive. They have excellent contacts within the retail trade, including important chain store buyers. The disadvantage for the microbrewer is that he or she is a small fish in a very large pond. First and foremost, these distributors are selling their main brand. They may have a hard time dealing with a small brewery's baggage — the many line extensions, seasonals, older style kegs, limited POS (point-of-sale), and promotional support. Additionally, they often don't understand the time-intensive hand selling required of craft-beer products. Main brand houses are also very selective in choosing new brands.

Most markets may also contain one or two specialty or miscellaneous brand houses. A miscellaneous brand house carries many products other than one of the big three, such as regional breweries, popular imports, and nonalcoholics. Although they do not dominate the marketplace like a main brand house, they usually have a high level of service and can be a good home to the small brewer. They typically have very large portfolios, and it is easy to get "lost" in the price sheet.

Also present in some markets is a specialty distributor or "microdistributor" who sells only handcrafted, authentic products — usually imports as well as microbrewed domestics. This is a relatively new concept, and although there are currently few distributors of this nature, there are many new start-ups coming on-line soon. Microdistributors typically offer great enthusiasm, have a sales staff that know and care about microbrewed products and beer in general, and are good at taking the time to hand sell your products. However, they can be understaffed, with tendencies to highlight the account base.

Liquor/wine distributors are also options now that they are entering the craft-beer segment in increasing numbers. Wine distributors will customarily cover a much broader territory, which is usually statewide, while beer distributors commonly confine themselves to a single metropolitan area. Wine distributors are good at product knowledge and hand selling but have a very large portfolio, larger than any other type of beverage wholesaler. They are normally very strong onpremise and weak off-premise. Because of the slow pull through of wine and liquor products, they may call on most accounts only every two weeks, whereas a major house may call on a high-volume account as often as five to six times per week. Specialty houses ordinarily have a call frequency somewhere in between. Because most liquor/wine houses are relatively new to beer sales, they either don't carry draft products at all or are very weak in draft sales and service.

It is often difficult to terminate a brewery/distributor agreement. When shopping for a distributor, choose one that not only suits your needs now, but that will also be appropriate in five or even ten years from now. Spending time in the marketplace in which you are searching for distribution is the most effective way of selecting a distributor best suited to your needs. Obtain a price sheet from each wholesaler so you know which distributors carry the various brands in the market. Talk to retailers to gain insight into which distributor they prefer dealing with. Ask questions about call frequency, draft service, product knowledge, enthusiasm of the salespeople, and which distributor understands and sells craft beers the best. Look around the retail accounts as well. Find out which distributor seems to put up the most POS, has the most draft handles and best shelf positioning for craft beers. Talk with other craft brewers in that market to get their opinion from the supplier side.

Once you narrow it down to two or three distributors, call each one and set up an appointment to show your products. Distributors are approached constantly by various suppliers looking for distribution, so it is important to sell your product, even on the first call. Depending on the market, many distributors are very selective in looking at new brands. Make sure you are well prepared and have a convincing proposal when meeting with the distributor. You should know your pricing, shipping costs and arrangements, what your advertising and promotion plans are, post-off programs, and in what way you will assist the distributor in selling the brand. Be sure to take samples of both product and POS into the interview. Try to also gain some insight about the distributor during the interview. Some questions to ask are: Do they know craft beers and how to sell them? Do they carry other specialty brands, and what has their success been with those? Do they have a brand manager or specific person responsible for your product line? Are they willing to carry all of your line extensions and draft? Do they have refrigeration space for your brand? Do they have good draft support and service? Do they seem financially strong?

Try to get a commitment on pricing. Although you cannot dictate to a distributor what they will sell your beer for, you can get an understanding prior to signing a contract of what margins the distributor will be working on. Typically, distributors work on a 25 percent gross margin for craft beers.

Additionally, it is very important to choose a distributor that you feel comfortable with. The "comfort factor" should be high on your list when you make the final decision. Each beer wholesaler has its own personality, and you will want a company you can trust and feel confident with so that a lasting, mutually beneficial relationship is built.

Once you have chosen a distributor willing to carry your products, be sure to have your attorney draft a contract agreement. As the product supplier, it is your responsibility to provide such a contract.

Working with the Distributor

It is now time to work closely with the wholesaler in rolling out the product. The wholesaler's sales staff is essentially the brewery's sales staff, so it is imperative that they are excited and educated about your brand. You should hold a "kick-off" meeting with the sales staff and tell them the story behind your brands, how they are made, how they are unique and different, and how to sell them. Remember that the sales staff has a lot of other brands to sell; you want to somehow make your brand special so each salesperson aggressively sells your brand every time they walk into an account.

In today's competitive craft-beer market it is essential to keep in touch with each distributor. Many small brewers fail to realize how much time and effort this requires. Depending on the size and intentions of your brewery,

salespeople should be budgeted to work directly in the distribution network. Each distributor should be contacted on nearly a weekly basis to make sure they have adequate POS and are using it to monitor inventory levels and ordering projections, to discuss key accounts, etc. It is common practice for the brewery sales representative to do "riders" with the distributor staff, where they spend a day with one salesperson on their daily route to help present and discuss your products to the retailers. It is also very helpful for brewery representatives to spend time in the market, independent of the distributor's sales staff, to make new placements and generally promote the brand. Remember that distributors have many brands to sell. Be respectful of their other brands when in the marketplace. One of the most difficult tasks is to maintain appropriate "mind share" from your distributor. If your brand only accounts for perhaps 2 percent of the distributor's revenue, it is very difficult to get more than 2 percent of their time. By staying in touch with the principles of the company, spending time with the sales managers and staff, and spending ample time in the market yourself, you will help ensure adequate representation of your brand.

Rules and Regulations

The rules and regulations pertaining to the distribution and advertising of beer products are highly regulated and are enacted and enforced primarily on the state level. Therefore, each state has its own set of laws which the brewer is responsible for knowing and abiding by. It is incumbent on you, the brewer, to know the specific regulations of each state in which you sell. Generally, most states don't allow the brewer to give any items of value (T-shirts, mirrors, glassware, etc.) to a retailer or consumer. There are often regulations as to what a brewer may supply to the distributor, payment terms between brewer and distributor, and very specific, often restrictive terms for terminating a distributor. Contact the state regulatory agency and beer wholesaler trade organization for the specific laws before doing business in that state.

Summary

Beer distribution — with its own personality, language, and terms — is very different from the beer business. It is, however, intrinsic to the beer industry. As essential as distribution is to the success of a brewery, it is important to learn this industry so that you are comfortable and knowledgeable enough to make it work for you. You can brew the very best of products and have great packaging and pricing, but without good distribution, it will be not be enjoyed by the end consumer.

Chapter 18
Trademark Licensing and Premium Promotion

by Peter Hexter
President of CUI Inc.

Trademark licensing and promotion may be one of the least understood areas in the brewery business. Each aspect of this topic could be a seminar. Careers are made and sometimes destroyed by how these sensitive aspects are handled within a corporate brewery structure. They should be considered an important part of the grass-roots foundation of any successful brewery operation no matter what its size.

"No time and no money" is the cry of every understaffed, undercapitalized brewery when it contemplates or begins to implement license trademark guidelines or promotional programs. But you may be surprised to learn that it takes just a little of both resources to create the professional image and controls that the biggest breweries maintain. Here I will give some simple guidelines to help you create a straightforward, cost-effective approach to protecting your trademark, discovering some hidden revenue, and building simple and successful promotions. I emphasize, however, that one should always consult an attorney for the final implementation of any documents pertaining to trademarks or licensing agreements.

Trademarks

First and foremost, we need to understand a little about trademarks. What are trademark rights and how does one protect them?

The use of trademarks is over two thousand years old, and today there are more than 450,000 actively registered trademarks. A *trademark* is any word, name, slogan, symbol, or design used by a manufacturer or seller to identify the source of a product and to distinguish that product from the products of others. A trademark also serves as a guarantee of consistent quality and as an aid in product advertising and sales.

In the United States, the rights to a particular trademark are established by the first person or commercial entity to use it. The rights are maintained by continuous, consistent, and proper usage. These rights are recognized under common law as property rights. Additional advantages and enhanced rights can be obtained by registering the trademark with the U.S. Patent and Trademark Office. Such registration is somewhat like a birth certificate — it merely provides official recognition of what has already come to pass.

Unlike copyright and patent rights, rights to a trademark can last forever, so long as the mark is still in use and used properly. Likewise, trademark rights can be lost forever through improper use.

Exclusive rights to a trademark are usually lost through careless and incorrect use with the result that the trademark becomes a descriptive or generic word for a product. Many common words were once valuable trademarks — aspirin, mimeograph, trampoline, yo-yo, cellophane, escalator, linoleum — but were lost through improper usage or lack of diligence. It is no wonder that present-day companies with exclusive rights to such trademarks as Kleenex®, Band-Aid®, Xerox®, Coke®, Levi's®, and Dacron® spend tremendous amounts of time and money to protect their trademark rights. Loss of those rights would mean that any competitor could use the trademark as a description name for a product and take advantage of all the advertising dollars spent and the goodwill established by the original owner.

Trademark Protection

Responsibility for the proper use of a trademark rests with the trademark owner. The company's trademarks should always be used in a consistent manner in all printed materials emanating from the company: product labels and packaging, advertising, catalogs, point-of-sale materials, annual reports and publications, speeches, press releases, and letters.

Likewise, when the company's trademarks are misused in print by others, such as the media and licensees, it is the company's responsibility to alert the offender and request that the trademark be properly designated in the future.

You must decide how far you wish to go geographically to protect your trademark. Short term, you need to register on a state-by-state basis where you presently conduct business and where your future expansion is planned. Additional options are to register it nationally, but this form of registration does not afford the same protection as that of state-by-state registrations.

In summary, take the time now to confirm that your trademarks are protected. Once that has been completed, begin to develop clear guidelines as to their proper usage.

Licensing:
Promoting the Hidden Assets

Many of you may not realize it, but there could be revenue in your trademarks. Make sure before you attempt to realize profit from that revenue that you have in place all the instruments required to protect these assets. The most concise way to protect your trademark and begin to generate revenue is through the development of a simple licensing program. At the base of every successful licensing program is a strong agreement and a clear, concise statement from you, the licenser.

In formulating a license agreement, keep in mind the following points:

* Use simple, straightforward language.
* Let your suppliers know in a cover letter with the agreement that you are serious about your trademarks and the rights and restrictions that accompany their use.
* Be prepared to back up your license agreement or trademark with legal action if violations occur.
* Send out quarterly request forms for royalties and make sure someone follows up on cases of nonpayment. (See following sample.)

Educate Your Licensee

To minimize your risk of misunderstandings with your licensee, make certain that he understands the practical conditions of your agreement. This can be accomplished by the following:

* Provide a "how-to" kit for trademark reproduction.
* Keep it simple: show examples of what is acceptable and what is not.
* Refer to specifics in your format; generalization leads to abuse.
* Use PMS color reference whenever possible.
* When developing new brand logos, keep in mind the expense of reproduction, screening, embroidery, printing, etc.

Sample

State of North Carolina County of New Hanover License Agreement
THIS AGREEMENT, made this _____ day of _____, (year), by and between _____, a corporation organized under the laws of _____ (hereinafter," _____ "), _____,

and CUI Inc., a Delaware corporation with a place of business at 1502 North 23rd Street, Wilmington, North Carolina 28405 (hereinafter, "CUI").

WITNESSETH:

WHEREAS, _____ is the owner of and has the exclusive rights to the trademarks _____, and the _____ logo (hereinafter "trademarks"); and WHEREAS, CUI desires to design and manufacture thematic steins and other merchandise items named herein, bearing said trademarks and desires to obtain a license therefore; and WHEREAS, CUI also desires to design and manufacture thematic steins and other merchandise items described herein depicting a species _____ or other thematic artwork which may not be the subject of any trademarks of_____.

NOW, THEREFORE, in consideration of the promises and of the covenants contained herein, and other valuable consideration, the receipt of which is hereby acknowledged, the parties hereto agree as follows:

1. LICENSE:

Subject to all terms, conditions, and limitations contained in this agreement, _____ hereby grants to CUI a limited, exclusive license to use the trademarks. Said trademarks shall be used only in conjunction with the design and manufacture by CUI of _____ thematic steins, hereinafter referred to as _____, and any other merchandise items created pursuant to this agreement, which items may include, but shall not be limited to, ceramics, glassware and clocks, as well as on the depiction or portrayal of such merchandise appearing in or on any media used by CUI to exploit or promote the sale thereof.

It is expressly understood that this agreement constitutes an exclusive right to CUI and _____ is prohibited from granting to any other party a license to use the said trademarks in conjunction with the design and manufacture of the same or similar items.

_____ will use its best efforts to register and maintain, or cause to be registered and maintained, the trademarks to enable the goods to be distributed and sold under the trademarks as provided herein.

2. DESIGN AND MANUFACTURE OF MERCHANDISE:

CUI will design and manufacture a thematic stein depicting a species of_____, in accordance with the following requirements and conditions:

(a) Both lidded and unlidded steins may be used.
(b) Art and graphics will be provided by CUI and reviewed by _____.
(c) There will be new thematic steins designed and manufactured as determined by CUI, with the intention of creating a collector's series of thematic steins.
(d) The edition size and style will be determined by CUI and reviewed by _____.
(e) CUI will bear all inventory risk.

CUI may also design, develop, manufacture and market a complete line of thematic merchandise items for _____, including but not limited to, ceramics, glassware and clocks. _____ shall have the right to review each item of merchandise prior to its being offered for sale.

3. INDEMNIFICATION:

CUI agrees to indemnify, defend, and hold _____ harmless from and against any and all costs, charges, expenses, disbursements, claims, demands, judgments, and liabilities of any nature, including attorney's fees which in any way arise from CUI's manufacture, distribution, exploitation, or merchandising of the items to be manufactured hereunder, or the purchase or use of the same, excepting, however, claims for infringement, copyright, trademark, or the like which relate to the trademarks.

CUI assumes no liability for trademark infringement and _____ hereby indemnifies and holds harmless CUI from and against all losses, damages, and expenses, including attorney's fees, incurred as a result of or related to claims of third persons involving use of the trademarks.

4. TERM OF LICENSE:

The license granted hereunder to use the trademarks in conjunction with the manufacture and sale of _____ steins and merchandise shall remain in effect for a period of _____ ( ) years from the date of execution hereof. CUI shall have the option to renew said license for an additional _____ ( ) years by giving written notice of the exercise of said option on or before thirty days prior to the end of the initial five-year term.

The license granted hereunder to use the trademarks shall not be assigned, transferred, pledged, or otherwise encumbered by CUI without prior written authorization of _____.

5. ROYALTY:

In addition to any other consideration recited herein, CUI agrees to pay _____ a royalty, payable on a quarterly basis, for the license to use the trademarks as follows:

_____ of all net sales on all consumer sales of _____ steins or other merchandise items.

_____ of all net sales on all wholesale sales of all _____ steins or other merchandise items.

CUI shall provide _____ with a statement of all consumer and wholesale sales together with payment of the fee as provided herein, on a quarterly basis, within ____ ( ) days after the end of the preceding calendar quarter.

CUI shall at all times keep complete and accurate business accounts and records showing sales of any item or items provided for. _____ shall have the right, at its own expense and with reasonable notice, for it or a designee to audit such accounts and records.

6. MARKETING:

(a) The sale of these ____ steins and merchandise is not limited to retail sales to _____ members.

(b) _____ shall provide at least one full-page ad for the stein each year in its official membership magazine at no cost to CUI.

(c) _____ shall endorse the program both verbally and in written form when requested by CUI, which endorsements may be used by CUI in its marketing efforts.

(d) _____ shall provide to CUI a full list of names and addresses of ____ members and other potential clients at no cost to CUI on an annual basis.

(e) _____ shall assist CUI with marketing ideas, creative sources, and actively promote the program.

(f) Except as herein provided, CUI shall bear all product development and marketing costs.

Notwithstanding anything herein to the contrary, CUI shall have the sole authority to determine the mode and method of advertising, merchandising, promoting, manufacturing, selling, and distributing all products subject to this agreement, and the sole authority to fix the prices, discounts, and terms of sale to all purchasers, whether consumers, dealers, or distributors.

7. TERMINATION:

In the event of any breach or default by either party of any obligation under this agreement, the other party, at its sole discretion, may cancel this agreement by giving to the other _____ ( ) days' written notice.

If CUI becomes insolvent in that its liabilities exceed its assets, or is adjudicated insolvent, or is the subject of a bankruptcy proceeding, or is involved in a reorganization, or takes advantage of or is subjected to any insolvency act, or makes an assignment for the benefit of creditors, then in such event, this agreement shall forthwith terminate and the license herein granted shall not constitute an asset or property in any such proceeding which may be assigned or which may accrue to any bankruptcy estate, any creditor, any court, or to any creditor or court appointed committee, or any receiver.

Upon expiration of the term of this agreement, or termination as otherwise provided, CUI shall immediately cease to use the trademarks. CUI agrees that upon such expiration or termination it will not claim any right, title, or interest in or to the trademarks which are the subject hereof.

8. CHOICE OF LAWS:

This agreement shall be interpreted and construed in accordance with the laws of the state of North Carolina.

9. ENTIRE AGREEMENT:

This instrument contains the entire and only agreement between the parties hereto relating to the subject matter hereof and no oral statements or representations or prior written matter not herein contained shall have any force or effect. This agreement may not be modified or amended except by a written agreement duly executed by both parties.

10. NOTICES:

Any notices required or permitted to be given under this agreement shall be deemed sufficiently given if mailed by registered mail, postage prepaid, addressed to the party to be notified at its address shown at the beginning of this agreement, or at such other address as may be furnished in writing to the notifying party.

(CORPORATE SEAL)
BY:_____
(SEAL)
ATTEST:
_____ PRESIDENT
_____
_____ SECRETARY
CUI, INC.
(CORPORATE SEAL)
BY:_____
(SEAL)
ATTEST:
_____ PRESIDENT
_____
_____ SECRETARY

Qualify Your Suppliers

To minimize hassles with your suppliers, make certain that you also follow a few, simple guidelines:

- Choose reputable suppliers who represent a quality image.
- Remember that their treatment of your trademark will create an impression of your product with the public.
- Make sure you maintain tight control and final sign-off on all promotional and or license merchandise.
- Whenever possible, visit your suppliers. Let them know you are serious about the relationship, confirm their legitimacy, and confirm they are in accordance with your agreement.

Corporate Gift Shop

The corporate gift shop should be a consideration for every brewery, regardless of its size. It is a great incentive for your licensee to realize he has an additional outlet for his product, and it also generates strong revenue from your loyal patrons. Start out with small quantities and, when possible, items that do not differ in size (i.e., adjustable banded hats versus hats in five sizes). Try to be creative in your display of the merchandise; remember, your customer will form his impression of value from that initial image.

I believe that we must acknowledge an uncertain era ahead. As in all alcohol categories, beer licensing — and ensuing sales of retail merchandise — face a great deal of uncertainty in the next decade. They remain, however, some of the least expensive ways to gain strong secondary brand impressions. Every item sold generates revenue, it becomes a potential billboard for your establishment, and it is still an inexpensive way to get secondary brand impressions.

If you wish, you may tie in a theme of responsibility with your licensed and trademark materials. The big breweries have done this to some extent: Miller's "Think When You Drink," and Budweiser's "Know When to Say No." You can let the public know you are aware of the potential problems with irresponsible beer consumption.

Along these same lines, make sure your licensed products are tasteful. Avoid associations with children or underage drinkers (i.e., baby bottles, bibs, etc.).

The Four Ps of Promotions: Purpose, Plan, Product, and Placement

I realize that you have limited dollar and manpower resources for promotions, but there are niches in your markets which you can exploit. This is especially true if you can find the right companies to help you execute these promotions.

First and foremost, when you consider any promotion, ask yourself, how can this help me sell more beer? To answer that question, you need to understand promotional merchandising and accept the fact that there is seldom a time when the total impact of a promotion can be measured in the short term.

Purpose. Set a goal or objective to target a new town, state, or region, or perhaps to capture a specific category on-premise or to boost sales at a specified time of year.

Once you have done that, remember that the more clearly you define the purpose behind the promotion, the clearer the value of the project will become.

Second, don't build false hopes for a particular promotion for yourself or your retailer by setting unrealistic goals.

Third, realize that there are some results from a promotion that can be measured only with time.

Plan. Plan ahead, and build in a long lead time to develop sources and place your promotion. Most large breweries work a year in advance. Communicate your plan internally to those involved in the execution, as well as externally, to those who will be part of the promotion. A yearly promotional planner is ideal to give to your distributors if you plan to run a series of promotional opportunities.

Test or research your promotion before making a major commitment. Has it been done before? What was its level of success? Make sure the promotion is in place when you promised it. Always review the legality of your promotion on a state-by-state basis. After the promotion is over, critique it. Get feedback from your retailers and on-premise people. Many times their suggestions will help make the next promotion more successful.

Product. Your product should obviously tie into the objective and theme of your promotion.

Remember quality and image. Your promotional product is a reflection on your beer product. It should have a higher perceived value to the consumer than what he is actually paying.

As with licensed products, consider promotional products that do not have a sizing requirement.

Work with suppliers who can provide low minimums, quick turnarounds, and enough inventory to support a highly successful campaign. Look to a supplier who can provide turnkey opportunities, which make the most of your money and manpower.

Use products that carry "the billboard" concept: hats, steins, sunglasses, etc.

Placement. Make sure your driver or salesperson understands the importance of promotional placement.

Point-of-sale materials should communicate a clear, concise message. It is important that you make sure that your displays are maintained and are not sabotaged by competition.

If a promotion is being done "live" on-premise for a particular night or event such as Monday night football, be sure that it is executed in a manner that brings anticipated results.

Conclusion

In the final analysis, there are a number of companies, both large and small, who have the ability to help you plan and execute your promotions. Many of these companies will work on a cost-plus basis or simply as an opportunity to sell promotional merchandise.

Their compensation is built into the merchandise margin. Check them out thoroughly. Make sure they have the ability to live up to all elements of the promotional agreement. The more vertical they are as a company, the more unlikely you are to experience complications before and during your promotion.

Chapter 19
Brand Building with Draft or with Bottled Beer

by Pat Meyer
General Sales Manager of the Rockies Brewing Company

Whenever there is a gathering of beer salespeople, a conversation about brand building usually occurs. Brand building in the context of beer sales refers to the ways in which a sales force can take a new brand of beer and put it in front of the consumer so that he or she will try it, like it, and become a regular customer. The main point of debate in conversations about brand building is usually whether brands are built on-premise (in bars and restaurants) or off-premise (in liquor and grocery stores). Since draft beer is primarily an on-premise package and bottled beer is primarily an off-premise package, the discussion tends to be about the ways draft beer can be sold versus the ways bottled beer can be sold to generate brand loyalty. Selling draft beer and selling bottled beer each pose unique challenges and reap unique benefits. Hopefully, the following information will at least acquaint you with some of the techniques that can be employed to maximize your results as you begin formulating a sales strategy for each of your packages.

Having a fairly clear idea of how you want to see your product sold is essential to its success. Either a distributor or your own sales force can usually secure the initial distribution and sales. It is important that these initial sales be strategic in order to build your brand for the future. It is far easier to have a successful initial product launch than to try to revive a brand if it does not catch on immediately. It's in your best interest to thoroughly think through your sales goals and strategies before you take your product to market. Of course no matter how completely you plan your sales effort, you will have to make some changes on the fly. Depending on your personality, that's the part that you will either have the most fun with or get the most gray hairs from.

Selling Draft Beer to Create Brand Awareness

About 15 percent of all the beer sold in the United States is sold in kegs. Within the craft-brewing segment the actual percentage of draft beer is most likely higher than that, perhaps in the 30 percent range. Gaining draft lines is not as easy as simply walking into your local pub and asking the manager to put your beer on draft. Unfortunately most bars and restaurants have a limited number of draft lines available, and those limited lines represent a good portion of the retail bar profit. However, while there is a limited number of lines, there seems to be no limit to the number of competitive salespeople calling on each account, most of them offering several quality products.

With such a competitive draft market, it is necessary to add value to what you offer the retailer. Retailers want to maximize sales and subsequent profit. This is an area where your interest and those of the retailers generally mesh well. Most retailers will encourage you to engage in brand building activities. It's how

e the sell through on your
their profit. You will find
ne specific brand-building
retailer when you make
tion, you will have much
nber and complexity of the
can offer to increase con-
d sales in the on-premise
our imagination and state
er, the following are some
activities that you can
pon the dynamics of your

aff volunteers. Bartenders
me of the best salespeople
can find a way to get the
and recommending your
tten the upper hand in the
e consumer's attention.
wonderful tool for getting
nd in touch with a new
of hours and a few free
t in showing the wait staff
truly unique and interest-
ff. On many occasions the
g a large wait staff that
urs can be daunting. Your
f you cannot get the wait
is to bring the brewery to
s can usually be accom-
t changes when you have
the building at the same
agination to make these
If the laws in your state
ntives, they work well to
ormation you have given
consumer. You might be
le you have to offer in the
way of incentives to get the staff excited.
Simple wearables or free food and drinks can
go a long way. Above all, if you use your imagination to make things fun and exciting for the
wait staff, they will treat you right.

Interaction with the consumer. Sometimes
you have to take your information directly to
the final consumers. Promotional nights give
you the opportunity to meet with the people
whom you want to introduce to your product.

The basic premise of all promotional nights is
to have an attractive price for your product
and some sort of giveaway items to capture the
customer's interest. It is best if you can find
some way of giving your goodies away that promotes interaction between yourself and the
patrons. You want to make sure that the information you give the customers makes them
want to buy your product at regular price.
Imaginative promotions will get customers
talking about your beer and hopefully asking
questions. Beer dinners as promotions are
becoming very popular across the country.
However, the people who attend these events
are usually the ones who will try every new
beer that comes to the market. This doesn't
mean you shouldn't aggressively pursue beer
dinners. Many of the people at these dinners
are self-styled beer connoisseurs. They are the
people who will talk about beers to anyone
willing to listen. Take every opportunity to
make sure that these people are talking from a
knowledgeable basis. Any way that you can figure out to get people to listen to the story of
your product is time and effort very well spent.

Brand presence. No matter how effective
you have been with promotions and wait-staff
training, you can't reach every customer personally. It is imperative you find other ways of
getting your message across. Most restaurant
patrons don't ever see your tap knob, so you've
got to find some way to get your logo in front
of them. Screened glassware, coasters, table
tents, and neons represent just a few of the
tools you can use. Since each establishment
has different policies regarding what kind of
point-of-sale items you can utilize, you have to
have a variety to offer. Even if you have an eye-
catching logo, it helps if you can find a way to
incorporate a few lines of text or a catch
phrase. Try to find a way to let the customer
know what to expect when ordering your product. Also, make sure you're the one to put up
all your point-of-sale-items — don't count on
distributors, bar owners, or on anyone else to
do it. And be prepared because you will always
go through at least twice as many point-of-sale
materials as you thought you would.

Selling bottled beer to create awareness. Bottled beer accounts for the majority of beer sold. Whether you bottle in twenty-two-ounce single bottles, twelve-ounce six-packs, or some other size container, the off-premise is where you can expect to find a good percentage of your volume. The selling strategies and techniques do not vary too much from package to package. Generally speaking, it is much easier to gain initial distribution off-premise than on-premise. The crunch for space is not as severe. While this is good for gaining simple distribution, it is not so great for brand building. With so many different products, retailers have less incentive to help you in building your brand. If your brand doesn't sell like hot cakes something else will.

There are a number of pricing schemes that can be used to make retailers more receptive to your product and your goals. But the legality of pricing schemes varies from state to state, so you'll have to devise a program that works for your market. For the most part brand building in the off-premise comes down to good salesmanship, price positioning, packaging, and thank goodness, a good product. A large percentage of sales and consumer sampling in the off-premise initially comes from impulse buys. Good brand building in the off-premise means putting your product in a position to get those impulse buys. Besides flashy packaging, there are some basic mechanics you can focus on to encourage those impulse purchases.

Shelf positioning. Perhaps the most important aspect of off-premise sales is shelf positioning. With the rapid growth of the craft-brewing industry, many stores have begun to use warm shelves for beers as well as their traditional cold shelves. Ideally you would like to be at eye level: you want people to see your product without really looking for it. Additionally it is important that you are in the right segment of the cooler. People usually focus their attention to where there are a number of choices in the price range that they are comfortable with or familiar with. Don't let yourself be grouped in with a lot of beers that are not your price competitors.

Getting as much shelf space as possible has two benefits. First, the "billboard effect" gives your product more visual presence. Secondly, it may help you avoid out-of-stock situations during busy periods. Focus on these items on both the cold and warm shelves, but pay the most attention to the cold shelf. Cold beer is what sells. The more you accomplish these goals, the more people will try your beer.

Floor displays. Getting your product displayed on the floor is a powerful brand-building tool. A floor display gives your product a large visual presence in a store. By examining the natural traffic flow in a store, you will find the best location for your floor display. Ideally, you would like everyone who shops in the store to pass by your display. A display in a corner of the store that no one ever sees is really just a stack of beer. Always remember to make your displays shopable. If it is a hassle to grab a bottle or a six-pack, some people won't bother. Also, a good display provides the customer with some information. Displays are natural billboards for getting a message to the consumer. Find short, concise sentences or phrases to explain to the customer just what they are looking at.

Cooler point-of-sale material. Once you have established a good shelf position, it is important to make the most of the attention you receive from the customer. Display the price of your product so consumers can decide if it is in their price range. Cooler statics or channel strips are inexpensive and easy ways to convey this information. If your product is offered at some type of temporary price reduction, make sure customers know they are getting a bargain. People will buy almost anything if they feel they are getting a value. It is a definite plus if you can put some sort of accolade at the point of purchase. Many consumers need the extra information provided by a couple of lines of text. The wine industry, by anyone's rights, has done a wonderful job at just this. Any positive information you can put in front of the customers at this critical juncture when they are about to make a decision is going to weigh in your favor. The bottom line is to put new customers at ease with the idea of spending their hard-earned money trying something new rather than going with something they already know they like.

Handselling. On occasion you may have the opportunity to reach the public personally. Some states allow for in-store tastings. Sampling product at the point-of-purchase is the name of the game in brand building. Research the laws in your state to find out if this is legal. In-store tastings provide you with the opportunity to tell people your story face to face and give them an opportunity to see and taste for themselves. If you can't do tastings, you still may be allowed to come into the store and set up a handsel. While it is not as effective as doing tastings, it still gives you the opportunity to get your message across to the public. Handselling can also ingratiate you to the retailer. To achieve the most success, you should have something to catch the customer's eye or something to give away. The cost of give-away items can be a small price to pay for the opportunity to get people to try your beer and listen to your story.

Profit Considerations

A vital question in planning a sales strategy is, how much profit is involved in different products? On the surface it appears that draft beer is a far more profitable package than bottled beer. I would make the argument that when draft beer is sold effectively, it is roughly at parity with bottled beer in terms of profit per barrel. Your cost structures will be unique to your operation and economies of scale. Your revenue structures will vary depending on wholesale and retail margins in your particular market. Here are some generalizations based on averages that I have observed in different markets around the nation. There are much higher costs of packaging associated with bottled beer, but there are also much higher revenues per barrel. By the time that you add the extra costs associated with supporting your sales at retail in the on-premise market, the gap between keg profit and case profit is very small. Typically a 15.5-gallon keg of beer is sold to retail for around $80. At a 27 percent wholesale margin price, the keg, not

including shipping and tax, is $58.40. Gross profit per barrel, depending on economies of scale, is in the neighborhood of $80 per barrel. For a case of six-pack bottles, sale to retail is around $18. At 25 percent wholesale margin price, the case of six-packs, not including shipping and tax, is $13.50. Gross profit per barrel, depending on economies of scale, is in the neighborhood of $70 per barrel. The on-premise market is very expensive to support in terms of sales effort and expected point-of-sale support. The extra dollars of revenue that you gain selling kegs can easily be invested in maintaining your draft lines.

Putting It All Together

While most beer sale professionals agree with the basic brand-building premises outlined above, they usually disagree on how much focus should be put on selling bottled beer versus selling draft beer. Unless you have an unlimited amount of resources, some choices have to be made regarding how to focus your sales efforts. There are two basic schools of thought regarding where sales emphasis should be placed. One school argues that bottled beer in the off-premise should be the main focus of sales effort. The other school argues that on-premise draft should be the main focus.

The reason for focusing on bottled beer in the off-premise is driven by the sheer numbers of volume and customer exposure. On a daily basis more people will visit liquor and grocery stores than bars and restaurants. In the off-premise more people notice the brand presence that you create, resulting in more beer sales. It takes less effort to ensure you have distribution in the accounts that really matter.

The reason for focusing on draft beer is the quality of brand building that can be accomplished. It is much easier to gain retailer support for engaging in brand building in the on-premise. Consumer sampling usually can be accomplished more easily. Many people are more receptive to trying something new when they are out and they can purchase single servings.

Both of these lines of thought are valid. The trick comes in deciding how to balance your focus so your sales in on-premise do as much as possible to promote your off-premise sales and vice versa. There is no patented formula for accomplishing this. You have to do your homework to find out how your particular market functions. Get out on the street and talk to retailers and consumers. Examine your costs and make a realistic assessment of how much time and money you are willing to invest. Create target lists of the top accounts in your area and what you would like to accomplish in each of them.

But above all, remember that even though it seems hard, selling your product to retail is the easy part. Selling it to the ultimate consumer is the essential part.

Chapter 20
Using Used Dairy Equipment

by Randy Sprecher
Founder of Sprecher Brewing Company

As most brewers will attest to, you can never have too much money when starting your brewing venture. However, it sometimes turns out that you do not have adequate financial backing and must cut some corners. Purchasing and modifying used stainless-steel equipment can help when you are short on cash and do not wish to seek additional investors.

Dairy equipment and tanks are the most commonly sought-after items. Actually many process vessels, not just dairy-industry pieces, can be found with varied configurations and sizes suitable for brewery use. Purchasing used dairy equipment can save you large sums of capital, and the equipment has a reasonable resale or collateral value. However, this type of purchase must be done with considerable forethought as this approach can present many problems. No one wants to bring home, at any cost, an enormous paperweight.

Some of the skills, knowledge, and experience necessary to utilize used dairy equipment include the basic equipment and construction knowledge, rigging and moving, tools to do the work, and the dedication to see the project through. In short, the less outside work to be done, the cheaper you can get underway, and of course, the shorter the time line to realize the resulting profits.

There is the question of whether or not you can produce quality products from such equipment, and the answer is yes. Actually, seemingly inferior equipment has been used without problems and with exceptional results by

brewers both here and abroad. The technique, skills, and experience of the brewer are more important in the final analysis.

In brewpubs the importance of appearance may outweigh the cost — commercially manufactured equipment has the edge in appearance. However, handcrafted vessels can be attractive and exhibit a superior finish.

The simplest way to get started is to have a used stainless-steel yard prepare a tank for you. They may have the ability to modify a tank suitable for use as a fermenter or storage (lager) tank. This usually entails adding a sight line and top fitting for blowoff/vacuum breaker devices to the tank. These tanks usually come horizontal with insulation, a set of legs, and an outer mild-steel jacket. However, some tanks will be single-wall stainless (i.e., without any insulation or jacket). These tanks are of 1950s

One-hundred-barrel, gas-fired, agitated brew kettle.
Photograph by Randy Sprecher.

to 1970s vintage and of ten-gauge (one-eighth-inch) thickness for both body and ends.

I have experience converting used stainless tanks (usually 304-type) into both gas-fired and agitated mash and kettle vessels, chill water holding tanks, hot wort tanks, and fermentation and lager tanks. Modifications to the tanks usually include additions of manways, legs, outlets, pressed or spun domes, cones, and flat tops. Of course additions like sight lines, zwickels, CO_2 stones, CIP, and vacuum breaker/blowoff units are also included.

Key considerations to vessel selection are dimensions, strength, and interior finish. In regard to tank dimensions, consider whether the tank fits your brew size and if it is suitable to your operation. Also, if you are planning on a used dairy tank as a fermenter, for instance, make sure there's extra room for the foam head which occurs during fermentation.

Strength involves a much more involved consideration and should be trusted to an experienced person or firm. This is especially true when making production vessels with legs or flame heat. However, understand the following points: Pay attention to the attachments. Most leg attachments situated underneath vessels are best when they have additional mounting plates installed between the vessel and the legs. Check for warpage. Stainless steel has a very high thermal conduction, and when it's heated unevenly, permanent warpage can result. Expect some minor warpage for vessels subjected to high temperatures (i.e., a boiling kettle). When checking for warpage look for slight undulations which usually appear on the side walls. After several heating cycles, additional changes should cease unless a design and/or heat flow problem is involved.

And for the interior finish, often a 2B (almost mirrorlike) finish is satisfactory. In certain pieces (i.e., yeast receivers and propagators) a polished or electroplated finish is desirable.

A new major expense consideration is in the retrofitting of bevelseat-type connections. The older bevelseats have become increasingly expensive as they become obsolete. There are many outlets and fitting connection sites on any tank. For large diameter pieces, cutting out old fittings and welding in newer tri-clamp

Forty-barrel, gas-fired, agitated mash mixer with PC controller (on left) and a lauter tun from a Canadian brewery (upper right). *Photograph by Randy Sprecher.*

fittings may be more cost effective. Of course, attention to interior fit and finish is a must.

The typical dairy tank is horizontal, usually with insulation, and has a mild-steel outer jacket, legs, and a manway in the lower front position. Sizes range from 500 to 6,000 gallons, with tanks rarely exceeding 6,000 gallons. Usually the actual stated capacity on the manufacture plate is larger than the stated working capacity on many plates. With the exception of a large-diameter, short-length tank, most tanks will occupy more floor space than the popular vertical type. Horizontal tanks are my choice for fermenters because they provide a shallower depth for the yeast to work in. For the subsequent aging, I prefer vertical tanks, but because of cost savings I opt for horizontal tanks.

Another desirable feature is a double wall, or flood wall, on the tank for cooling purposes. This type of tank may have anything from a portion of the bottom, sides only, or 50 percent of the cylindrical area for cooling. The second wall may be high pressure for freon or low pressure for chill water. Either case is suitable for use with glycol chill water — provided the integrity of the interior sections of the double wall has not been sacrificed. Interior sections can be tested by forcing compressed air or tap water in one side of the tank and then out the other side.

It is also possible, but involves a bit more work, to turn a vertical tank on end, plasma cut the manway to reinstall it on a sidewall, and add a leg set. This will produce a vertical tank with a valley bottom and top and also a side manway.

Although this is just an exposure-level treatment of this topic, certain things should be obvious. Only people who must save money should attempt utilizing used dairy equipment. Also, you should always have as much experience with using used dairy equipment as possible, or have a shop or individual work closely with you in getting the job done right. This should include a well-defined plan for your production needs and detailed drawings of any piece to be substantially modified. With these considerations covered, you are now ready to put together a facility which can be efficient, sanitary, durable, and capable of producing a quality product. As with all things, Murphy's Law gets involved, and a little luck is always appreciated. So good luck in your endeavor.

Chapter 21
Sample Business Plan

Previous sections of this book have covered basic information about what you need to consider when opening a brewery. The next step in your adventure is putting your ideas on paper and developing a business plan.

Here we have taken an actual brewery's business plan and deleted information relevant only to this particular brewery. When you review this business plan, keep in mind that the information it contains applies to 1993, which is when it was written. Figures and other information that, based on their age might be confusing, have been deleted. Many thanks to the donor of this particularly detailed and clear business plan. They did, however, ask that we warn you about the amount of capital they began this venture with: "We got lucky. If we did this over, we would aim for $100,000 more in the beginning."

Changes to this business plan are to the company's name (we're calling it the Craft Brewing Company) and certain figures and names, which we've changed to "XX."

Remember that this is only a sample plan. We strongly recommend that you carefully tailor your own plan to your own business. *Your* business plan should reflect the unique personality and characteristics of *your* business.

Remember also that your business plan is the culmination of all the time spent thinking, researching, compiling, and learning about this industry. If you put time and effort into researching your opportunities in the microbrewing industry, you owe it to yourself to spend the time preparing an effective and thorough business plan. Convincing people that your plan is one that will work is never easy, but the more you put into your plan and it's presentation upfront, the less difficult convincing those people will be in the long run.

TABLE OF CONTENTS

Executive Summary

Description of the Business: The Craft Brewing Company Inc. is a privately held corporation owned and managed by the president and vice president. The business of the company is the production of high quality, fresh beer for the local and regional markets. The Craft Brewing Company will be located at XX, which is a warehouse less than a five minute walk from the center of XX. A five year lease, renewable for an additional five years at the same rate is being negotiated. The Craft Brewing Company will initially produce three different styles of beer: a dark ale, an amber ale, and a golden ale. These products will be distributed in kegs to licensed retail outlets. The products of the Craft Brewing Company will be wholesaled to premium pubs, taverns and restaurants in the city of XX, throughout XX County, and then to the broader regional market. In addition, the Craft Brewing Company will have its own tap room where retail customers may come to view the operation of the brewery, while purchasing beer by the glass, beer to go, snacks, and retail items such as T-shirts and glassware with our logo printed on them.

The Craft Brewing Company will produce beer with a 14-barrel, stainless-steel brewing plant. Production capacity of our 14-barrel brewing plant with five fermenters is approximately 700 barrels a year (1 barrel equals 31 gallons, which equals two standard 15.5-gallon kegs). The addition of more fermentation tanks at regular intervals will increase capacity to approximately 2,800 barrels annually, which is the estimated limit imposed by the size of the space being leased. The management team intends to produce and sell approximately 670 barrels in the first year and then double production and sales in the second year. Thereafter, the management team will increase production and sales by approximately 500 to 600 barrels annually, until the approximately 2,800-barrel limit imposed by the space we are initially renting has been reached.

Management Responsibility: As president, XX is responsible for the overall implementation of the Plan of Action and the daily operation of the business. The president will oversee the tenant improvements and installation of the brewery. The president will carry out the licensing process, secure financing of operational expenses, acquire and service retail accounts, and direct the daily start-up operations. The president will also be head brewer, and will be responsible for all tasks related to daily beer production.

As vice president and general manager, XX will assist the president in all areas related to the business start-up and the daily operation of the brewery. The vice president/general manager will specifically be responsible for advertising, promotions, purchasing, inventory control, and the management of the tap room and its retail sales.

Marketing and Distribution: The Craft Brewing Company produces beer in kegs for wholesale to the licensed liquor retail market. Kegs will be self distributed by the Craft Brewing Company to its local clients. In the first year, the president will market the company's products and be personally responsible for acquiring local retail accounts and distributing kegs to those accounts. The president is the individual most familiar with the company's products and with the local market for these products. The president is therefore the best qualified person to represent the company to its customers. The marketing strategy will consist of direct person to person sales calls by the president to local premium retail outlets. Craft Brewing Company products will also be advertised in the local printed media.

The Craft Brewing Company will also have a tap room on the site where customers may come to purchase our products at retail prices. This retail outlet will allow us to receive pint price on the sale of beer, which will make an important contribution to our profit margin. Snacks and promotional merchandise such as glassware and T-shirts will also be sold to increase our public exposure and profit margin.

Professional Support: The following personnel will be used as needed. See Attachments for professional references and resumes.

Brewing Consultant:	XX
Business Consultant:	XX
Master Brewer:	XX
Accountant:	XX
Finance:	XX
Attorney:	XX

Estimated Production, Sales, and Income: The following numbers are our projections of production levels, gross sales, and net income for the Craft Brewing Company, during the first three years of operation.

Year	Production	Gross Sales	Net Income
One	671 bbl.	$181,508	$46,121
Two	1,077 bbl.	$256,741	$70,534
Three	1,558 bbl.	$329,387	$88,508

BUSINESS PLAN INTRODUCTION

Microbreweries are a historic means for satisfying the public's demand for a greater variety of fresh quality beer. In the late nineteenth and early twentieth centuries, the United States supported nearly four thousand breweries, the majority being independent local and regional operations producing a vast array of Old World beer styles. Without question, Prohibition nearly destroyed this brewing tradition.

Today America is experiencing a revival of its brewing tradition. Microbreweries are defined by the industry as small breweries which produce less than 15,000 barrels of beer annually and distribute their beer for off-premise consumption. Currently there are more than three hundred microbreweries and pubbreweries operating in the United States and Canada. In 1991 the microbrewery and pubbrewery industry in the United States experienced a 14 percent annual increase in barrels of beer produced, when compared to production for 1990. The Canadian industry experienced 20 percent annual growth for 1991. In spite of the troubled economy, the microbrewery industry has demonstrated remarkable growth. Early industry forecasts for 1992 are equally encouraging.[1]

The current demand for a greater variety of more flavorful beers originated with the import beer market. As the imported beer market grew, beer drinkers had an opportunity to further educate their tastes to the great variety of world beer styles. As a result the microbrewery and pubbrewery industry in the United States has benefited from the public's increased awareness of and demand for more flavorful beers. Imported beers account for more than 4.5 percent of beer sales in the United States, which represents a significant market share. However, while the microbrewery industry demonstrated significant growth in 1991, America's import beer market experienced a 10 percent decline for 1991.[2] This decline is partly due to a rise in the Federal Excise Tax on imported beer which has made domestic microbreweries much more price competitive with imports.

Beer drinkers are clearly demonstrating their demand for a greater variety of full-flavored beers. Unfortunately, beer does not transport well, and most styles of beer begin to deteriorate in quality if they are not consumed within a few weeks of having been brewed. While this is clearly a disadvantage for imported beers, microbreweries are at a clear advantage in being able to deliver the freshest product to the consumer.

Advantages of Microbreweries: One of the advantages of a microbrewery is its ability to supply its product to the consumer when it is at its peak of freshness. Microbreweries are brewing a handcrafted product on a more limited scale where quality is the most important concern. For this reason, using the highest quality traditional ingredients — malted barley, hops, yeast, and water — is justified, rather than the chemicals and cheaper adjuncts such as corn and rice which are used by large scale brewers to cut costs. Fresh quality beer produced locally, without chemicals in processing or for preservation is the key note of the micro-brewing industry.

The microbrewery has the additional advantage of bringing the beer drinking public into immediate contact with the equipment and operation associated with beer production. A well designed microbrewery with a tap room allows the public to witness first-hand the creation of the handcrafted beer they are drinking.

The Market: XX has a growing population which supports a variety of restaurants and pubs. Many of these restaurants and pubs are carrying microbrewed beer on several taps and enjoying significant sales of these products. These currently operating licensed retail outlets are our primary targets as customers. Our microbrewery will be identified with the local community and will appeal to the city resident who, with friends, family members, and business associates, is eager to support a locally produced beer. Having once tasted our fresh ale, these consumers will be sure to ask for our product at their favorite local restaurant or pub.

Specialty beers can be produced for seasonal holidays, community events, and local bars which desire to offer a unique, specially contracted beer to their customers. To increase our market exposure, table tents, beer menus, T-shirts, decorative keg tap handles, and other promotional materials will be utilized at the brewery and distributed to our licensed liquor retail clients.

Since our product will be sold to licensed retail outlets, promotions will be handled at the point-of-sale using these low cost promotional items, which will be provided free of charge to our accounts. Direct advertising to the general public will be on a regular but limited scale in the local printed media. We will earn the confidence of our retail licensees and their beer drinking customers by providing a consistent quality product and supporting that product with point-of-sale promotional items.

Production Process: The Craft Brewing Company will initially produce three styles of traditional British ale. Brewing begins by cracking the highest quality malted barley with a roller mill. This grist is then mixed with hot water in the mash tun, producing mash. A sweet liquid called wort is filtered out of the mash and transferred to the brew kettle. The wort is then brought to a rolling boil and hops are added to contribute bitterness, flavor, and aroma. After boiling, the wort is transferred through a heat exchanger, cooling the liquid down to fermentation temperature. The wort is then pumped into the primary fermenter where yeast is added. After one week of fermentation the fresh ale is transferred to a cold conditioning tank where it is clarified and carbonated for a second week. Now at the height of freshness, the ale is racked to kegs where it is ready to be distributed to the market and served. (See attached designs for the specifications on the major brewing equipment.)

Management Team: Craft Brewing Company is a privately held corporation managed by the president and vice president. All decisions will be made by the management team, officers, and shareholders, in compliance with the Company's articles of incorporation and bylaws.

President: XX is an accomplished homebrewer with seven years of experience. XX has been researching and preparing for this project for more than six years and has a solid understanding of the brewing process and the market for microbrewed beer.

Vice President: XX is likewise an experienced homebrewer who is capable of managing the brewing plant unassisted. The vice president has ten years of experience in the retail sales and restaurant industries, working as a cashier, hostess, bartender, and waitress in many fine establishments.

Consultant: The management team will be assisted by XX, a highly qualified professional brewing consultant. Mr. XX is the managing consultant on several successful brewing projects.

The management team is committed to the success of this plan. All decisions will be made with the best interest of the business and other investors in mind. Whenever necessary, the management team will rely on the assistance of professionals on a contractual basis.

Plan of Action: Having signed the Letter of Intent on the building lease and opened the corporate general account with an initial capital contribution of $75,000, as discussed in the Executive Summary above, the following tasks in order of priority will be completed. First, the management team will pursue the required equity capital by means of this business proposal and a share offering circular form which will be delivered to prospective investors.

Once the share offering has been delivered to prospective investors, the president and his brewery consultant, XX, will complete the final building utility and brewery layout designs. Once these plans have been finalized, the president and brewery consultant will place an order for the capital brewing equipment. The capital equipment for the brewery will be delivered ten to twelve weeks from time of order. The brewery consultant will personally supervise the installation of the brewery once the equipment has been delivered.

While the capital equipment is being fabricated, the president will complete the process of acquiring all permits necessary to begin capital improvements to the space being leased. Once a building occupancy permit has been issued, and while waiting for the main brewing plant to be fabricated and delivered, the management team will carry out the building improvements which have been designated as their responsibility in the lease Letter of Intent. At this time, the management team will also complete the process of filing for liquor and business license from the relevant federal, state, county, and city authorities.

The management team is seeking financing from private investors to contribute toward the costs of the capital equipment, improvements to the building, and the first several months operating capital. See the Use of Proceeds section in the Share Offering Circular for a more detailed discussion of these expenses.

Approximate Expenses — Start-Up (1993):

$ 91,000	Brewery Equipment, Delivered, Installed, and Operational
$ 55,000	Building Improvements
$ 146,000	Total Capital Improvements
$ 10,000	Start-up Professional Fees
$ 19,000	Operating Capital
$ 175,000	Total Capital Investment

PRODUCTS

Initial Products: The Craft Brewing Company will initially produce three flagship beers; a dark ale, an amber ale, and a pale ale. The dark ale, brewed within the general porter style parameters which have proven so popular on the West Coast, will have a distinct roasted-chocolate flavor, nicely balanced with the mild-spicy hop nose characteristic of premium hops. This ale will be fairly dry, medium bodied, and quite dark with ruby-red tints around the edges. Our experience with the many different porters and dark ales being produced throughout the United States, leads us to anticipate that this ale will be very popular with beer drinkers who enjoy traditional, dark British porters, stouts, and brown ales.

Our second flagship product will be an amber ale brewed within the style parameters commonly known as pale ale, which includes amber-colored ales. This amber ale will have a lightly sweet, malty flavor, balanced by the aroma hops. This ale will have a fruity-hop flavor in the finish and the hop nose, which is so characteristic of amber ales. It will be light to medium bodied and amber-red in color. Pale ales are one of the most popular of traditional

British beer styles being produced by microbreweries in the United States. It is a beer which is both satisfying to the experienced ale drinker and yet not too overpowering as to frighten off the neophyte.

Our third flagship product will be a golden ale, a light bodied, only slightly sweet and lightly hopped ale, with a rich golden color. This golden ale is a style of beer which is designed to be light and thirst quenching, with a more moderate alcohol content than our other beers. It will be an excellent accompaniment to an afternoon lunch or the evening meal when the beer drinker chooses to have two or three beers without becoming filled up or intoxicated. This beer is intended to appeal to experienced ale drinkers, as well as novice beer drinkers who have not yet experienced the ale revolution.

Future Products: In addition to these three flagship beers, other styles are being planned as limited, seasonal offerings. For example, barley wine, raspberry stout, brown, special bitter, and India pale ale. All of these are popular specialty styles enjoying steady seasonal demand.

The production of specialty beers will depend on local demand as expressed in customer surveys conducted by the management. They will be produced on a limited rotating basis, depending on the availability of fermenters. The management will actively pursue contract brewing accounts with local licensed retailers who are interested in having a special beer produced solely for sale to their own customers. In addition, our tap room will allow us to offer new products on our own taps to test the public's response to these new products before offering them for wholesale to other retailers.

Although our beer recipes will be designed to meet certain style parameters which have been proven to be popular by other brewers in the industry, our beer recipes will be adjusted so that the final products have their own unique quality. We are not attempting to imitate the products of other brewers. On the contrary, we will produce our own unique ales within style parameters which have a demonstrated track record of success.

Suppliers: One important element of our beers which will help to ensure their popularity will be the use of the highest quality, traditional ingredients. All of our ingredients will be purchased from the most reputable local suppliers. Our malted barley will be supplied by XX. They carry the finest domestic and imported specialty malts which are needed for making traditional British ales. Our hops will be supplied by XX. They carry all of the premier hops produced in the Pacific Northwest, and many of the noble hop varieties of Europe which are essential for producing original versions of traditional ales. Finally, our yeast will be supplied by XX. They specialize in storing and shipping yeast cultures in such a variety that brewers have the opportunity to craft beers to their own particular flavor profile.

As the growth of the industry indicates, there is an increasing variety of handcrafted beers being made available to the American public. The advantage our beers enjoy in this market will stem from using the finest ingredients provided by the most reliable local suppliers. In addition, our beers will have their own unique flavor profile and be the freshest available to our local customers. Finally, our products will benefit from the additional demand which is generated by the customers knowledge that these beers have been produced within the community with local pride.

Bottling and Export: When starting a microbrewery, it is necessary to consider all available options. This is especially true when it comes to the issue of how the product will be packaged for sale. The issue of packaging is largely dependent on the amount of capital available and the nature of the local market. While there are some benefits to bottling a portion of the brewery's capacity for local retail sales, a top-quality bottling line entails a large initial capital investment and a much larger input of labor.

After having carefully researched the local market, we have determined that our best option is to initially concentrate solely on draft sales. We have concluded that a sufficient demand exists to support our business with draft sales alone. Our strategy is based on the belief that the most important task is to first concentrate on developing a sound local base of satisfied retail accounts and loyal draft beer drinkers, before diversifying our product line.

Despite our decision to initially concentrate on local draft sales, we recognize that a bottled product on local grocers' shelves would help to raise our public profile and increase our profit margin. For this reason, the management team of Craft Brewing Company is carefully examining the option of hiring another brewery to produce for us sometime after the second year of operation. Many small scale brewing companies in the United States have enjoyed tremendous success by contracting with a different brewery to produce a bottled product which the contracting company then distributes to its own customers. By contracting a bottled product from another brewery we will be able to service our own draft accounts without reducing our draft capacity. In addition, contracting would allow us to increase both market exposure and profit margins, without the great expense associated with owning and operating a bottling line.

Finally, we would like to raise the issue of exporting a contracted bottled product. We have carefully researched the beer market and developed several important relationships with beer importers and retailers. It is our firm belief that a specially designed product, contracted from a local brewery and then wholesaled by the Craft Brewing Company, would receive shelf space and enjoy steadily growing sales.

THE INDUSTRY

Industry History: Within the brewing industry, the Craft Brewing Company is considered to be a microbrewery and brewpub combination. A microbrewery is any brewery producing less than 15,000 barrels of beer per year. A brewpub is a restaurant or tavern which produces its own beer. Today these small breweries are proliferating rapidly, but they are a relatively new phenomenon which can be considered revolutionary.

The microbrewing revolution began in 1977 with the birth of the New Albion Brewing company in Sonoma, California. The primary characteristics, which distinguished New Albion and other new craft breweries from the established industrial breweries, were their small size, limited financing, and concentration on producing premium, specialty lagers and ales rather than the standard pale lagers. The most significant difference was the fact that most new microbreweries were built from the grass roots by homebrewers with more enthusiasm than formal training.

Today there are nearly three hundred microbreweries and pubbreweries operating in the United States (1993). Most of these enterprises were established in the 1980s, but the industry's growth remains strong. Industry statistics demonstrate that while the major brewing companies are flat-to-declining in sales, the market for premium specialty products is expanding. Tastes are changing, and quality, variety, flavor, and freshness are what the beer drinking public is coming to demand. The brewing renaissance taking place in North America has proven that it is more than a temporary fad. On the contrary, it is becoming increasingly evident that every city, even small communities, have the potential to support at least one local brewery, and larger cities such as Portland and Seattle are already supporting many more.

As the microbrewing industry has grown and prospered, a whole host of associated industries has sprung up to meet the needs of microbrewers. Brewing consultants, equipment fabricators, ingredient suppliers, publicists, distributors, and even educational programs are now catering to the special needs of microbrewers and, as a result, making the business of small-scale craft brewing much easier today than it was just ten years ago. These enterprises are now devoting large sales staffs and significant resources to servicing the microbrewing industry, because they are confident that this is a growth industry for the future.

Institutional Support: As the microbrewing industry has grown and prospered a variety of new professional organizations, trade associations, and educational programs have been established to assist microbrewers and educate the public.

Professional and trade associations include: the Institute for Brewing Studies (a division of the Association of Brewers), Brewers Association of America, and the XX Small Brewers Association.

These professional organizations perform many essential tasks for the microbrewing industry including: publishing industry statistics and information; representing the industry in legislative lobbying efforts; conducting trade shows and conferences; undertaking public relations with the media; and developing programs for brewery insurance, quality control, and continuing education for brewers.

Some important examples of the quality publications provided by these organizations include: *Zymurgy*® (American Homebrewers Association®), **The New Brewer** (Institute for Brewing Studies), the *North American Brewers Resource Directory* (Brewers Publications), the *Brewery Planner: A Guide to Opening Your Own Small Brewery* (Brewers Publications), the *Brewery Operations Series* (Brewers Publications), and the *American Brewer* (Owens Publications). These and other publications are an invaluable resource for starting and successfully operating a microbrewery.

The ever-increasing number of trade conferences and microbrewing festivals which help to improve the quality of our product and educate the beer drinking public about our products includes: the Institute for Brewing Studies' Craft-Brewers Conference, the American Homebrewers Association National Conference, the Great American Beer Festival®, and a rapidly growing number of local and regional beer festivals.

Finally, in any discussion of institutional support we can not neglect the educational programs which recently have been designed specifically to further educate microbrewers. These programs include: the Beer Judge Certification Program; courses on quality control and brewing technology at the Siebel Institute of Technology in Chicago; and a variety of programs on sanitation, microbiology, brewing business management, etc., at the University of California at Davis.

The sources above represent only a portion of the proliferating number of institutional resources available to microbrewers today.

Industry Prospects: Well into the second decade of the microbrewing revolution, a variety of statistical evidence clearly demonstrates that this industry is much more than a temporary fad. We are at this time witnessing a proliferation of microbrewing enterprises, trade associations, institutional support, and beer festivals, organized specifically to celebrate craft brewing. Likewise, the great number of associated industries which view the microbrewing industry as an important market for their products and services is a strong indication that the microbrewing phenomenon has matured into a stable industry.

Industry statistics on annual production levels, malt beverage sales, tax assessments, and contemporary trends in the sales and consumption of various alcoholic beverages, indicate a growing consumer preference for microbrewed beers. In both the United States and Canada, beer is the alcoholic beverage of choice. However, while the production of major domestic brewers and the volume of imported beers has declined recently, the specialty beer market shows no signs of losing momentum. In one interesting recent development, a number of microbreweries have even begun to export their products to Europe and Asia, with Japan being a particularly promising market.[3]

Two potentially negative trends which may affect the industry are neo-Prohibitionism and tax increases. Neo-Prohibitionist legislation which cuts into the profit of brewers or restricts their market (i.e., alcohol warning label requirements and restrictions on the sale and consumption of alcoholic beverages) will always remain a threat in a pluralistic society. However, lately a greater amount of information has become available proving the healthful aspects of moderate drinking. In addition, the microbrewing industry and support institutions such as the Institute for Brewing Studies are working to protect their interests.

Unfortunately, in times of economic instability many governing bodies may look at the success of today's and tomorrow's brewers as a way to increase revenues by raising taxes on beer. One answer to this threat are the lobbying associations which have been organized to protect the interests of small brewers. One important example of these lobbying efforts is the exemption won by small brewers (less than 60,000 barrels production) from the new Federal Excise Tax on beer, imposed in 1991. In our region, the XX Beer and Wine Wholesalers Association is actively lobbying the State government.

Growth in Adversity: Despite the important efforts of these groups, the potential for new taxes will continue to be the greatest threat to the microbrewing industry. Although small brewers have been exempted from the latest Federal Excise Tax increase, this exemption could be lifted, or other state and local taxes could be imposed. It is important for this reason to consider the potential impact of higher taxes on our industry.

Recent statistical analysis of beer sales have reached the conclusion that beer sales are relatively price inelastic and respond more slowly to increases in the price of beer. These studies would seem to indicate that a not unreasonable rise in taxation on beer would only result in a minor drop in beer sales. Although the determination of who bears the cost of a given price increase is complicated, these studies indicate that with a product as price inelastic as beer, the increase will probably be paid by the retail customer.[4]

One additional set of conclusions from these studies concerns price increases and product substitution. The evidence indicates that there is probably little substitutability, among consumers between beer, wine, and distilled spirits. This means that (all other factors remaining constant) an increase in the price of one category, should not result in the substitution of another category of alcoholic beverage. Consequently, we may conclude that the growth in sales of specialty beers, which are priced as a premium product, is the result of changing consumer tastes, not changes in the price structure of beer.[5]

Studies of income elasticity also demonstrate that beer sales are relatively inelastic with respect to the consumer's income. Recent industry reviews, which consider the impact of the recession and the business cycle on beer sales, have reached the conclusion that the business cycle has little discernible influence on the microbrewing industry. Finally, industry statistics clearly show that throughout the last recession, the microbrewing industry continued to grow at an impressive rate.[6]

Clearly there are threats to our industry, but statistics demonstrate that consumer tastes and preferences are changing. In such a market the best strategy is to provide the consumer with the highest quality product. Beer drinkers are also voters who will go to great lengths to reject unreasonable attacks on their favorite beverage.

THE MARKET AND COMPETITION

Potential Customers: The most important customers of the Craft Brewing Company are the owners and managers of local licensed liquor retail outlets. These local outlets consist of pubs, taverns, and restaurants in the cities of XX, XX, and XX. However, since it is our marketing strategy to concentrate on satisfying the demand of a core group of customers in the first year, a select number of retail outlets in these cities will receive priority.

All of the establishments listed above are located in our core local market. Most of these establishments have at least four taps allocated to specialty and microbrewed beers, several have more than six microbeer taps.

The president has spoken with the owners of all of these establishments, and they have all expressed strong interest in featuring a quality local product once it is available.

An important part of our marketing strategy is to concentrate on providing our customers with the best possible, most responsive service they have ever received when purchasing beer. Consequently, it will be necessary to take on new accounts carefully, so as to have enough beer in stock to meet the demand of our core accounts. One potential mistake would be to try to provide beer for more customers than our initial capacity allows. For this reason we will prioritize our accounts according to certain criteria which we would like to see our retail customers meet. The fact is that we do not want to sell our product to simply any retailer that expresses an interest. We want our products in the right places, along side of other quality beers, and receiving the proper attention necessary for serving microbrewed beer at its peak of quality. For this reason we will initially concentrate our sales efforts on establishments which are already serving microbrewed beers, before offering our products to bars which are not yet carrying microbrewed beers.

There are additional licensed retail outlets in XX, which would be satisfactory retailers of our products. The fact is that there has been a very positive response from licensed retailers in our local market. Our only problem will be to decide which outlets may carry our products in the early months when production is still limited, and which will have to wait. We will make this decision carefully so as to develop a core group of satisfied, loyal clients, while planning for a much broader distribution in the future. Eventually we intend to introduce our products in local restaurants and taverns which have not yet begun to offer their customers microbrewed beer.

Competition: Our competitors in the local market are primarily those microbreweries in XX and XX who distribute their products to this region, in addition to the super-premium draft imports being offered. The local breweries include: XX

All of these breweries distribute their products to licensed retail outlets in our local market, through licensed liquor distributors. These local distributors include: XX

First let us begin this evaluation of our competition with a brief discussion of the super-premium imported draft beers which we consider to be our competitors because many of them are similar in style and price to domestic microbrewed beers. Although these beers are by and large excellent products, the fact remains that they find it difficult to compete with domestic microbrewed beers. The imports do have strong name recognition in many cases, but they can not compete in the areas of freshness, direct and personal service to local retailers, or local brand loyalty. Furthermore, shipping costs and advertising for these products usually place them several dollars above microbrewed beers in price, and these beers are subject to the new, higher Federal Excise Tax rate. Statistics demonstrate that while microbrewed beers are enjoying steady annual growth in sales, the market share of super-premium imports has recently begun to decline.[7]

By and large, the domestic microbreweries listed above all consistently produce quality products. For this reason, it is the responsibility of the individual brewing company to make some effort to help consumers distinguish their beers from those of their competitors. Some brewing companies rely on the excellent quality of their products and word of mouth as their strongest marketing point. This strategy is often used by new brewing companies which in the early years have less capital available for advertising. Other pioneer microbreweries benefit from greater brand recognition, due to their longer operating history and easily recognizable logos.

Another way to win loyal consumer support is to develop a distinctive flavor profile, such as a characteristically assertive hop flavor. In contrast to these methods, some brewers spend thousands of dollars on a strong advertising campaign through the local and national media to increase their market share. Others with smaller advertising budgets may choose to rely on less expensive, but often equally effective, point-of-sale promotional materials.

Finally, the most fundamental marketing strategy which may be employed is through pricing. Some brewers choose to underprice their competition to gain market share. Others, choose to price their products above the market average, in order to capture an image as the brewer with the most premium products. Still others may price their products near the industry average. This strategy helps them to avoid being seen as a discount brewer, while at the same time avoids driving off potential customers who refuse to buy beer which is priced significantly above that of the competition.

All of the brewers competing in our market rely on some mix of the above marketing strategies to acquire a base of loyal local support and then increase their market share. The Craft Brewing Company will likewise pursue a marketing strategy appropriate to its production goals, financial means, and the particular characteristics of our local market. Our marketing strategy will be carefully discussed in the next section of this business plan. However, it should be emphasized here that the demand for microbrewed products is growing and as the statistics demonstrate, the microbrewing industry's share of the beer market is also growing.[8]

Most microbrewers are in agreement that competition is healthy. The great variety of microbrewed products available to consumers has only served to further educate the beer drinking public to the quality of our products, creating ever greater demand. Although we are in competition with other microbrewers, our share of the market will not come so much at their expense, as it will at the expense of imported beers and domestic industrial brewers whose customers are gradually shifting to fresher and more flavorful microbrewed products.

Market Size and Trends: The size of our local microbrewed and specialty ale market in XX is sufficiently large to provide us with a market share which will ensure the initial success of the Craft Brewing Company Likewise, this market has been steadily growing at a rate which is more than adequate to achieve our projected growth in sales. Our market research and conclusions are based on statistical analyses of beer sales volumes by individual breweries, which are reported to the State Liquor Control Board each month. These sales reports have also been analyzed and reprinted in a more comparative form published monthly by the State Wholesalers Association. In addition to these reports, we have carefully questioned brewers, local licensed retailers, and local licensed beer distributors to determine the average monthly level of microbrewed beer sales and the growth in sales which have occurred over the last several years.

Using the above sources, we have determined that for 1992, average sales of microbrewed beers in our local market, was approximately XX kegs each month. In addition, approximately another XX kegs of imported ales and other specialty beers were sold in this market each month. We consider specialty imported beers such as Guinness Stout, Bass Ale, Heineken, etc., to be our competitors because these are also considered to be super-premium, specialty products which are priced in a similar range as microbrewed beers. It is these imports, as well as other microbrewed beers, which we will be competing with for tap-handle space at the businesses of local licensed retailers. Consequently, a careful analysis of our local market leads us to the conservative estimate that the size of the local market for our products in 1992 was approximately XX kegs of specialty beers each month, on average. At the average super-premium keg price of $XX, the total dollar-unit market for our products in 1992 was approximately $XX each month on average, or $XX for the year.

The same sources, which we relied on to determine the size of our local market, have also helped us to determine that for the last several years this market has been growing by approximately 30 percent annually. When questioned on their expectations for future growth, local beer distributors expressed the opinion that they anticipate that our local market will continue to grow at or near the present level of 30 percent annually. If we trust the experts who are most familiar with our market, we can anticipate that with 30 percent growth in 1993, sales of beers in our market should reach approximately XX kegs of specialty beers each month on average. Given the demographic and economic growth trends of our local region, we believe this estimate to be on the conservative side.

Regional Demographic Growth: In a national study of population changes, XX County was projected to be the fifth fastest growing county in the United States between now and the end of the century. In XX County, employment has increased XX percent since 1980, which compares favorably with the State's employment growth rate of XX percent during the same period. During the recession years of 1990, 1991, and 1992, although the unemployment rate in XX County rose, it remained below the state and national averages. XX County may not be impervious to recession, but the large number of government officials who are employed and live in this area make our local market less vulnerable to business fluctuations.

One consequence of having government as the largest employer in our local market is reflected in the volume of retail sales. When we examine retail sales levels, it becomes apparent that XX County has developed into a regional consumer market. While retail sales have increased by XX percent since 1970, the population has increased by XX percent. These two figures indicate that a large nonresident population is making purchases in XX County. XX County's retail sales are clearly being augmented by the large number of persons who daily visit the State's center of government. Regardless of who these persons may be, many of them stop to do a little shopping, have some lunch, and even drink a beer, while they are in XX. Of the XX billion in retail sales that occurred in XX County in 1991, XX percent occurred in XX, and XX percent occurred in the city of XX.[12]

We are still a relatively small urban area, but it is our smallness and the quality of our environment and living which continue to attract new residents. Retail sales can be expected to grow along with XX County's population. More and more restaurants and pubs will be opened to serve the needs of our growing community. Consequently, local restaurant and bar sales of specialty beers can also be expected to grow with the State, its government, and the city of Olympia.

Regional Market Growth: XX and XX States are considered to be our broader regional market, which is an important sales region once our local market demand has been satisfied. The following are sales reports posted with the Liquor Control Board and XX Beer and Wine Wholesalers Association for 1992 that provide the following annual percentage growth rates in beer sales.

Brewery % Change During a One-Year Period
(List primary craft/microbrew competitors in your market.)

This annual growth in sales figures is a good indication of the overall health of the industry that we propose to enter and compete in. Clearly, the XX microbeer market and our local market have sufficient growth potential to accommodate many new microbreweries.

Estimated Local Market Share and Sales: Sales, distribution, and tax records can help us to determine the relative market share and popularity of our competitors and their products. Our research, counting taps and questioning licensed retailers as to their levels of sales, also gives us a good picture of which microbreweries have the largest shares of our local market. For example, the microbreweries with the most popular products and largest market shares in our local market are the XX, XX, and XX.

XX is perhaps the most successful craft brewer in our local market, selling approximately

XX kegs a month on average. As a percentage of the approximately XX kegs of super-premium, specialty beers sold each month in this market in 1992, XX currently controls a little more than XX percent of the local market we intend to compete in. The other market leaders each control from XX percent to XX percent of the specialty beer market.

The management team of the Craft Brewing Company is determined to produce approximately XX kegs (XX barrels), during the first twelve months of production. Of these XX kegs, approximately XX kegs of beer will be marketed and sold in our local market in this first year of production. These approximately XX kegs will be sold in our local market through the following three marketing channels:

1. Wholesale distribution to local licensed retailers: $XX per keg
2. Retail keg sales to the public from our warehouse: $XX per keg
3. Retail pint sales to the public in our tap room: $XX per pint

The following is the estimated breakdown of sales in our local market through these three channels in the first year of production:

1. Wholesale distribution to local licensed retailers: XX kegs
2. Retail keg sales to the public from our facility: XX kegs
3. Retail pint sales to the public in our tap room: XX kegs

If we include the XX kegs being sold through our own tap room, this means we will be marketing approximately XX kegs or approximately XX kegs each month on average during the first year. If we assume a total local market of approximately XX kegs each month on average for 1993 through 1994, then the Craft Brewing Company intends to capture from 12 to 14 percent of the local market in 1993 through 1994.

Clearly we intend to be a very competitive market-share leader in our local market.

Therefore, let us examine what we believe to be the important advantages which we have over our competitors in the local market which will help us to win a 12 to 14 percent market share.

First, the Craft Brewing Company intends to price its products slightly below the level of our strongest competitors. Specialty draft imports and other microbreweries must absorb the additional costs associated with delivering their products to the XX area, often over great distances. The Craft Brewing Company, on the other hand, will handle its own distribution and save on delivery and storage costs in its local market. In addition, it is simply part of our strategy to always price our products slightly below those of other market leaders, since this is what our local licensed retailers have told us would be of particular importance when they are making decisions on trying a new beer on their taps.

Second, the Craft Brewing Company will be a local entity in which the community can take special pride. Our brewery and tap room will create jobs and enhance the atmosphere of the downtown area. It is common sense to assume that given everything is nearly equal in the areas of price, style, and quality, people will choose to patronize local producers rooted in their community.

Third, the Craft Brewing Company will be able to provide the very freshest beers to our local market. Other microbreweries must rely on beer distributors to deliver their products to the XX market, and these beers may spend some time sitting in local warehouses before being distributed to licensed retailers. Our products, on the other hand, will be distributed directly from our own cold room in our own delivery van. Consequently, kegs of our ales will never reach the market beyond their peak level of maturity, nor before they are perfectly matured either.

Fourth, we are committed to making the best beers possible, using the highest quality ingredients available. We are serious when we make this commitment. We would not be entering this market if we were not certain that we could make excellent ales which will be highly competitive. Brewing beer is what we do and we believe that a commitment to quality will go a long way toward assuring our long term success. Consistently high quality beer can sell itself without much promotion, but a poor quality beer will not succeed for long, no matter how actively it is promoted.

Fifth, the Craft Brewing Company will be able to serve its products on its own taps in a tap room which will be named XX. Our own retail outlet will permit us to try new products before offering them for distribution to the wholesale market. In addition, a tap room will allow us to receive the full retail pint price on a significant percentage of our barrel production. Every keg sold at retail pint price rather than wholesale keg price, will significantly increase our profit margin, while at the same time helping us to reach our 12 to 14 percent market-share target. XX will be a casual drinking room separated from the brewery by a large glass window which will allow customers to view the activities on the production floor while enjoying their favorite beverage. XX will also be the display and sales center for retail promotional items which will bear our corporate and product logos. Although the cash profit on these items is only 50 percent, they represent a much greater value as free advertising by increasing our exposure in the community.

By bringing the management team into direct contact with the customers in our local community, our own retail outlet will help us to increase our market share as well as compete more effectively with outside microbrewers. Two-way communication between the management team and our customers will provide us with invaluable feedback on our products. Furthermore, as beer drinkers make themselves comfortable at our establishment, the Craft Brewing Company's image as a local community enterprise will be enhanced.

Finally, and most importantly, we believe that our commitment to service will assure that we earn a leading share of our local market and increase that share into the future. No other brewer has the potential to provide the level of prompt service to the licensed retailers in our local market that the Craft Brewing Company has. We have already begun to develop close relationships with the licensed retailers in our local market. We know them by name, we have visited them and purchased beers in their establishments, we have questioned them as to their priorities when deciding which beers to put on their taps, and we have carefully observed the preferences of their customers. We at the Craft Brewing Company are committed to the relationships we have begun to develop with our future customers and their customers. By using consumer surveys, delivering our own beer, serving our beer in their establishments, working closely with their employees, and carefully listening to licensed retailers and beer drinkers in XX, we are sure to earn a leading share in our local market and keep it.

As the local market and demand for draft specialty beers continues to grow, the Craft Brewing Company will expand its production to satisfy that demand and increase our market share. The following is a graphic representation of our market-share projections based on the previously stated assumptions concerning our industry's prospects for growth, our estimated monthly sales, and the marketing strategy which we will discuss in the next section.

ASSUMPTIONS

Total local market for microbrewed and specialty draft beer in 1992 equaled XX kegs a month per XX kegs a year.

Annual growth rate in local market of 30 percent for next three years.

Total local market for specialty draft beer from summer 1993 through summer 1994 equals XX kegs a month per XX kegs a year.

Craft Brewing Company's market share of XX to XX percent.

Average wholesale keg price of $XX a unit.

Average retail keg price of $XX a unit.

Average retail pint price of $XX a unit, at 120 pints per keg.

LOCAL MARKET-SHARE PROJECTIONS

Production Year	(1) 93/94	(2) 94/95	(3) 95/96
Estimated Total Annual Sales in Local Market (Kegs)	XX	XX	XX

Craft Brewing Company

	(1) 93/94	(2) 94/95	(3) 95/96
Estimated Share of and Annual Sales in Local Market	13.5%	13.5%	12%
(Kegs)	XX	XX	XX

The following is the dollar value breakdown in local beer sales through our three marketing channels for the first three years:

LOCAL SALES PROJECTIONS BY DOLLAR VALUE

Production Year	(1) 93/94	(2) 94/95	(3) 95/96
Local Sales Wholesale Kegs	756	926	1,108
Dollars ($85)	$64,260	$78,710	$94,180
Local Sales Retail Kegs	40	140	160
Dollars ($110)	$4,400	$15,400	$17,600
Local Sales Retail Kegs by the Pint	294	336	336
Dollars ($300 per keg)	$88,200	$100,800	$100,800

Estimated Regional Sales: Thus far, this discussion of market share has only concerned the local market for which the management team will be personally responsible for promotions, sales, distribution, and service. In the fifth month of operation, the demand from our local market will no longer be sufficient to absorb all of the barrels being produced by the Craft Brewing Company. At that point, we will begin to market our products through a distributor to the broader regional market. For this purpose we will rely on XX to distribute our beer in the XX market. In the seventh, eighth, and twelfth months of operation we will purchase additional fermentation tanks and kegs in order to increase our production capacity to approximately 1,200 barrels a year. Further equipment purchases will be made in the second and third years of operation in order to increase our production capacity to approximately 1,800 barrels a year as the demand for our products in the local and regional markets continues to expand. All barrels produced above the level which our local market can absorb will be sold in the regional market through licensed wholesale distributors at an average price of $XX a keg.

The following chart indicates the estimated number of kegs which will be sold in the regional market after satisfying the local demand.

REGIONAL SALES PROJECTIONS

Production Year	(1) 93/94	(2) 94/95	(3) 95/96
Estimated Total Regional Sales Kegs	252	752	1,512
Dollars ($68)	$17,136	$51,136	$102,816

Total Sales Projections: The following chart indicates the estimated combined total of local and regional sales for the first three years of operation.

TOTAL SALES PROJECTIONS

Production Year	(1) 93/94	(2) 94/95	(3) 95/96
Local Sales Wholesale Kegs	756	926	1,108
Dollars ($85)	$64,260	$78,710	$94,180
Local Sales Retail Kegs	40	140	160
Dollars ($110)	$4,400	$15,400	$17,600
Local Sales Retail Kegs by the Pint	294	336	336
Dollars ($300 per keg)	$88,200	$100,800	$100,800
Regional Sales Wholesale Kegs	252	752	1,512
Dollars ($68)	$17,136	$51,136	$102,816
Total Sales Kegs	1,342	2,154	3,116
Gross Beer Revenue	$173,996	$246,046	$315,396

These figures are based on the previously stated assumptions and represent our projections of sales targets to be achieved by the management team of Craft Brewing Company In the fourth and fifth years we will continue to expand production by the amount of 500 to 600 barrels a year. By the fifth year of operation (1998 to 1999) the Craft Brewing Company will be producing at near the 2,800-barrels-a-year capacity which the space in our brewing facility can accommodate.

MARKETING PLAN

The Fundamentals: It is the intention of the management team to establish the long term profitability and success of the Craft Brewing Company by carefully concentrating on building a core group of satisfied local customers. This core group consists of the licensed liquor retailers operating pubs, taverns, and restaurants in the cities of XX, XX, and XX. While it is these licensed retailers who are our direct customers, we recognize that ultimately our customers are the beer drinkers within our local market who patronize the establishments of our licensed retail customers and our own tap room. Consequently, the key to our marketing strategy is to make the highest possible quality beers which will satisfy the tastes and demands of beer drinkers in our market, while providing our licensed retail customers with the best service possible.

Our effort to make the best beer possible will be achieved by the following means. First, all beer profiles and recipes have been selected after careful market research to determine exactly what is popular among beer and ale drinkers in our market. The most important part of our research consisted of many long conversations with local licensed retailers, who were eager to tell us what their customers preferred when ordering a microbrewed beer and what they were looking for when buying beer to stock their bar taps. In addition, interviews with local beer distributors have been particularly helpful in pointing out which beers sell well in our local market, why they sell well, and what styles will compete well in this market. Having made the decision as to what flavor profiles we would like to reproduce in our beers, the president as head brewer will rely on his brewing consultant, XX, to determine the exact balance of ingredients and specific brewing techniques necessary to achieve those flavor profiles.

Our three initial products have been designed specifically to satisfy local tastes and demands, as they have been identified by our market research. However, we believe that ale drinkers in our local market have similar preferences to ale drinkers throughout the XX beer market, and we expect our products to be competitive throughout that broader market. As a final note regarding the design of our recipes, we intend to carefully monitor the responses of beer drinkers to our products when they first reach the local market and long after. Consumer feedback will be the means be which we gauge the reactions of beer drinkers to our products, so that we may make any necessary adjustments.

Another key aspect of our marketing strategy, which is intended to ensure we make the best beer possible and then sell that beer, is our determination to use the finest brewing ingredients available. Only premium ingredients will be used, without exception. We have made certain that our suppliers all have excellent reputations among the microbrewing community in our region. Nevertheless, as our operations progress, XX as head brewer, and XX as general manager, will continue to demand the highest quality from our suppliers and will be prepared to find new sources of brewing materials whenever our current suppliers fail to meet the exacting standards of the Craft Brewing Company.

Brewing the best beer possible is our motto, and we will not cut corners to save a few dollars at the expense of beer quality. We will use the finest ingredients, top quality brewing equipment, and well-proven brewing methods to establish our market share. Only a quality product will create consumer loyalty in our core local market and ensure regular growth in sales as that market expands.

Distribution: In the first year of operation, it is our strategy to concentrate on winning the loyalty of licensed retailers in our local market. In this effort the president as head brewer, will have primary responsibility for local sales and for distributing beer from our cold room by delivery van when our customers place an order. We believe that only through close personal contact with our local customers can lines of communication and a long term business relationship be established. Once this relationship has been firmly established, a properly trained employee of the company will assist in making daily deliveries so that the president can concentrate on acquiring new accounts and increasing sales in the local market.

In the fifth month of operation, while the president maintains the accounts in our local market, the Craft Brewing Company will seek the help of a professional beer distributor to reach out beyond the local XX market. Of the three major liquor distribution companies operating in our region, XX carries XX percent of the microbrewed beers being distributed to licensed retailers in the city of XX. In XX County, XX is represented by import and microbreweries manager, XX. Mr. XX and the company he represents are spoken of highly by local licensed retailers and by the local brewers whose products they distribute. In a meeting with Mr. XX, the president and XX reached a verbal understanding that XX would represent and distribute Craft Brewing Company products at selected retail outlets in XX County and the city of XX. XX is clearly the distributor of choice in our region and will be relied on to distribute our products outside of the city of XX when capacity is being expanded in the second year.

Once full capacity with our five initial fermenters has been achieved, additional fermenters will be added to increase capacity. At this time, with increased capacity, we will more intensively promote sales of specialty and contract beers in our local market while arranging for XX to begin to distribute our flagship products to the XX, XX, market.

Once we are satisfied that we have achieved a competitive market share in XX and that our accounts in that market are being serviced properly by XX, we will then consider a further stage of expansion. While adding additional fermenters and kegs to our production line, we will begin to offer our products to the broader regional market, including the XX area. At this stage we will carefully consider which distributor we want to represent us and which accounts we would like to see our products in.

On-Premise Retail Sales: The tap room is another important distribution and sales outlet for our products. Our tap room has been designed to accommodate a maximum occupancy of fifty persons. The space will contain a serving bar, a display cabinet for retail promotional items, and seating for approximately thirty to forty persons, with some additional standing room available. The XX is designed to be an extension of the brewery where patrons can witness the brewing operation first hand and talk to the brewery staff, while enjoying some of our quality ales.

Our tap room is intended to enhance the experience of drinking a quality ale, when all of one's senses are brought into play. There

will be no smoking in the XX because tobacco smoke would interfere with the beer drinkers ability to fully appreciate the flavor and aroma of the beers being served. Furthermore, we believe that a no smoking environment will be greatly appreciated since there are no other nonsmoking drinking establishments in town. The dimensions of our tap room are not large, so we have chosen to light the space well and to paint the walls in light colors in order to avoid the impression of being closed in, and so that customers may appreciate the clarity and rich colors of our products. Decorations will be limited to a few plants, one large fish tank behind the serving bar, wall displays of our corporate and product logos, and a few tasteful posters with aquatic themes. A variety of comfortable chairs and tables will be provided for casual seating. In addition, game boards will be available for those who wish to play a little chess, backgammon, etc., while they visit with friends. A small sound system will provide music whenever appropriate.

In our tap room customers will be able to make a variety of retail purchases. Initially we will have a small selection of T-shirts for sale. But as cash flow permits, we will include other promotional items to increase our merchandise sales. A small selection of snacks, such as nuts, chips, and locally baked pretzels, will also be available to our customers. In regard to beer sales, customers will be able to purchase beer in a variety of volumes. Besides pints and 10-ounce schooners, a sampler of beer which includes a small glass of each of our products will be offered for sale. In addition, customers will also be able to have the take-out vessel of their choice filled for off-premise consumption. Finally, customers in the XX may also purchase a keg of beer at retail price from our cooler, for off-premise consumption.

Pricing: As mentioned previously, our pricing strategy is designed to make our beers competitive and to achieve a profit, while at the same time positioning our products amongst the best beers being produced by our competitors. A keg price of approximately $XX is the median price now being asked by competitors in our local market. Consequently, we intend to ask $XX for our kegs, in order to make our products just slightly less expensive than those of our competitors. When questioned as to their views on pricing, local licensed retailers indicated that this price for a quality product would be one incentive for carrying Craft Brewing Company products.

A further aspect of our pricing strategy is our determination to maintain stable prices over a substantial period of time. Although we can not be certain that significant changes to our cost structure will not occur, it is our plan to maintain prices at the $XX a keg level for at least two years. In this way we will provide our customers with a degree of predictability when purchasing our products. Changes in price will only take place when our own costs rise appreciably and thereby threaten the minimum profit margin we require to meet our operating costs and achieve our projected growth targets. Price changes will also be considered whenever our products fall significantly out of alignment with the median price being asked by our major competitors.

Our discussions with local licensed retailers and with other brewers have also made us aware that when a new brewery is starting up, it is necessary to offer the kegs from the first production runs at a price which is just below the standard price for those products. The first several production runs of any new brewery can be expected to produce excellent beers, but not necessarily the exact style of beer which is being aimed at. It may take two or three adjustments to the start-up recipe before the desired flavor profile is achieved. It may also take several production runs before consistency of flavor for a particular recipe is achieved.

Local retailers have told us that they would be willing to try these early beers, understanding that the recipe may still need some adjustment before we are all satisfied

with the finished product. However, they have also expressed the opinion that these early beers should be offered at a discount, below the level that they will be priced at when the desired flavor profile is achieved. This pricing practice is typical of start-up breweries in our market, and we can not ignore the expressed views of our customers. Consequently, our first kegs to be produced in the recipe adjustment phase will be offered to our customers at a price of $XX a keg, which is near the bottom of the price range which our products will compete in. In the effort to achieve the desired flavor profiles with the smallest number of test production runs necessary, the president will be assisted by brewing consultant, XX, and former head brewer of the XX Brewery, XX. Between these three experienced brewers, it is expected that it will require two test runs for each recipe, before the desired flavor profile is achieved with the third production run. At that time we will be justified in pricing our kegs at their full market rate of $XX.

The following is the projected price breakdown of the wholesale and retail items to be sold by the Craft Brewing Company.

ITEM	PRICE
Beer:	
Wholesale Kegs (1/2 bbl.) — Self Distributed	$85.00
Wholesale Kegs (1/4 bbl.) — Self Distributed	$50.00
Wholesale Kegs (1/2 bbl.) — Distributor	$68.00
Wholesale Kegs (1/4 bbl.) — Distributor	$38.00
Retail Kegs (1/2 bbl.) —	$110.00
Retail Kegs (1/4 bbl.) —	$60.00
Pint	$2.50
Schooner	$1.50
Sampler	$2.50

Pint and schooner glasses will be of the standard size prevailing in our industry. The "Sampler" will consist of several small glasses, each containing one of the various products available on our taps.

Promotional Merchandise and Snacks: Promotional merchandise, such as T-shirts, glassware, lapel pins, etc., and snacks, such as fresh baked goods, nuts, chips, etc., will be priced at twice our cost in order to realize a consistent and reasonable profit.

Advertising and Promotions: As general manager, XX is responsible for point-of-sale promotions and advertising. Initially, point-of-sale promotions will consist of table tents, coasters, and tap handles, provided free of charge to our customers. When cash flow permits, other items such as neon signs, bar towels, and mirrors, all displaying our logo will be given to local retailers who have demonstrated a strong sales record with our products. All promotional items are considered to be an advertising tool since they will display the corporate logo and logos of individual products.

The vice president's experience working in the restaurant and bar industry has taught her that the owners of these establishments and their service employees are especially grateful when promotional materials are maintained by the company distributing them. Consequently, we will take full responsibility for the display of our point-of-sale promotional items, placing them on tables, and replacing the supply at regular intervals.

Our research of the food and beverage service industry has also led us to conclude that only a knowledgeable bar and wait staff can properly represent our products to the consumer. Consequently, both the president and vice president will provide brief, yet informative, introductions to our products for the wait staff of our licensed retail customers. These product introductions are intended to familiarize these important representatives of our products with the brewing methods used by Craft Brewing Company. In addition, our licensed retail customers and their wait staffs will be invited to visit the brewery and witness first hand the production of the beer they will later be selling. These brewery tours are intended to help develop a special relationship between the Craft Brewing Company and those who serve our products to beer drinkers in our core market.

The vice president is also responsible for carrying out all direct advertising of Craft Brewing Company products, to the consumers in our local market. Advertising will be conducted through the local printed media. Throughout the year we will run weekly, Friday and Saturday ads in XX newspaper, the paper with the largest circulation in our local market. When XX College is in session, we will also run weekly adds in the college's XX Journal. We believe that this advertising strategy will provide the greatest exposure for our products, in the most cost effective manner. However, we will regularly survey our customers to determine whether or not they learned of our products through these printed ads. Depending on the results of these surveys, certain changes in our advertising strategy may be considered.

In regard to surveying our customers and the general beer drinking public, the following method will be employed. The president and vice president will design a survey sheet to determine the public's response to our products and our advertising campaign. These survey sheets will be distributed and collected by president and vice president in the establishments of our licensed retail customers. In addition, both president and vice president will conduct regular visits to these establishments to maintain contact with our licensed retail customers, their employees, and their customers. These fact-finding visits will be most frequent in the first year of operation, particularly in the first months when product evaluation and recipe adjustments will take place. It is our determination to never lose touch with the needs of our customers and the tastes of the beer drinking public.

Finally, in regard to the issue of public relations, we at the Craft Brewing Company believe that an ounce of prevention is worth a pound of cure. What this means in a practical sense, is that the vice president will actively pursue a strategy of meeting with local groups which are concerned about issues related to excessive drinking. It is our intention to develop an open dialogue and positive relationship with local citizen groups which advocate responsible drinking. Likewise, we will take the initiative to foster a cooperative relationship with local law-enforcement agencies, to show them that we are as concerned about alcohol misuse as they are. At the Craft Brewing Company we advocate the enjoyment of quality beer in moderation, not the consumption of alcohol in large quantities. In order to avoid any potentially harmful publicity in the future, which may stem from the misuse of our products, we will make certain that the relevant interest groups understand that we take the issue of alcohol misuse as seriously as they do.

COMPANY STRUCTURE

Management Team: The following is a list of the key management roles and the individuals who will be responsible for them.

President. XX has overall responsibility for the start-up and daily operation of the Craft Brewing Company. In the start-up phase, the president will choose and supervise all utility subcontractors; the president will approve, supervise, and assist in all construction; the president will approve the design and purchase of all brewing equipment; and the president will supervise and assist the installation of all brewing equipment.

Head brewer. In the daily operations phase of the project, XX will be responsible for all tasks related to the production of beer. The president will supervise the design of all product recipes and any necessary adjustments to those recipes. The head brewer will perform the regular brewing routine and all tasks associated with preparing Craft Brewing Company products for the market.

Sales and distribution manager. As previously indicated, the president will be responsible for acquiring and servicing accounts in our local market. Likewise, the president will be responsible for distributing full kegs and picking up empty kegs from clients. The president will be assisted in sales calls by the vice president and in distribution by corporate employees.

Vice president. XX will act as vice president which involves providing assistance to the president at every level of the brewery start-up and daily operations. Should the president be temporarily unable to perform his roles as president and head brewer, the vice president will be sufficiently familiar with all aspects of the business that the vice president will be able to train and supervise any employees needed to assist her in the full operation of the business.

General manager. XX will be responsible for all tasks associated with purchasing, inventory control, accounts receivable, accounts payable, record keeping, and the preparation of all production and sales reports required by the relevant licensing agencies. In these tasks, the general manager will be assisted by the president who will provide information on sales, beer inventory, and the status of raw materials' stocks. In addition, XX of XX will review our books regularly in preparation for the quarterly tax filing which is required. As general manager, XX will also be responsible for managing the operations of our retail outlet, XX. The general manager will be responsible for maintaining the retail inventory and tracking sales. The general manager will also be responsible for overseeing the employee hired to run the bar. When time permits, the general manager and president will take over at the bar, and the employee can be assigned to other tasks, such as brew-house sanitation and deliveries.

XX's final area of responsibility as general manager is that of promotions, advertising, and public relations for Craft Brewing Company. The general manager will supervise the design and creation of all corporate and product logos. The general manager will manage the advertising account and evaluate the influence of our advertising strategy on sales.

The general manager will act as public relations officer to the community in order to enhance our image as a community entity concerned with the welfare of our community. The general manger will also assist the president in working with our customers to promote sales and maintain open lines of communication.

The president and vice president believe it is important to be personally involved with every facet of the company's operation. No task will be assigned to an employee before we have repeatedly performed that task ourselves and can then instruct and oversee the employee properly. This same philosophy extends to the management of our corporate accounting, which we intend to be directly involved in.

The president and vice president feel confident that with the assistance of the employees discussed below, they can perform the tasks outlined above. They have a long-standing relation of eleven years and a well demonstrated record of working together to solve problems. In addition, the management team will be assisted in many areas by the specially contracted professionals discussed below. For further information on the credentials and experience of the management team, see their attached resumes.

Management Compensation: For his responsibilities as head brewer, XX will draw an initial monthly salary of $XX. For her responsibilities as general manager, XX will draw an initial monthly salary of $XX. These salaries are the minimum income which XX and XX require to pay for their living expenses. At this time the management team is receiving no compensation or payments from the company. Wage payments will begin at the end of the first month of production and sales of 28 barrels or more, which is projected to be July 1993. All future wage increases or bonuses will be granted to the president and general manager/vice president as a reward for significant production and sales increases, but only after due consideration by the Board of Directors.

Board of Directors: The Craft Brewing Company has been established by its founders and management team, XX and XX, as a corporation under the laws of XX State. The Board of Directors meets monthly to conduct any such business as may come before it. The activities and affairs of the corporation are managed by the Board of Directors. The Board of Directors has delegated responsibility for management of the day to day operation of the business to the management team, XX and XX. Members of the Board of Directors receive no compensation for their services and all directors hold office until the next annual meeting of the shareholders or until their successors have been elected and qualified. Executive officers are appointed by the Board of Directors and serve at the pleasure of the Board of Directors.

The management team has decided to provide themselves with the most reliable professional support and counseling available, in order to acquire the breadth of experience which is necessary to ensure the success of the Craft Brewing Company. Toward this end, the following individual has accepted our invitation to join the Board of Directors so that she can lend her experience to and question the decisions of the management team.

XX has accepted the management team's invitation to join the Board of Directors as a financial advisor, director, and executive secretary. Among her many responsibilities at this position, XX, has been involved in working with small businesses in the areas of finance and the preparation of commercial loan packages. XX is also currently a board member of the XX, a nonprofit corporation of XX State. XX is a community development loan fund, which pools investment dollars from individuals and organizations in order to provide loans for small businesses and nonprofit organizations that benefit the region.

XX's primary responsibilities involve providing the management team with financial advice and recommendations during Board meetings. In addition, XX will perform the role of executive secretary, preparing the company's annual reports and maintaining regular communications with shareholders. XX will not receive a salary for her efforts, but the Board of Directors may vote her a bonus for exceptional performance.

XX has demonstrated her commitment to the Craft Brewing Company by purchasing 5,000 shares of Company's stock for $XX. As an incentive to join our board and perform the responsibilities of executive secretary, XX has been awarded 5,000 matching shares in addition to the 5,000 shares the executive secretary purchased.

Executive Officers: The directors, executive officers, and significant personnel of the Company are as follows:

XX	Chairman of the Board President Brewery Manager Director
XX	Executive Treasurer Vice President General Manager Director
XX	Executive Secretary Director

Employees: The Craft Brewing Company is scheduled and budgeted to hire employees at regular intervals. The first full-time employee will be hired in July so as to have sufficient time to properly train that employee before full brewing and sales operations commence.

The first employee will be hired primarily as a beverage server and retail sales person in the tap room. However, this individual must be flexible and prepared to perform a variety of additional tasks, including cleaning, brewing assistance, and deliveries. The management is already talking with individuals they believe can be trusted to fill this position and who would be an asset to the Company as well.

In the twelfth month of operations an additional employee will be hired. Once again this person must be flexible and prepared to perform a variety of assignments on the production floor and in the tap room. However, it is anticipated that the primary responsibility of this second employee will be as a brewing and delivery assistant.

At the beginning of the nineteenth month of operation and again in the twenty-eighth month, additional employees will be hired and trained to perform a variety of tasks associated with beer production and deliveries. The need to hire these additional employees at regular intervals is anticipated because of the work load associated with projected increases in brewing capacity and sales in our local market. This brings our total number of full-time employees to help with retail sales and beer production at near full-production capacity to a total of four employees by the end of year three of operations. It is not anticipated that any additional employees will be required beyond this number.

It is the management teams philosophy that employees are an asset to the company, not a drain on resources. We intend to train our employees thoroughly, treat them well, and provide them with responsibility when they earn it. All full-time employees will be given a starting salary of $XX a month or approximately $XX per hour. Employees who perform well and demonstrate an interest in long term employment with Craft Brewing Company will be compensated for their efforts in year-end bonuses to be decided by the management team and Board of Directors. Eventually we hope to develop a profit-sharing program to properly reward all those employees of the Craft Brewing Company who make a significant contribution toward the Company's success.

Supporting Professional Services: The following individuals will be contracted by the Craft Brewing Company to provide services during the start-up and operational phases of this project. See Attachments for their resumes and references.

Technical advisor. XX will draw up the plans for formal approval by the city and will assist the president in directing the building improvements to be carried out by the Craft Brewing Company. The technical advisor will also help to choose utility subcontractors and coordinate their activities with the overall construction project.

Accounting. XX has assisted the Craft Brewing Company in identifying our tax responsibilities. During the operational phase, the accountant will also help the management team to implement their own accounting software program and periodically review tax reports.

Legal representation. XX will act as attorney for the Craft Brewing Company. XX will review our lease; prepare the initial articles of incorporation, bylaws, and subscription agreement; and provide legal council whenever necessary.

Business consultant. XX, director and business development specialist with the Small Business Development Center in XX, XX, has worked closely with the management team since the initiation of this project. XX has personally reviewed and critiqued our business plan and pro formas. XX is personally as well as professionally interested in this project, and the business consultant has offered to continue to provide business and financial counseling at no cost, whenever requested.

Master brewer. XX will act as a local resource to the president in the early stages of brewery operation. The master brewer has worked closely with our brewing consultant at XX as head brewer and manager. XX will be involved in the initial recipe formulation, and since the master brewer lives in XX, the master brewer will be available to troubleshoot any problems or assist the president whenever his services may be required.

Brewing consultant. XX will act as consultant in all matters related to designing, purchasing, and installing the brewing plant. The brewery consultant will assist the president in designing the brewery layout, choosing equipment, ordering equipment, and arranging for its delivery. The brewery consultant will supervise the installation of the brewing plant and work with utility subcontractors to connect equipment to all necessary utilities. The brewery consultant will also help design the product recipes and supervise the initial production runs.

Banker. XX is a vice president and commercial loan officer for XX, XX, XX. Primary area of expertise is small-business loans and SBA guarantees.

The management team comes to this project with a variety of important skills and experiences which will benefit the Company. In those areas where they lack experience, the management team has wisely decided to contract on a temporary or part-time basis with qualified professionals. In this way the Craft Brewing Company will be provided with all the necessary professional support, and costly mistakes will be avoided.

BUILDING AND CONSTRUCTION PLAN

Leased Facilities: The facilities being leased by the Craft Brewing Company are comprised of the following three distinct sections: (refer to the attached building and site drawings)

1. The Production Floor, 1,800 square feet (60 by 30) of open-floor warehouse, with a 19-foot high ceiling, containing the brewing plant, a cool room for fermentation and keg storage, and a loading dock for shipping and receiving
2. XX, 570 square feet (19 by 30) of ground floor retail sales space, adjacent to the Production Floor
3. The Corporate Office, 285 square feet (19 by 15) of second story loft above the retail sales space, including a space for grain storage and milling

These spaces have been acquired in accordance with the conditions specified in the enclosed lease.

Building Improvements: In accordance with the attached lease agreement, the following building improvements will be carried out in order to prepare the leased space for brewery operations. Likewise, the cost of these building improvements will be born in accordance with the terms of the attached Letter of Intent to Lease:

1. Removal of all extraneous hardware from the leased space
2. Power washing the interior of the leased space
3. Painting the interior of the leased space
4. Building of a demising wall between the leased space and the remainder of the building
5. Framing and finishing the loft and ground-floor retail space
6. Installing two handicap accessible bathrooms
7. Moving the stairs from the northwest to northeast loft
8. Cutting an access door in the northeast wall of the warehouse
9. Improving the sliding doors on the north end of the building
10. Installing drains at certain points on the production floor
11. Installing an insulated cool fermentation room
12. Painting the exterior of the warehouse
13. Preparing the public alley on the north end of the building to be paved by the city

The above list represents the primary building improvements which must be completed to prepare the leased space for operation. These improvements must be completed before the brewing plant can be installed and connected to the necessary utilities. The president will be assisted by the technical adviser in the planning, coordination, and execution of these building improvements. The estimated costs of these improvements are included in the financial plan cost schedule.

Subcontracting: In addition to the building improvements listed above, the following utility upgrades will be carried out by licensed professionals:

1. Plumbing: Installation of drainage system, connecting of all sinks and bathroom facilities to the drainage system, all welding necessary to prepare the brewing plant for operation, installation of separate utility meter.

2. Electrical: All wiring necessary to install appropriate lighting, all wiring necessary to prepare the brewing plant for operation, all wiring necessary to bring newly constructed walls and rooms up to code, installation of separate utility meter.
3. Gas: Installation of forced air gas heater, connecting of burners to the brewing kettle and hot liquor tank, installation of separate utility meter.
4. Refrigeration. Installation of cool room refrigeration unit and primary fermenter glycol system.
5. Telephone. Installation of business phone lines.

The subcontractors listed above will be chosen by the president through a competitive bidding process. The president will be assisted in this choice and in the overseeing of the work of these professionals by the technical adviser.

THE LEASE AGREEMENT

The management team has negotiated and executed a Letter of Intent to lease a piece of commercial real estate at XX. The Letter of Intent was signed by all parties in March 1993. This letter is the foundation from which the final lease will be drafted, and therefore, it represents the main points of agreement between the landlords and the tenants. See the attached Letter of Intent for full details of the lease agreement.

The total area being leased is 2,365 square feet of floor space and 285 square feet of loft space. In addition, the Letter of Intent guarantees the Craft Brewing Company "first right of refusal" on any additional space which may become available in the future.

The lease is to commence on May 1, 1993, with the rent commencement date set for July 1, 1993. A provision delaying our full responsibility for the lease has been included, which states that should financing not be acquired by the Craft Brewing Company by December 31, 1993, then the lease will be invalid. This clause is intended to protect the Company should the necessary start-up capital not be raised.

The lease is for five years, with a one-time option to renew the lease at the same terms and conditions for an additional five years. Rent is $XX a month, plus the triple nets (NNN) which represent our pro-rata share of the landlords taxes, insurance, and maintenance costs on the building.

OVERALL SCHEDULE

The following is an outline of the specific tasks which must be performed or milestones which must be achieved during the start-up phase of operation. This outline represents our projections of the time required to perform these tasks. These tasks have been ordered both chronologically and by priority.

MILESTONES

Period — March 15 to 31:
Mail Out Business Proposal and Share Offering
Begin to Raise Investor Equity Capital
Prepare for Building Permit Plan Review
Seek Bids on Fabricating Brewing Vessels
Complete Bidding Process on Building Improvements
Complete Final Licensing Applications
Clean and Prepare Building Interior
Approve Graphic Designs for Logos
Finalize and Sign Lease Agreement

Period — April 1 to 15:
Raise Investor Equity Capital
Meet with Potential Investors to Promote Share Sales
Choose Fabricator for Brewing Vessels
Receive Building Permit
Seek Bids on Utility Subcontracting

Period — April 16 to 30:
Raise Investor Equity Capital
Achieve Minimum Investment Level
Notify Investors of Minimum Level
Transfer Investor Capital to General Funds Account

Begin Building Improvements
Have Interior Washed and Painted
Cut Cement Floors for Drains and Plumbing
Disassemble Existing Stairs and Loft
Begin to Design the Interior of the Tap Room

Period — May 1 to 15:
Order and Make Down Payment on Brewing Vessels
Continue to Raise Investor Equity Capital
Building Improvements
Rough In Plumbing
Inspect Hook-up to Sewer System
Grade and Pave Alley
Pour New Cement Floor Slab
Cut Exterior Door Openings
Begin to Frame in Demising Wall Exterior Doors

Period — May 16 to 31:
Continue to Raise Investor Equity Capital
Building Improvements
Continue Framing in New Walls
Frame In Bathrooms
Build New Loft Floor and Ceiling
Schedule Framing and Wiring Inspections

Period — June 1 to 15:
Continue to Raise Investor Equity Capital
Purchase Miscellaneous Brewing Equipment
Continue Building Improvements
Complete Framing of New Walls, Doors, Etc.
Install Heating Systems
Framing and Wiring Inspections

Period — June, 16 to 30:
Continue to Raise Investor Equity Capital
Continue to Purchase Miscellaneous Brewing Equipment
Install Cold Room and Refrigeration
Receive Delivery of Brewing Plant
Install and Hook-up Brewing Plant
Complete Building Improvements
Have Exterior of Building Painted

Period — July 1 to 15:
Sell Final Shares for Equity Capital
Final Occupancy and Health Inspection

Receive Final Permits and Licenses to Operate
Complete Brewery Installation and Hook-up
Make Final Equipment Purchases
Begin Installing Fixtures and Furnishings for
   Tap Room
Install Tap Room Bar and Sink
Final Utility Inspections
Purchase Brewing Ingredients
Begin Test Recipe Brewing
Begin Advertising in Local Printed Media
Meet with Local Licensed Retailers to Discuss
   First Sales

Period — July 16 to 31:
Complete Tap Room Preparations
Paint Corporate Logo on North Frontage
Plant Sidewalk Trees
Keg First Brew Runs
Begin to Market Products

We believe these tasks can be completed within the scheduled time periods above. However, one serious potential delay would be in achieving the minimum level of investors equity capital which is necessary for us to begin ordering brewing equipment and scheduling building improvements. Further delays might arise in acquiring a building permit and in coordinating the work of the subcontractor with the overall project and with city inspectors which review many stages of the building improvement process. Any such delays would influence the timing of the entire project and could potentially delay start-up by as much as several months. A delay in our start-up of beer production would entail certain additional expenses until sales of beer began. Nevertheless, we are confident that even should certain reasonable delays occur, the overall success of this project would not be jeopardized.

THE FINANCIAL PLAN

Assumptions: The following information has been provided in order to fully identify the assumptions which the management team has made in projecting the growth in sales, expenses, revenue, and profit of the Craft Brewing Company for the first three years of operation.

Revenue: The Revenue section is broken down into several categories: wholesale through distributor, wholesale self-distributed, retail keg sales, and retail pint sales. All beer sales are based on barrel volumes where one barrel equals 31 gallons or two 15.5-gallon kegs. There is also a separate revenue line for food and merchandise sales. First year production and sales levels are based on our research of the local market and are considered to be relatively conservative projections of local demand. In following years, wholesale self-distributed sales are projected to increase by 1.5 percent each month, wholesale through a distributor sales are projected to increase by 6 percent each month, and retail keg sales are projected to flatten out at approximately 14 kegs each month on average. Retail pint sales are projected to flatten out at 28 kegs each month since they will be limited by the size of our tap room. See the sections on projected local, regional, and total beer sales in the business proposal.

Cost of Goods Sold: This figure includes the ingredients, energy, water, excise and business taxes required to produce beer. The numbers for brewing ingredients are based on actual costs from suppliers and correspond with the given production levels and historical production cost averages. Utility costs are based on estimates of local energy and water rates for a given level of production. Tax rates are based on current rates of $XX per barrel federal excise tax, approximately $XX per barrel state excise tax, and a nominal local business and occupation tax. These excise taxes could be subject to increases in the near future. Costs of food and merchandise sold in our retail outlet are taken to be 50 percent of the retail sales price. Costs of brewing ingredients, water, energy, and supplies are projected to remain relatively constant over time as a proportion of the costs of producing a given volume of beer (approximately $17.50 per barrel). We anticipate that rising prices for these ingredients will be offset by the savings realized through larger volume purchases.

Gross Profit: When the Total Cost of Goods Sold is subtracted from Gross Sales, the resulting figure represents our Gross Profit. Our Gross Profit percentage from year to year will decrease slightly as the ratio of beer sales through a distributor (which have the smallest profit margin) increase, while our ratio of retail beer sales (which have the largest profit margin) remain relatively stable.

Operating Expenses — General and Administrative Expenses: Refer to the Pro Forma General and Administrative Expense Schedule-First Year Supplement. These numbers are based on cost estimates from suppliers and service providers. In some cases, irregularly billed payments are spread out over the twelve months of the year as average monthly payments. The different expenses on the General and Administrative Schedule are projected to increase by 1 percent each month. The exceptions are rent and parking which remain constant, and salaries and payroll taxes which will be increased in accordance with the discussions in the sections of this proposal on employees and management compensation. The costs of all employees hired after the first year and their corresponding payroll taxes appear on separate lines in the Second and Third Years Income Statement.

The final expense which is factored into the Company's Operating Expenses is the depreciation rate on certain assets. The assets being depreciated include: start-up leasehold improvements (building construction costs), brewery equipment, handling equipment (the delivery van, keg dolly, etc.), cooperage (kegs), fixtures and furnishings (tap-room furnishings, office equipment, lighting, etc.), and other capital assets purchased during the operational phase to expand production capacity. Depreciation is based on a straight line method over a period of seven years.

EBIT (Earnings Before Income Taxes): When Operating Expenses are subtracted from the Gross Profit, the resulting figure represents the Company's Earnings before corporate income taxes. Interest Income from cash in the Company's general account at

Centennial Bank is then added to the EBIT line, with the resulting sum being the Company's Profit before corporate income taxes. Corporate Income Taxes are calculated at current rates and when subtracted from the Profit before taxes, result in the Company's Net Income or Loss.

Net Earnings: This line represents the Company's earnings once paid out dividends, any loan principle, and any new equipment purchases have been subtracted from the Company's Net Income/Loss.

NOTES

1. The Institute for Brewing Studies, *North American: Brewers Resource Directory, 1992–93* (Boulder: Brewers Publications, 1992), 90.
2. Ibid. 11.
3. Barbralu Cohen, "A Yen to Sell in Japan," *The New Brewer* 8 (May–June 1991): 32–33. Angela LoSasso, "Tap into a Thirsty Market: Hop to It, Start-Up Microbrewery," *Entrepreneur* (June 1992): 134–138. Rick Lyke, "On Premise Sales: Proof of Changing Lifestyles," *Beverage Industry* (1990): 14–16.
4. Buddy Kilpatrick, "The 'T' Word and Beer," *The New Brewer* 7 (September–October 1990): 33. Stanley L. Ornstein, "Control of Alcohol Consumption through Price Increases," *Journal of Studies on Alcohol* 41 (1980): 807–818.
5. Buddy Kilpatrick, "The 'T' Word and Beer," *The New Brewer* 7 (September–October 1990): 32.
6. Buddy Kilpatrick, "The Recession and Beer," *The New Brewer* 9 (September–October 1992): 40–41.
7. The Institute for Brewing Studies, *North American: Brewers Resource Directory, 1992–93* (Boulder: Brewers Publications, 1992), 29.
8. Ibid. 19–27.
9. XX State Liquor Control Board, *Report of Beer Sales in the State of XX by Individual Breweries* (September 1992). XX Beer and

Wine Wholesalers Association, *Total Beer Sales in XX Including Imports for the Period January 1, 1992, through September 30, 1992.*

10. XX State Liquor Control Board, *Report of Beer Sales in the State of XX by Individual Breweries* (September 1992). XX Beer and Wine Wholesalers Association, *Total Beer Sales in XX Including Imports for the Period January 1, 1992 through September 30, 1992.*

11. XX Regional Planning Council, *XX County Statistics* (September 1992), V-1–V-11 and VII-1.

12. XX Regional Planning Council, *XX County Statistics* (September 1992), V-1–V-11 and VII-1.

13. XX State Liquor Control Board, *Report of Beer Sales in the State of XX by Individual Breweries* (September 1992). XX Beer and Wine Wholesalers Association, *Total Beer Sales in XX Including Imports for the period January 1, 1992, through September 30, 1992.*

Chapter 22
Characteristics of the Microbrewery Industry

The following statistics were collected and analyzed by the Institute for Brewing Studies (IBS) and reflect finance and sales ratios and brewery operations data from the brewing industry for the year 1994. The IBS annually surveys all microbreweries and brewpubs in North America to collect this information. These statistics are taken from the 1995–96 edition of *Industry Revealed*. This book, as well as the annual *North American Brewers Resource Directory,* both published by Brewers Publications, contain vital information for your business.

The statistics presented here can be a basis for projections for your brewery and will certainly enhance your business plan. This is the most comprehensive information available on this unique and burgeoning industry.

Key

Mean: The "average" value of the survey. Computed by all responses divided by the number of responses.

Median: The "middle" response. An equal number of larger and smaller values were given as responses.

Mode: The most common response to a question. U.S. responses are in barrels and U.S. dollars; Canadian responses are in hectoliters and Canadian dollars.

Brewpubs: more than 50% beer sales on-site

Microbrewery: less than 15,000 bbl. (17,600 hL) sales

Regional Brewery: between 15,000 bbl. (17,600 hL) and 500,000 bbl. (586700 hL) sales

Note: Contract brewing companies were not mailed a survey during the past year. We will publish contract brewing information in next year's report.

Regions

Mountain West: Arizona, Colorado, Idaho, Montana, Nevada, New Mexico, Utah, Wyoming

North Central: Illinois, Indiana, Iowa, Kansas, Michigan, Minnesota, Missouri, Nebraska, North Dakota, Ohio, South Dakota, Wisconsin

Northeast: Connecticut, Delaware, Maine, Maryland, Massachusetts, New Hampshire, New Jersey, New York, Pennsylvania, Rhode Island, Vermont, Virginia, Washington, D.C., West Virginia

Pacific: California, Hawaii

Pacific Northwest: Alaska, Oregon, Washington

South: Alabama, Arkansas, Florida, Georgia, Kentucky, Louisiana, Mississippi, North Carolina, Oklahoma, South Carolina, Tennessee, Texas

Eastern Canada: New Brunswick, Newfoundland, Nova Scotia, Ontario, Prince Edward Island, Quebec

Western Canada: Alberta, British Columbia, Manitoba, N.W. Territories, Saskatchewan, Yukon Territories

Demographics of Survey Respondents

Total Number of Survey Respondents: 232
Total Number of Survey Respondents, by Country:

United States:	203
Canada:	29

Number of Total Respondents per Type and Sales of Brewery (According to Sales):

Type of Brewery	Responses
U.S. Brewpub (0–750 bbl.)	42
U.S. Brewpub (751–1500)	44
U.S. Brewpub (1501+)	28
U.S. Micro (1–1000)	26
U.S. Micro (1001–7500)	40
U.S. Micro (7501–15,000)	15
U.S. Regional (15,001–75,000)	8
Can. Brewpub (0–880 hL)	9
Can. Micro (1174–8800)	8
Can. Micro (8801–17,601)	6
Can. Regional (17,602–88,005)	6

Number of Total Respondents per Region:

Region	Brewpub	Micro	Regional
United States			
Mountain West	23	23	0
North Central	20	11	1
Northeast	21	18	0
Pacific	19	15	1
Pacific NW	8	11	5
South	23	6	1
Canada			
Eastern	5	6	1
Western	2	3	5

General Information

Number of Years in Business:

Type	Responses	Mean	Median	Mode
U.S. Brewpub	101	3.0	2.5	1.0
U.S. Micro	70	3.6	3.0	1.0
U.S. Regional	6	8.4	N/A	N/A
Can. Brewpub	5	4.9	N/A	N/A
Can. Micro	8	4.1	N/A	N/A
Can. Regional	6	12.5	N/A	N/A

Majority of Volume of Beer Sold Fermented Using:

Type	Responses	Ale Yeast	Lager Yeast
U.S. Brewpub	113	88%	12%
U.S. Micro	81	75	25
U.S. Regional	8	75	25
Can. Brewpub	5	60	40
Can. Micro	9	56	44
Can. Regional	7	57	43

Total Number of Brands Brewed Year-Round:

(Excluding "Duplicate" Beers Sold as Different Brands)

Type	Responses	Mean	Median	Mode
U.S. Brewpub	106	7.2	5.0	5.0
U.S. Micro	84	4.1	3.5	4.0
U.S. Regional	8	6.1	N/A	N/A
Can. Brewpub	7	3.3	N/A	N/A
Can. Micro	9	4.2	N/A	N/A
Can. Regional	7	5.4	N/A	N/A

Total Number of Brands Brewed Seasonally:

Type	Responses	Mean	Median	Mode
U.S. Brewpub	102	8.4	7.0	6.0
U.S. Micro	73	3.2	3.0	1.0
U.S. Regional	8	3.9	N/A	N/A
Can. Brewpub	7	4.9	N/A	N/A
Can. Micro	7	1.4	N/A	N/A
Can. Regional	3	3.3	N/A	N/A

Average Number of Beers Offered at a Time at Brewpubs and Brewery-Restaurants:

Type	Responses	Mean	Median	Mode
U.S. Brewpub	113	5.8	5.5	5.0
U.S. Micro	17	6.1	5.8	6.0
U.S. Regional	5	7.0	N/A	N/A
Can. Brewpub	7	4.1	N/A	N/A

Distribution

Number of Distributors (Excluding Self):

Type	Responses	Mean	Median	Mode
U.S. Brewpub	46	1.8	1.0	1.0
U.S. Micro	81	9.8	4.0	4.0
U.S. Regional	6	64.7	N/A	N/A
Can. Micro	8	3.0	N/A	N/A
Can. Regional	5	4.2	N/A	N/A

Percentage of Sales Distributed by Self vs. Distributed by Distributors:

Type	Responses	Mean	Median	Mode
U.S. Brewpub	46	48/52%	48/52%	100/0%
U.S. Micro	78	30/70	5/95	0/100
U.S. Regional	8	9/91	N/A	N/A
Can. Micro	8	84/16	N/A	N/A
Can. Regional	7	71/29	N/A	N/A

Number of States/Provinces in Which Your Beer Is Currently Available:

Type	Responses	Mean	Median	Mode
U.S. Brewpub	42	1.4	1.1	1.0
U.S. Micro	82	4.8	2.0	1.0
U.S. Regional	8	15.5	N/A	N/A
Can. Micro	8	3.4	N/A	N/A
Can. Regional	7	3.4	N/A	N/A

Physical Plant

Average Batch Size (in Barrels/Hectoliters):

Type	Responses	Mean	Median	Mode
U.S. Brewpub	112	9.9	8.8	7.0
U.S. Micro	84	20.2	16.7	20.0
U.S. Regional	8	78.9	N/A	N/A
Can. Brewpub	7	8.8	N/A	N/A
Can. Micro	9	39.7	N/A	N/A
Can. Regional	7	125.0	N/A	N/A

Total Capacity of Fermenting Tanks (in Barrels/Hectoliters):

Type	Responses	Mean	Median	Mode
U.S. Brewpub	108	49	42	7
U.S. Micro	81	502	77	30
U.S. Regional	8	2,057	N/A	N/A
Can. Brewpub	6	24	N/A	N/A
Can. Micro	8	2,825	N/A	N/A
Can. Regional	7	2,419	N/A	N/A

Total Capacity of Serving Tanks (in Barrels/Hectoliters) at Brewpubs and Brewery-Restaurants:

Type	Responses	Mean	Median	Mode
U.S. Brewpub	96	53.7	68.4	17.5
U.S. Micro	10	50.0	37.5	15.0
Can. Brewpub	6	17.5	N/A	N/A

Brewing Process and Ingredients

Percent Using Following Carbonation Method(s):

Method (Responses)	U.S. Brewpub (113)	U.S. Micro (76)	U.S. Regional (7)	Can. Brewpub (7)	Can. Micro (9)	Can. Regional (7)
Carbonating Stone	80%	43%	2%	3%	7%	2%
Naturally/ Spundig	45	31	3	4	3	5
Inject CO_2	38	23	2	1	1	3
Keg Conditioning	17	12	0	1	1	1
Kraeusen	6	8	1	1	0	2
None of These	0	1	0	0	0	0

Brewing Method: Mash or Extract?

Type	Responses Full Mash	w/Partial Mash	Malt Extract Extract	All Malt
U.S. Brewpub	114	95%	3%	3%
U.S. Micro	79	95	3	3
U.S. Regional	8	100	0	0
Can. Brewpub	7	71	0	29
Can. Micro	9	100	0	0
Can. Regional	7	100	0	0

Percent Using Other Fermentable Ingredients Besides Barley Malt and Wheat Malt:

Ingredient (Responses)	U.S. Brewpub (109)	U.S. Micro (75)	U.S. Regional (7)	Can. Brewpub (6)	Can. Micro (7)	Can. Regional (7)
Fruit	48%	21%	14%	33%	29%	0%
Oats	40	15	0	33	0	0
Honey	31	20	14	67	14	14
Flaked Barley	22	5	0	33	0	0
Rye Malt	19	7	0	0	0	14
Sugars	14	7	0	50	0	29
Vegetables (incl. pumpkin, potatoes etc.)	13	1	0	0	0	0
Malt Extract	10	8	0	33	0	0
Maple Sap/Syrup	8	3	0	50	14	14
Torrified Wheat	6	8	0	17	14	0
Apples/ Apple Cider	6	1	0	0	14	0
Corn	4	1	0	17	14	29
Rice	2	1	0	0	0	0
Corn, Rice or Barley Syrup	2	0	0	0	0	0
Other	6	11	0	0	0	0
None	20	39	71	0	43	43

Percent Using Other Non-Fermentable Ingredients Besides Hops and Hop Products:

Ingredient (Responses)	U.S. Brewpub (97)	U.S. Micro (69)	U.S. Regional (6)	Can. Brewpub (5)	Can. Micro (8)	Can. Regional (7)
Herbs/Spices (incl. chile peppers)	51%	32%	33%	80%	0%	14%
Clarifying Agents	38	33	0	80	38	14
Fruit Essences	27	13	17	20	0	0
Coffee	3	1	17	0	0	0
Enzymes	0	3	0	0	0	13
Other	4	10	0	20	0	0
None	27	32	67	0	56	63

Shelf Life and Quality Assurance

Estimated Shelf Life of 1/2-Barrel Keg (Days After Kegging):

Type	Responses	Mean	Median	Mode
U.S. Brewpub	76	64.5	59.8	60.0
U.S. Micro	72	93.4	89.9	90.0
U.S. Regional	7	100.7	N/A	N/A
Can. Micro	9	63.2	N/A	N/A
Can. Regional	7	75.7	N/A	N/A

Estimated "Tap-Life" of 1/2-Barrel Keg (Days After Tapping):

Type	Responses	Mean	Median	Mode
U.S. Brewpub	66	29.6	29.7	30.0
U.S. Micro	64	38.0	30.1	30.0
U.S. Regional	3	35.0	N/A	N/A
Can. Micro	8	15.9	N/A	N/A
Can. Regional	6	17.2	16.0	14.0

Estimated Shelf Life of Bottled Beer (Days After Bottling):

Type	Responses	Mean	Median	Mode
U.S. Brewpub	22	72.4	60.8	60.0
U.S. Micro	55	118.4	91.3	90.0
U.S. Regional	6	130.0	N/A	N/A
Can. Micro	9	116.1	N/A	N/A
Can. Regional	6	117.5	N/A	N/A

Percent Using Following Method(s) to Help Achieve Microbiological Stability in Bottled Products:

Method (Responses)	U.S. Brewpub (45)	U.S. Micro (69)	U.S. Regional (8)	Can. Brewpub (4)	Can. Micro (9)	Can. Regional (7)
Standard (Coarse) Filtration	71%	58%	63%	25%	89%	100%
Sterile (Micro)Filtration	20	30	50	25	67	71
Bottle Conditioning	2	13	13	25	0	29
Tunnel Pasteurization	0	6	13	0	0	14
Flash Pasteurization	0	4	0	0	0	14
Stabilizing Additives	0	3	0	0	0	0
Other	9	7	0	0	22	0
None	22	12	0	25	0	0

Percent of Breweries that Date-Code Bottled Beer:

Type	Responses	"Yes"
U.S. Brewpub	27	37%
U.S. Micro	62	74
U.S. Regional	8	88
Can. Brewpub	4	25
Can. Micro	9	78
Can. Regional	7	100

Packaging

Percent of Beer Sold in:

Packaging	U.S. Brewpub (88)	U.S. Micro (80)	U.S. Regional (8)	Can. Brewpub (6)	Can. Micro (9)	Can. Regional (7)
Bottles	6%	48%	54%	1%	46%	61%
Draft (incl. "To Go")	94	52	46	99	54	39

How/Where Sales Occur

Percent of Beer Sold at:

Account (Responses)	U.S. Brewpub (102)	U.S. Micro (65)	U.S. Regional (5)	Can. Brewpub (7)	Can. Micro (9)	Can. Regional (7)
Brewery or Brewpub	88%	10%	1%	94%	11%	1%
On-Premise Accts	7	44	35	6	27	23
Off-Premise Accts	5	46	64	0	62	76

On-Premise: bars/restaurants/taverns/sports venues
Off-Premise: beer/liquor/grocery/convenience stores

Pricing — Bottles

Note: Retail Prices Are Not Including Sales Tax

Case of 24 12-Ounce Bottles, Price Paid by Wholesaler/Distributor:

Type	Responses	Mean	Median	Mode
U.S. Micro	32	$15.01	14.50	14.00
U.S. Regional	7	14.63	N/A	N/A

Case of 24 12-Ounce Bottles, Wholesale Price:

Type	Responses	Mean	Median	Mode
U.S. Brewpub	3	$25.11	N/A	N/A
U.S. Micro	34	20.40	20.00	21.00
U.S. Regional	5	20.43	N/A	N/A
Can. Micro	4	31.90	N/A	N/A
Can. Regional	3	28.84	N/A	N/A

Case of 24 12-Ounce Bottles, Retail Price:

Type	Responses	Mean	Median	Mode
U.S. Brewpub	4	$31.54	N/A	N/A
U.S. Micro	38	26.30	25.00	24.00
U.S. Regional	4	27.11	N/A	N/A
Can. Micro	5	32.90	N/A	N/A
Can. Regional	3	33.62	N/A	N/A

Case of 12 22-Ounce Bottles, Price Paid by Wholesaler/Distributor:

Type	Responses	Mean	Median	Mode
U.S. Brewpub	10	$21.50	21.11	25.00
U.S. Micro	26	19.70	20.02	20.02

Case of 12 22-Ounce Bottles, Wholesale Price:

Type	Responses	Mean	Median	Mode
U.S. Brewpub	13	$26.60	26.40	26.40
U.S. Micro	22	25.03	25.24	26.00

Case of 12 22-Ounce Bottles, Retail Price:

Type	Responses	Mean	Median	Mode
U.S. Brewpub	13	$37.70	36.03	36.00
U.S. Micro	24	33.23	34.00	35.90
Can. Micro	4	35.00	N/A	N/A
Can. Regional	3	40.33	N/A	N/A

Pricing — Kegs

Note: Retail Prices Are Not Including Sales Tax

1/2-Barrel Price Paid by Wholesaler/Distributor:

Type	Responses	Mean	Median	Mode
U.S. Brewpub	25	$69.20	69.52	70.00
U.S. Micro	59	66.42	65.00	65.00
U.S. Regional	5	59.20	N/A	N/A

1/2-Barrel Wholesale Price:

Type	Responses	Mean	Median	Mode
U.S. Brewpub	27	$86.11	89.01	90.00
U.S. Micro	59	85.50	85.00	85.00
U.S. Regional	5	82.80	N/A	N/A

1/2-Barrel Retail Price:

Type	Responses	Mean	Median	Mode
U.S. Brewpub	41	$94.63	95.00	100.00
U.S. Micro	49	96.30	91.02	90.00
U.S. Regional	5	87.20	N/A	N/A

1/4-Barrel Price Paid by Wholesaler/Distributor:

Type	Responses	Mean	Median	Mode
U.S. Brewpub	11	$39.42	37.00	35.00
U.S. Micro	19	34.50	35.01	35.00
U.S. Regional	3	32.33	N/A	N/A

1/4-Barrel Wholesale Price:

Type	Responses	Mean	Median	Mode
U.S. Brewpub	11	$45.11	45.00	45.00
U.S. Micro	20	45.10	45.00	45.00
U.S. Regional	3	43.00	N/A	N/A

1/4-Barrel Retail Price:

Type	Responses	Mean	Median	Mode
U.S. Brewpub	25	$52.02	50.01	45.00
U.S. Micro	26	51.03	48.02	45.00
U.S. Regional	5	49.00	N/A	N/A

Pricing — Brewpubs and Brewery-Restaurants

(Including Microbrewery Tasting Rooms)
Note: Prices Include Sales Tax

10-oz. Glass Price:

Type	Responses	Mean	Median	Mode
U.S. Brewpub	41	$1.95	1.95	1.75
U.S. Micro	6	1.82	N/A	N/A
Can. Brewpub	7	2.29	N/A	N/A

12-oz. Glass Price:

Type	Responses	Mean	Median	Mode
U.S. Brewpub	29	$2.26	2.25	2.25
U.S. Micro	8	2.08	N/A	N/A

16-oz. Pint Price:

Type	Responses	Mean	Median	Mode
U.S. Brewpub	89	$2.78	2.75	2.75
U.S. Micro	11	2.80	2.65	2.50
U.S. Regional	4	2.19	N/A	N/A
Can. Brewpub	4	3.56	N/A	N/A

20-oz. "Imperial" Pint Price:

Type	Responses	Mean	Median	Mode
U.S. Brewpub	18	$3.38	3.26	3.50
U.S. Micro	3	3.07	N/A	N/A
Can. Brewpub	4	4.31	N/A	N/A

Brewery Employees

Total Number of Full-Time Brewery Employees:

Type	Responses	Mean	Median	Mode
U.S. Brewpub	96	2.2	2.0	1.0
U.S. Micro	75	5.3	3.0	3.0
U.S. Regional	5	23.6	N/A	N/A
Can. Brewpub	7	1.0	N/A	N/A
Can. Micro	9	9.3	N/A	N/A
Can. Regional	5	50.4	N/A	N/A

Number of Full-Time Brewmasters/Head Brewers:

Type	Responses	Mean	Median	Mode
U.S. Brewpub	98	1.1	1.0	1.0
U.S. Micro	70	1.2	1.0	1.0
U.S. Regional	7	1.9	N/A	N/A
Can. Brewpub	4	1.0	N/A	N/A
Can. Micro	9	1.0	N/A	N/A
Can. Regional	6	1.3	N/A	N/A

Average Number of Hours Worked by Full-Time Brewmasters/Head Brewers:

Type	Responses	Mean	Median	Mode
U.S. Brewpub	97	47.3	45.2	40.0
U.S. Micro	67	51.0	49.8	50.0
U.S. Regional	6	44.8	N/A	N/A
Can. Brewpub	6	35.0	N/A	N/A
Can. Micro	8	50.4	N/A	N/A
Can. Regional	5	55.8	N/A	N/A

Average Annual Salary of Full-Time Brewmasters/Head Brewers:

Type	Responses	Mean	Median	Mode
U.S. Brewpub	88	$29,149	28,800	30,000
U.S. Micro	57	29,202	29,982	30,000
U.S. Regional	4	36,250	N/A	N/A
Can. Brewpub	7	32,629	N/A	N/A
Can. Micro	8	38,000	N/A	N/A
Can. Regional	5	56,600	N/A	N/A

Number of Full-Time Assistant Brewers:

Type	Responses	Mean	Median	Mode
U.S. Brewpub	76	1.2	1.0	1.0
U.S. Micro	65	1.8	1.0	1.0
U.S. Regional	7	5.4	N/A	N/A
Can. Micro	8	2.9	N/A	N/A
Can. Regional	5	4.4	N/A	N/A

Average Number of Hours
Worked by Full-Time Assistant Brewers:

Type	Responses	Mean	Median	Mode
U.S. Brewpub	62	36.0	39.7	40.0
U.S. Micro	55	43.2	40.4	40.0
U.S. Regional	6	41.7	N/A	N/A
Can. Micro	8	41.9	N/A	N/A
Can. Regional	5	43.8	N/A	N/A

Brewpub/Brewery-Restaurant Employees

Total Number of Full-Time Restaurant Employees:

Type	Responses	Mean	Median	Mode
U.S. Brewpub	69	27.5	20.2	10.0
U.S. Micro	11	13.1	5.0	18.0
U.S. Regional	3	21.7	N/A	N/A
Can. Brewpub	4	18.0	N/A	N/A

Number of General Managers:

Type	Responses	Mean	Median	Mode
U.S. Brewpub	81	1.2	1.1	1.0
U.S. Micro	11	1.0	1.0	1.0
U.S. Regional	3	1.0	N/A	N/A
Can. Brewpub	5	1.2	N/A	N/A

Brewery Financials—Start-up

Total Start-up Costs (x $1,000):

Type	Responses	Mean	Median	Mode
U.S. Brewpub	76	648	500	500
U.S. Micro	53	417	250	100
U.S. Regional	6	1,175	N/A	N/A
Can. Brewpub	4	451	N/A	N/A
Can. Micro	5	968	N/A	N/A
Can. Regional	6	553	N/A	N/A

Total Investment in Brewing Equipment (x $1,000):

Type	Responses	Mean	Median	Mode
U.S. Brewpub	84	199	150	150
U.S. Micro	55	280	145	100
U.S. Regional	5	540	N/A	N/A
Can. Brewpub	4	191	N/A	N/A
Can. Micro	5	540	N/A	N/A
Can. Regional	4	874	N/A	N/A

Income Statement

(For Fiscal Year Ending in 1994)

Annual Gross Revenues (x $1,000):

Type	Responses	Mean	Median	Mode
U.S. Brewpub	61	1,592	1,498	1,000
U.S. Micro	35	1,093	502	500
U.S. Regional	6	4,750	N/A	N/A
Can. Brewpub	4	1,250	N/A	N/A
Can. Micro	4	2,500	N/A	N/A
Can. Regional	4	5,425	N/A	N/A

Marketing/Public Relations Expenses (x $1,000):

Type	Responses	Mean	Median	Mode
U.S. Brewpub	29	55	30	15
U.S. Micro	15	30	26	26
U.S. Regional	4	399	N/A	N/A
Can. Micro	4	200	N/A	N/A

Balance Sheet

Total Liabilities (x $1,000):

Type	Responses	Mean	Median	Mode
U.S. Brewpub	20	389	319	436
U.S. Micro	15	355	240	369
U.S. Regional	4	2,838	N/A	N/A
Can. Micro	3	963	N/A	N/A
Can. Regional	3	1,966	N/A	N/A

Total Liabilities (x $1,000):

Type	Responses	Mean	Median	Mode
U.S. Brewpub	20	389	319	436
U.S. Micro	15	355	240	369
U.S. Regional	4	2,838	N/A	N/A
Can. Micro	3	963	N/A	N/A
Can. Regional	3	1,966	N/A	N/A

Cost of Goods Sold per Barrel/Hectoliter:

Type	Responses	Mean	Median	Mode
U.S. Brewpub	25	$67.76	45.25	45.00
U.S. Micro	13	76.23	77.00	20.00
U.S. Regional	5	102.60	N/A	N/A

Did You Expand Capacity More
Than 15% within the Past 12 Months?

Type	Responses	Yes	No
U.S. Brewpub	49	33%	67%
U.S. Micro	39	72	28
U.S. Regional	5	60	40
Can. Micro	5	60	40
Can. Regional	5	80	20

If Yes, Percent Expansion of Capacity within the Past 12 Months:

Type	Responses	Mean	Median	Mode
U.S. Brewpub	15	70.7%	30.3	100.0
U.S. Micro	25	92.4	75.0	50.0
U.S. Regional	3	61.0	N/A	N/A
Can. Regional	4	33.8	N/A	N/A

For How Many Quarters Have You Shown an Operating Profit?

Type	Responses	Mean	Median	Mode
U.S. Brewpub	29	7.5	6	4
U.S. Micro	32	9.3	5	4
U.S. Regional	3	17.0	N/A	N/A
Can. Micro	3	2.7	N/A	N/A
Can. Regional	5	7.2	N/A	N/A

Seating

Seating Capacity, Bar/Lounge:

Type	Responses	Mean	Median	Mode
U.S. Brewpub	87	71.5	59.7	100.0
U.S. Micro	18	59.4	40.2	40.0
U.S. Regional	4	83.5	N/A	N/A
Can. Brewpub	5	133.0	N/A	N/A

Seating Capacity, Dining:

Type	Responses	Mean	Median	Mode
U.S. Brewpub	87	141.1	125.3	200
U.S. Micro	16	108.0	105.0	200

Seating Capacity, Outdoor:

Type	Responses	Mean	Median	Mode
U.S. Brewpub	61	59.4	50	50
U.S. Micro	13	66.0	50	50
U.S. Regional	3	51.3	N/A	N/A
Can. Brewpub	3	50.0	N/A	N/A

Sales Ratios

Number of Turns per Table — Lunch:

Type	Responses	Mean	Median	Mode
U.S. Brewpub	56	1.7	1.5	1.0
U.S. Micro	16	1.9	1.5	1.0
Can. Brewpub	4	1.8	N/A	N/A

Number of Turns per Table — Dinner:

Type	Responses	Mean	Median	Mode
U.S. Brewpub	59	2.7	2.6	2.0
U.S. Micro	17	2.9	2.9	3.0
Can. Brewpub	3	2.7	N/A	N/A

Average per Customer Check Total — Lunch:

Type	Responses	Mean	Median	Mode
U.S. Brewpub	55	8.41	7.75	6.00
U.S. Micro	12	7.79	7.00	6.00
Can. Brewpub	4	9.25	N/A	N/A

Average per Customer Check Total — Dinner:

Type	Responses	Mean	Median	Mode
U.S. Brewpub	57	13.40	12.98	15.00
U.S. Micro	14	12.88	10.48	9.00
Can. Brewpub	4	13.50	N/A	N/A

Percent of Sales — Food vs. Bar:

Type	Responses	Mean	Median	Mode
U.S. Brewpub	75	57/43%	56/44%	50/50%
U.S. Micro	15	56/44	60/40	60/40
U.S. Regional	4	23/77	N/A	N/A
Can. Brewpub	4	21/79	N/A	N/A

Beer "To Go"

Average Estimated Breakdown of Total Bar Receipts:

Type	Responses	House Beer	Guest Beer	Wine	Spirits	Other
U.S. Brewpub	76	77.9%	6.4%	6.5%	6.0%	2.5%
U.S. Micro	17	84.6	6.4	4.6	6.5	1.2
Can. Brewpub	6	52.3	22.0	5.3	13.8	6.8

Average Estimated Package Breakdown of Total Amount Sold for Take-out:*

Type	Resp.	Bottles	Trad. Kegs	Non-Trad. Kegs	Draft To Go
U.S. Brewpub	46	12.5%	23.0%	13.3%	43.6%
U.S. Micro	14	63.2	15.6	1.6	20.6

Traditional kegs are ½-bbl. and 50-liter. Nontraditional kegs are 5 gal., 3 gal., 5-liter and "party-pig" containers. Draft "To Go" is dispensed on demand for carry-out in 1 gal., ½-gal., and other size containers.

Guest Beers

Does Your State/Provincal Law Permit Sale of Guest Beers?

Type	Responses	Yes	No
U.S. Brewpub	86	95%	8%
U.S. Micro	20	80	20
Can. Brewpub	6	100	0

Contributors

Tom Anders of Petaluma, California, is vice president of sales for Scott Laboratories. For the seventeen years he has been with Scott, he has provided technical assistance to producers of valuable liquids. Previously, he was a brewing microbiologist, brewing chemist, and quality assurance special projects coordinator for Joseph Schlitz Brewing Company.

Keith Dinehart has ten years of experience in the public relations field in Chicago. Since his family started Chicago Brewing Company in 1990, he has been responsible for the creation, development, and implementation of the brewery's image through public relations. In addition, he is responsible for managing wholesaler relations for fifteen distributors in the state of Illinois. Prior to the brewery he was an account executive in charge of media relations at two public relations firms in Chicago, Financial Shares Corporation and Financial Communicators Incorporated. Keith is a graduate of Illinois State University with degrees in speech communications and public relations.

Jim Dorsch is editor of *American Brewer* and *Beer, the magazine*. He was a writer for Michael Jackson's Discovery Channel CD-ROMs, *The Beer Hunter* and *The World Beer Hunter*, and is senior editor of Michael Jackson's Beer Hunter Web Site. Jim is a contributing editor of *Ale Street News* and has written about beer for *The Washington Post, The Chicago Tribune*, **The New Brewer**, *Market Watch, Nightclub & Bar, Southwest*

Brewing News, Celebrator Beer News, Brew, and *Brewpub*. He coordinates beer classes for the Smithsonian Resident Associates Program in Washington, D.C.

Peter Egelston has been involved in three brewery startups. In 1987 he and his sister, Janet, opened the Northampton Brewery, a brewpub in western Massachusetts; in 1991 they opened New Hampshire's first brewpub, the Portsmouth Brewery; in 1994 they started the Smuttynose Brewing Company, a microbrewery in Portsmouth, New Hampshire.

Peter Hexter of Wilmington, North Carolina, is president of CUI Inc., designers and decorators of quality porcelain, stoneware, and glassware. Peter is a former college football and wrestling coach and has brought this sense of motivation to his family's business. He holds a bachelor of arts in economics.

John Hickenlooper was raised in the suburbs west of Philadelphia. He spent his salad days, green in judgment, as a geologist, until an untimely dismissal in 1986. The following two years he suffered the birthing of the Wynkoop Brewing Co., a three-hundred-seat home to profligate beer-lovers, within a massive historic warehouse in Denver, Colorado. He is single with a good dog.

Will Kemper has directed start-up and production for over a dozen craft breweries since 1984. He is a member of the Institute for

Brewing Studies, Master Brewers Association of the Americas, American Society of Brewing Chemists, and the Institute of Brewing. Will has a degree in chemical engineering from the University of Colorado, is a Siebel alumnus, and completed the Master Brewers Program from the University of California at Davis. He currently lives in Bellingham, Washington, and works as an independent contractor.

JIM KOCH started the Boston Beer Company in 1984 to brew Samuel Adams Boston Lager. He is the sixth consecutive eldest son to brew in America, dating back to the 1830s. Jim is brewing his beer in a renovated brewery in the Jamaica Plain neighborhood of Boston, in the former Haffenreffer Brewery. Jim was educated at Harvard University and taught in the Outward Bound program as a climbing and mountaineering instructor before he approached the beer industry.

MARCY LARSON is an accountant and office manager for the Alaskan Brewery, and her husband, Geoff Larson, is the brewmaster. Established in March 1986, the Alaskan Brewery is locally owned and operated. Marcy and Geoff are both managing general partners. Over eighty Alaskan investors with limited partnerships comprise the rest of the company.

TED MARTI, president and brewmaster of the August Schell Brewing Company, is also the great-great grandson of August Schell. He is the fifth generation to carry on the brewing tradition at the picturesque 136-year-old brewery. His brewing background includes attending Siebel Institute of Technology in Chicago and studying in Germany at several breweries. Over the past several years, Ted has worked with and developed many successful contract brewing relationships, further defining this format within the beer industry.

TOM MCCORMICK is the principle of McCormick Distribution & Marketing, a consulting company in distribution and marketing for the craft-beer industry. Previously he

opened and operated McCormick Beverage Co., a pioneering wholesale beer distributor of exclusively microbrewed beer. Tom has been involved in the industry since 1982, promoting the appreciation of craft beers. He can be reached at (916) 878-1214.

PAT MEYER has been the general sales manger at Rockies Brewing Company in Boulder, Colorado, since 1990. During that time he has been involved with planning and revising the brewery's sales strategies for all new and existing markets. Prior to joining Rockies Brewing he worked at the wholesale level for several years in both the Oregon and Colorado markets.

MICHAEL J. PRONOLD has a master's degree in natural resources. He currently is an environmental specialist with the Bureau of Environmental Services for the city of Portland, Oregon. He has over ten years of experience in dealing with wastewater and wastewater sludge issues.

SCOTT SMITH is the founder and president of CooperSmith's Brewing Company in Fort Collins, Colorado. CooperSmith's opened in 1989 and is considered one of the top-producing brewpubs in the country. In addition to involvement in the start-up of five additional brewpubs, Scott's work includes speaking at the Institute for Brewing Studies National Craft-Brewer's Conference, addressing the University of California at Davis' Masters Brewers Program, teaching a weekend course for the American Brewers Guild, writing for *The New Brewer* magazine, sitting on the editorial review board of *Brewpub,* and coauthoring the book *How to Open a Brewpub or Microbrewery,* published by the American Brewers Guild in Davis, California.

RANDY SPRECHER founded, financed with $40,000, engineered, and built systems for Sprecher Brewing Company in Glendale, Wisconsin, in 1985. Today Sprecher Brewing Company is a fast-growing $4-million-per-year beer and soda business, with projected 1996 sales of $4 million to $5 million.

JACK STREICH, a 1991 graduate of the diploma course in brewing studies at the Siebel Institute of Technology, is a Boston-based brewer who has consulted on the start up and/or operation of nine brewpubs in New England and New York.

JEFF WARE founded Dock Street Brewing Company in 1986. Today the Dock Street Brewing Company produces three bottled beers: Dock Street Amber Beer, Dock Street Bohemian Pilsner, and Dock Street Illuminator Bock. The company also owns and operates the award-winning Dock Street Brewery & Restaurant in downtown Philadelphia.

ERIC WARNER, born and raised in Denver, Colorado, successfully completed a degree in German studies at Lewis and Clark College in Portland, Oregon, before traveling to Germany to pursue a formal education in Brewing Science. After four years of extensive brewery, lab, and course work, Eric was awarded the degree Diplom-Braumeister from the Technical University of Munich at Weihenstephan. After returning to Colorado, Eric began planning the opening of Tabernash Brewing Company. Founded in 1993, Tabernash is a very successful Colorado microbrewery, producing award-winning German-style lagers and weiss beer. Eric authored the Classic Beer Style Series book, *German Wheat Beer* (Brewers Publications, 1992), and is regarded as an expert on the topic.

PETER WHALEN of Northampton, Massachusetts, is president of Goggins and Whalen Insurance Agency Inc. and a certified insurance counselor and licensed insurance adviser. Endorsed by the Institute of Brewing Studies, he has researched a specialized insurance program to suit the needs of small breweries. He received a bachelor of arts degree in economics from Trinity College in Hartford, Connecticut.

SHERI WINTER of Boulder, Colorado, is the marketing director for the Association of Brewers (AOB), a nonprofit educational association dedicated to disseminating information on beer and brewing. Before joining the AOB in 1995, she held various positions in software marketing, most recently as director of marketing for Visix Software Inc. Sheri is a homebrewer and an avid beer lover. She has visited numerous breweries and brewpubs throughout the United States.

Editorial Advisors

DAVID EDGAR began working for the Association of Brewers in 1987. He joined the staff of the Institute for Brewing Studies division in 1990 and became IBS Director in 1994. He served as managing editor of *The North American Brewers Resource Directory* (Brewers Publications) for three years. He has spoken at IBS' National Craft-Brewers Conferences, the Brewers Association of America convention, and at brewing classes sponsored by University of California at Davis and University of Colorado at Colorado Springs. He has written articles published in ***The New Brewer***, *Celebrator*, *All About Beer*, ***Zymurgy***®, and *Brauwelt*. A graduate of Siebel Institute's Short Course in Brewing Technology, David has visited more than 150 microbreweries and brewpubs in North America.

STEVEN FRIED graduated with a bachelor's degree in zoology from North Dakota State University in 1974 and a master in business administration from the University of West Florida in 1987. Steven started homebrewing while in the Navy in 1979. After serving in the Navy for ten years, he left to start a homebrew supply shop in 1985. Three years later Fried was hired as brewmaster at McGuire's upon installation of the brewery in the existing restaurant. Fried has used the original yeast strain for more than 925 batches through repitching.

BOB HAWKINS is proprietor and brewer of one of Oregon's newest craft breweries —

Bandon Brewing Company. Built along the southern coast of Bandon-by-the-Sea, Bob's traditional ale brewery uses only imported British malts to produce ales that are nonfiltered, naturally clarified, and top fermented.

CRAYNE HORTON and his wife, Mary, moved from Japan to Olympia, Washington, in 1992 with little more than a dream to open their own business and plenty of experience as homebrewers. They now own and operate the Fish Brewing Company, one of the Pacific Northwest's most successful and respected microbreweries. As president of Fish Brewing, Crayne is currently completing his second stock offering to fund a ten-thousand-barrel expansion of the company's annual production capacity and to begin bottling Fish Tail Ales in 1996. Crayne's future plans for the company are to simply continue to make authentically styled British ales with a robust character for true ale aficionados.

DANIEL KRAMER is a co-founder of the Hop Brewing Company in Amherst, Massachusetts, and has served as president, brewmaster, and a director since its inception. Prior to founding the Hop Brewing Company, Daniel served as head brewer of the River City Brewing Company in Jacksonville, Florida — one of the largest brewpubs in the United States. At River City Brewing Company, he was responsible for all phases of the brewery's start-up operations, including design, construction, and management. Prior to his employment with River City Brewing Company, Daniel was head brewer at Commonwealth Brewing Company, a brew-pub in Boston, where he was responsible for all day-to-day operations. Daniel holds a bachelor of science degree in management from the Rochester Institute of Technology and is a graduate of the diploma course at Siebel Institute of Technology.

FRED SCHEER'S brewing career began in 1968 in Germany where he worked an apprenticeship as brewer and maltster. In 1976 he received a brewmaster and maltmaster degree from the Technical Academy DOE-MENS in Munich, Germany. His work experience has included a variety of technical, packaging, and planning work as well as operating breweries (including one soft drink plant) in Europe and here in the United States. Fred is director of quality assurance for the Evansville Brewing Company in Evansville, Indiana. He is an active member of the German Master Brewers Association DOEMENS, the ASBC, and the MBAA, serving on the latter's international technical committee. In addition Fred is technical editor of **The New Brewer** magazine and a professional beer judge at the annual Great American Beer Festival®.

ERIC WALLACE grew up around the world as an Air Force brat and was exposed to good beer at a precocious age while in Germany. He graduated from the U.S. Air Force Academy in 1984 with a degree in international affairs, and spent eight years in the Air Force as a communications officer in Italy and Turkey before moving back to the United States in 1993. After noticing an obvious trend towards good beer brewing and drinking developing in the United States, he decided to get into the beer business with Dick Doore (another Air Force alumnus), forming Left Hand Brewing Company. They introduced their first beers in January 1994 and now have a brewing capacity of nine thousand barrels per year.

Index

with, 109
University of California, Davis: brewing manage-
ment at, 132
USA Today, on microbreweries, 51
Utility costs, 150

Val Blatz plant, 82
Vice presidents, responsibilities of, 128, 143, 144,
145
Volatiles, dealing with, 54

Wages, considerations about, 23
Wash-down procedures, 54
Waste issues, 5, 24–26, 52, 60
Wastewater
    characteristics of, 58–59, 59 (table)
    dealing with, 57–61
    pH of, 53, 59, 60
    treatment of, 25, 52–53, 55, 56
Wastewater treatment plants, 57, 60
Water, evaluating, 5–6, 20–21, 53
Wholesalers, 80, 105, 107
    packaging and, 104
Widmer, Kurt: on fund raising, 82
Widmer, Rob, 82
Wort, 11, 13

Yeasts, 41
    choosing, 21–22
    disposing of, 25, 60
    filtration and, 63
    wild, 6, 20

Zip City Brewing Company, growth of, 81
Zoning, 5, 51–52, 54, 55
Zymurgy, 131

OPENING A BREWERY?
THE INSTITUTE FOR BREWING STUDIES
WANTS TO HEAR ABOUT IT!

*Please fill out this form and send it to the Institute to make sure we know
about your new brewery and to help us serve the industry better.*

(please print or type)

Company Name _____

(dba) _____

Mailing Address _____

Street Address (if different) _____

City_____State/Province _____Zip/Postal Code _____

Country_____

Telephone _____

FAX_____E-mail_____WWW _____

Principals _____

_____

_____

_____

Head Brewer _____

Primary Contact _____

Names and styles of the beers you intend to produce _____

_____

_____

Date of first commercial sales (projected if not open yet) _____

_____

Check one only: ❑ Microbrewery   ❑ Brewpub   ❑ Contract Brewing

Annual production capacity (check one) _____ ❑ U.S. Barrels   _____ ❑ Hectoliters

Total square footage (including storage, offices) _____square feet

Number of seats (if applicable)_____

*Copy this form and send with any press releases, photographs suitable for printing or
newspaper clippings concerning your brewery to: Institute for Brewing Studies, PO Box 1679,
Boulder, CO 80306-1679, USA or FAX (303) 447-2825.*
Thank you very much.

BOOKS for Brewers and Beer Lovers

Order Now ... Your Brew Will Thank You!

These books offered by Brewers Publications are some of the most sought after reference tools for homebrewers and professional brewers alike. Filled with tips, techniques, recipes and history, these books will help you expand your brewing horizons. Let the world's foremost brewers help you as you brew. Whatever your brewing level or interest, Brewers Publications has the information necessary for you to brew the best beer in the world — your beer.

Please send me more free information on the following:
(Check all that apply.)

☐ Book and Merchandise Catalog   ☐ Institute for Brewing Studies

☐ American Homebrewers Association®   ☐ Great American Beer Festival®

Ship to:

Name _____

Address _____

City _____ State/Province _____

Zip/Postal Code _____ Country _____

Daytime Phone (   ) _____

Please use the following in conjunction with the order form when ordering books from Brewers Publications.

Payment Method

☐ Check or Money Order Enclosed *(Payable to Brewers Publications)*

☐ Visa   ☐ MasterCard

Card Number _____ Expiration Date _____

Name on Card _____ Signature _____

Brewers Publications, PO Box 1510, Boulder, CO 80306-1510, USA • (303) 546-6514 • FAX (303) 447-2825 • orders@aob.org • http://www.aob.org/aob

BREWERS PUBLICATIONS ORDER FORM

PROFESSIONAL BREWING BOOKS

QTY.	TITLE	STOCK #	PRICE	EXT. PRICE
____	Brewery Planner	500	80.00	_____
____	96-97 North American Brewers Resource Directory	505	100.00	_____
____	Principles of Brewing Science	463	29.95	_____
____	Beer Brand Index (Specify PC or Mac)	520	40.00	_____

THE BREWERY OPERATIONS SERIES from Micro- and Pubbrewers Conferences

QTY.	TITLE	STOCK #	PRICE	EXT. PRICE
____	Volume 6, 1989 Conference	536	25.95	_____
____	Volume 7, 1990 Conference	537	25.95	_____
____	Volume 8, 1991 Conference, Brewing Under Adversity	538	25.95	_____
____	Volume 9, 1992 Conference, Quality Brewing — Share the Experience	539	25.95	_____

CLASSIC BEER STYLE SERIES

QTY.	TITLE	STOCK #	PRICE	EXT. PRICE
____	Pale Ale	401	11.95	_____
____	Continental Pilsener	402	11.95	_____
____	Lambic	403	11.95	_____
____	Oktoberfest, Vienna, Märzen	404	11.95	_____
____	Porter	405	11.95	_____
____	Belgian Ale	406	11.95	_____
____	German Wheat Beer	407	11.95	_____
____	Scotch Ale	408	11.95	_____
____	Bock	409	11.95	_____
____	Stout	410	11.95	_____

GENERAL BEER AND BREWING INFORMATION

QTY.	TITLE	STOCK #	PRICE	EXT. PRICE
____	New Brewing Lager Beer	469	14.95	_____
____	The Art of Cidermaking	468	9.95	_____
____	Brewing Mead	461	11.95	_____
____	Dictionary of Beer and Brewing	462	19.95	_____
____	Evaluating Beer	465	19.95	_____
____	Great American Beer Cookbook	466	24.95	_____
____	Victory Beer Recipes	464	11.95	_____
____	Winners Circle	467	11.95	_____

BEER AND BREWING SERIES, for homebrewers and beer enthusiasts, from National Homebrewers Conferences

QTY.	TITLE	STOCK #	PRICE	EXT. PRICE
____	Volume 8, 1988 Conference	448	21.95	_____
____	Volume 10, 1990 Conference	450	21.95	_____
____	Volume 11, 1991 Conference, Brew Free or Die!	451	21.95	_____
____	Volume 12, 1992 Conference, Just Brew It!	452	21.95	_____

Call or write for a free Beer Enthusiast catalog today.

- U.S. funds only
- All Brewers Publications books come with a money-back guarantee.

*Postage and handling: Please include in payment $4 for the first book ordered, plus $1 for each book thereafter. Canadian and international orders please add $5 for the first book and $2 for each book thereafter. Diskette's nonreturnable.

Orders cannot be shipped without appropriate postage and handling.

SUBTOTAL	_____
Colo. Residents Add 3% Sales Tax	_____
Postage and Handling *	_____
TOTAL	_____

"We read it in *The New Brewer*."

CLEVELAND, OHIO

Incorporated in 1986, the Great Lakes Brewing Co. has won numerous national and international awards for both lagers and ales. The company's growing reputation is for producing consistently clear, lusty and full-bodied beers.

Pat and Dan Conway, Co-owners
Great Lakes Brewing Co.,
Cleveland, Ohio

"**W**hether we are looking for information concerning our day-to-day operation or guideposts for our ever expanding brewery, we refer *The New Brewer* for its highly informative material. It is indispensable reading for veterans and start-ups alike."

Industry leaders like Pat and Dan Conway know that only *The New Brewer* provides the inside information craft brewers from coast to coast depend Each issue is packed with vital statistics for business planning, the latest in brewing techniques, alternative technologies, beer recipes, legislative ale marketing and distribution ideas — everything you need to succeed in today's competitive market.

Whether you're an established brewery or just in the planning stages, our in-depth coverage will give you information you can put to work immediate After all, your business is our business.

See for yourself. Subscribe to *The New Brewer* today!

Please complete the following information. We'll rush subscription information your way!

NAME _____

TITLE _____

COMPANY _____

ADDRESS _____

CITY _____

STATE/PROVINCE _____ ZIP/POSTAL CODE _____

COUNTRY _____ TELEPHONE _____

Please return this coupon to: Institute for Brewing Studies, PO Box 1510, Boulder, CO 80306-1510, U.S.A. For faster service contact: (303) 447-0816; FAX (303) 447-2825; orders@aob.org or http://www.aob.org/aob **TNB**

The **New Brewer** · YOUR INSIDER'S VIEW TO THE CRAFT-BREWING INDUSTRY